ANTHROPOLOGICAL PAPERS

MUSEUM OF ANTHROPOLOGY, UNIVERSITY OF MICHIGAN

NO. 53

WHERE WOMEN WORK: A STUDY OF YORUBA WOMEN IN THE MARKETPLACE AND IN THE HOME

BY

NIARA SUDARKASA

ANN ARBOR

THE UNIVERSITY OF MICHIGAN, 1973

© 1973 by the Regents of the University of Michigan
The Museum of Anthropology
All rights reserved

ISBN (print): 978-1-949098-06-8
ISBN (ebook): 978-1-951519-18-6

Browse all of our books at
sites.lsa.umich.edu/archaeology-books.

Order our books from the University of Michigan
Press at www.press.umich.edu.

For permissions, questions, or manuscript queries,
contact Museum publications by email at umma-
pubs@umich.edu or visit the Museum website at
lsa.umich.edu/ummaa.

PREFACE

Eleven years have passed since the completion of the fieldwork upon which this monograph is based, and nine years have gone by since the original version of this study was written in the form of a doctoral dissertation.[1] During the interim, the dissertation has proven useful to a number of scholars interested in trade and markets in Nigeria and elsewhere, and with the recent growth of interest in "women's studies" the dissertation has attracted the attention of scholars seeking information on female roles in African societies. The publication of the study at the present time represents an effort to increase the availability of this modest contribution to the comparative literature on female roles and activities in different parts of the world.

It goes without saying that during the decade since this study was first written, the life of females in the areas studied has been affected by the enormous political, economic and social changes that have occurred in Nigeria.[2] In fact, some of the effects of these changes on the activities of females were apparent to me when I paid brief visits to Nigeria in 1969 and 1970. Also apparent, however, was the continued involvement of women in the world of the market. I did not remain in Nigeria long enough to make a systematic assessment of the extent to which the patterns of trade and the patterns of family life observed in 1961 and 1962 have changed over the past decade. For this reason, the original study is published here with relatively minor revisions rather than with the substantial additions that would have been made had I been able to conduct the field research necessary to up-date the earlier work. I can only hope that the present study will provide a useful baseline for those who do undertake an evaluation of the changes that have taken place in the life of Yoruba women over the past decade.

If there is one serious omission from the study, it is an analysis of the factors in the colonial situation that generated the impoverished conditions of the traders (and farmers, craftsmen, etc.) described in this work and that created the overall web of economic exploitation in which these people were immeshed. When I wrote this study a decade ago, I tacitly gave support to the social science fiction that what happened in Nigeria (and in all of Africa) in the 20th century could be sanguinely described in terms of "modernization," and that the processes of European entrenchment and exploitation

---

[1] See Gloria A. Marshall, *Women, Trade, and the Yoruba Family*, Ph.D. Dissertation, Columbia University, 1964.
[2] This has been a decade of many dramatic developments, the most publicized and tragic of which, and the most far-reaching in impact, was the Nigerian Civil War. Many volumes have been published on the war (also called the Biafran Revolution and the Biafran Conflict), however, this is not the publication in which to list a bibliography on the subject. Nonetheless, for an introduction to the issues, developments, and repercussions, see: Červenka, Zdenek, *The Nigerian War 1967–70*, Bernard and Graefe, Frankfurt, 1971. For a very comprehensive list of sources on Nigeria from "earliest times" to 1966, see: Ita, N. O. *Bibliography of Nigeria*, Frank Cass, London, 1971.

in Africa could be subsumed under the benign if not indeed benificent concept of "development." The fact that I did not delve into the factors underlying the conditions described in this study is perhaps an indication of the success of my training in Western social science. In any case, suffice it to say that I would bring a decidedly different perspective to such an undertaking if I were doing it today.

The acknowledgments that follow were written in 1964; to them I would add my deepest thanks to my husband, Delmer A. Sudarkasa, who has helped in various ways to make this publication possible and who had contributed profoundly to my intellectual development.

The publication of this book has been financed by The University of Michigan's Museum of Anthropology, with the generous assistance of The Center for Afroamerican and African Studies and The Center for Research on Economic Development.

Ann Arbor
July 1973

TO
ROWENA MARSHALL
AND
REV. AND MRS. A. E. EVANS

ACKNOWLEDGMENTS

The Ford Foundation, through its Foreign Area Training Fellowship Program, provided the financial support which enabled me to carry out the research on which this study is based. The Fellowship award made possible five and one-half months (January 1961–May 1961) of preliminary study in London, England, and 15 months (June 1961–September 1962) of field work in Western Nigeria. The Foundation also awarded me a Fellowship for the academic year 1962–63 during which much of the analysis of data for this study was undertaken. It is with deepest gratitude that I acknowledge this support.

I am also grateful to the Committee for the Comparative Study of New Nations, The University of Chicago, for having awarded me a Carnegie Study of New Nations Fellowship for the 1963–64 academic year during which the work on this report was completed. I thank the Nigerian Institute of Social and Economic Research for the use of its facilities while I was in Ibadan.

For their encouragement and their contributions to various phases of the work leading to this study, I extend my thanks to the anthropologists with whom I worked most closely at Columbia University. In this connection, I acknowledge my indebtedness to Professors Joseph H. Greenberg, Conrad M. Arensberg, Charles Wagley, and Abraham Rosman. I am especially indebted to Professor Elliott P. Skinner who first interested me in the study of women traders in West Africa and who guided me in the formulation of my research project. I had the benefit of his thoughtful criticism at every stage of the research and throughout the preparation of the manuscript.

My thanks also to Professors T. K. Hopkins, Robert Murphy, and William Hance for their critical reading of and helpful comments on this study. I am indebted to Professor Akin Magogunje of the University of Ibadan for invaluable criticisms of parts of this study, and to Professor Robert A. LeVine of the University of Chicago for having made available to me interview schedules which were used in the collection of some of the field data as well as for many fruitful discussions of my research findings. Professor Jacob Ajayi is to be thanked for having put at my disposal his unpublished manuscript on the Yoruba civil wars of the 19th Century.

Acknowledgment must also be made of my indebtedness to Professors

Raymond Firth and Alice Dewey with whom I had many useful conversations in London before going to the field. Professor P. C. Lloyd deserves my gratitude for his generous hospitality during my stay in Nigeria and for sharing with me his knowledge of Yoruba society.

There are many persons whose comments and experience helped me to better understand trade and markets in Yorubaland. Among these are: Professor Ojetunji Aboyade, Dr. B. W. Hodder, Mr. S. Edokpayi, and Mr. Tunji Antonio. I am especially indebted to Mr. J. A. Adediran for information gained from several reports which he prepared as a Trade Officer with the Western Regional Ministry of Trade and Industry.

I am grateful to a number of governmental officials for their assistance in collecting documents related to markets and trade. These officials include: Mrs. O. Obiogun of the Western Regional Ministry of Trade and Industry, Mr. M. Ikenze of the Federal Ministry of Commerce and Industry, Mr. J. A. Fakayode, and Mr. R. Fakorede of the office of the Ibadan City Council, and Mr. C. L. Labiyi and Mr. F. A. Oladele of the office of the Oyo Southern District Council.

Miss Toun Oguntade served as my interpreter and general assistant for seven months and deserves my deepest gratitude for her help. I also extend my thanks to Mrs. J. Ohu and Mr. Oyelayo Abiba who volunteered to act as my interpreters during some of the interviews conducted in Oyo and Awe. I am especially grateful to Mr. Oyeleke Abiba who assisted me in Awe and who gathered supplementary materials for me after I had returned to the United States.

Some of my friends in Nigeria made special efforts to arrange interviews for me and to find written materials which I needed. In this connection, I thank Mr. Olu Osigbogun, Dr. E. O. A. Bucknor, Mr. John Pepper Clark, Mr. Frank Aig-Imoukhuede, and Mr. Olusola Idowu. Particular thanks are due Mr. Dapo Falase who assisted me throughout the period of my research.

This book could not have been written without the cooperation of the women and men who permitted me to share in many aspects of their daily lives and who took hours of their time to answer the questions I had to ask. Were I to name them all, I should have to list hundreds of citizens of Awe and scores of women and men interviewed in the various markets which I attended. However, I thank Madame S. Adesesan, Mrs. F. Oparinde, and Mrs. O. Lawore for their continuous help, and I trust that the hundreds unnamed will not think my gratitude toward them wanting.

I am grateful to Oba Bello Gbadegesin, Ladugbolu II, Alafin of Oyo, for his kindness and his efforts to facilitate my research in Oyo. To the Bale and Chiefs of Awe and through them to the entire citizenry, I extend my deepest appreciation for their warmth and generosity toward me and their enthusiastic support of my research. Finally, I must thank Mr. S. Akinabi of Awe and Chief (Mrs.) H. T. Soares of Ibadan, neither of whom I can regard as "informants" but who, more than any other persons, helped me to understand the ways of the Yoruba.

In appreciation of their continuous moral and material support, this book is dedicated to my mother and my grandparents.

TABLE OF CONTENTS

Introduction
      The Problem: Definition and Scope 1

I.   The Setting: Urban and Rural Communities in Yorubaland 7

II. Division of Labor by Sex in Yoruba Society 25

III. Yoruba Markets: Centers of Women's Trade Activities 39

IV. Awẹ Women as Traders and Producers 65

V.   Residence and Kinship in the Town of Awẹ 97

VI. Female Employment and Family Organization in Yoruba Society . 117

Conclusions 155

Appendix 161

Bibliography 163

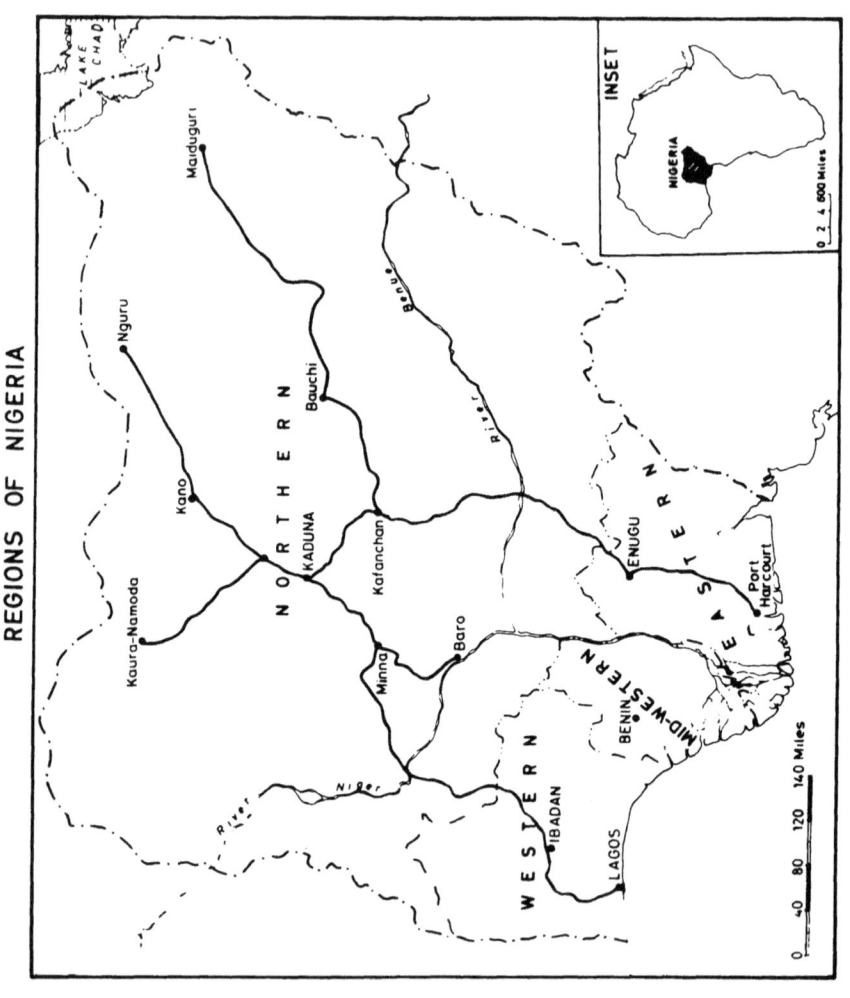

Fig. 1. Regions of Nigeria, 1964.

INTRODUCTION

THE PROBLEM: DEFINITION AND SCOPE

YORUBA women are well-known as traders within the internal marketing system of Nigeria. Indeed, they play an important part in the distribution of goods throughout West Africa for they are engaged in trade activities in most countries along the West African coast. The fact that these women have as one of their roles that of intermediary in the distribution network does not make them unique among West African women. Since the early twentieth century and, in a few cases, before that time, women of other West African societies have engaged in trade.

What is significant, however, is that in most societies other than that of the Yoruba, women are at least part-time cultivators. Where this is not the case, it can usually be demonstrated that the entry of women into the distribution sector of their economies began with the commencement of the Colonial Era. The Akan women of Ghana, for example, were cultivators prior to the twentieth century expansion of the exchange economy which greatly increased the number of positions available within the internal marketing system (McCall, 1956). An analogous development took place in Nigeria, but even so, some women of Nigeria—for example, a number of those belonging to the Ibo groups—have retained their roles as cultivators (Ottenberg, 1959).

Yoruba women were traders long before the twentieth century. There is no evidence of their ever having been cultivators, although women in some parts of Yorubaland did participate in some phases of farm work (Johnson, 1921: 101, 103). Today women rarely take part in any phase of agriculture even though many of them live in farmland areas. It can be said of the Yoruba women, as of the Nupe women, that "their sphere of work is, first, the 'refining' of agricultural produce to make it marketable, and secondly, the marketing itself" (Nadel, 1942: 252).

The large-scale participation of Yoruba women in modern trade activities cannot be attributed solely to the fact that they were traders in the traditional economy. Inasmuch as the men are cultivators of crops for the internal and external markets, it is not surprising that most of the tasks involved in the marketing of goods fall to women. Bauer (1954:22-34) has pointed out that in the economies of West Africa where there is an abundance of labor and a dearth of capital for expenditure in the distributive sphere of the economy (such as money for transport, bulking, and storage machineries), the distributive process necessarily involves large numbers of persons and the distribution chain includes a multiplicity of links. Where there are opportunities for employment in this sphere, it can be expected that persons who would otherwise remain unemployed would fill these positions. Thus, most Yoruba women, having few alternative employment possibilities due to their lack of specialized skills, are induced to trade in order to make any money at all. Trading, then, is a means of earning cash in a society where money is necessary for the procurement of services and goods.

Thus, the fact that trade by women is a phenomenon of long standing in Yorubaland, coupled with the expansion of trade avenues triggered by the growth of the modern economy, may be said to account for the fact that virtually all uneducated Yoruba women, and even many of those who are educated, are traders. Since women are engaged in trade pursuits which require that they move in the world of the market—and here "market" refers to the nature of the economy as well as to sites at which exchange of goods takes place—it can be expected that adjustments to this phenomenon would be evident in other spheres of the society.

This book examines the effect of trade by women on the structure of, and the behavioral patterns within, the kin and residential units to which women belong. It argues that the composition of the "domestic family" (Schwab, 1955) can be related to the involvement of women in trade, that the husband-wife relationship is adjusted to the realities of a situation in which women are independent wage earners, and that the process of socialization of children is directly related to the fact that women spend much of their time in their economic pursuits. Furthermore, it is argued that women's responsibilities to and dependence upon their wider kin network—the groups into which they are born and those into which they marry—are in part reflections of the fact that women are engaged in trade. Because of their independent incomes, women are expected to make separate contributions to the ceremonies undertaken by members of the lineages and compounds to which they belong. They are often called upon to render material assistance to their kinsmen in times of exigency, and the kin groups, in turn, provide structural support for the continued participation of women in trade.

There is no special class of women in Yoruba society that can be termed "traders." Virtually all women are engaged in some type of trade activity. No special code of ethics is referable to, no special prerogatives afforded, no special status accorded women traders as distinct from other groups of women. In this regard, Yoruba women differ from Nupe women traders as described by Nadel (1942). Trading is regarded as part and parcel of a Yoruba woman's overall role which includes first of all the roles of wife and mother.

THE PROBLEM

It is expected that by means of their trade activities, women will make some contributions to the upkeep of their families. At nearly all points in a woman's life cycle, she is engaged in one or more activities which afford cash remuneration. From their youths, most women are introduced into some line of trade and upon marriage, they begin trading on their own. This continues very nearly until the woman dies. In contrast to Nupe women, female traders in Yoruba society are not barren nor are they past childbearing age. Nonetheless, it will be apparent that the range of a woman's trade activities is, to some extent, a function of her age, the number and ages of her children, and her position among the wives married to her husband.

No attempt will be made in this study to provide general ethnographic data on the Yoruba peoples. Neither is this an exhaustive account of trade and markets in Yorubaland, or a general treatise on kinship and family among the Yoruba. Rather, this study points up the crucial areas of family life which have been affected by the fact that women are engaged in trade, and discusses trade only insofar as it is relevant to patterns within the family.

This study is divided into three parts. Part I presents general background data on Yoruba society, outlines the basic features of the town of Awe in which much of the field data was collected. Part II deals with the division of labor in traditional and contemporary Yoruba society, discusses the system of markets in which women carry on their trade, and presents a summary of the economic activities of Awe women. Part III is devoted to a discussion of the basic kin and residential unit in Yoruba society and to a consideration of the implications of women's involvement in trade for family life.

Much of the data presented was collected during 15 months of fieldwork in Western Nigeria. The materials on trade and markets were gathered in an area bounded by Ibadan, Oyo, Ogbomosho, and Iwo. From June to September of 1961, I lived in Ibadan, the capital of Western Nigeria, where I visited markets within the town, interviewed women traders, leaders of market women's associations, female chiefs, and several managers of European firms. In addition, I paid a few visits to markets in outlying small towns and rural settlements in order to obtain a general picture of the organization of the market network and of the patterns of trade. From September 1961 to September 1962, I lived in Awe, a town of some 5,000 inhabitants, located about one and one-half miles east of Oyo on the Oyo-Iwo road. It was in this small town that I gathered general ethnographic data, paying particular attention to the role of women in family and community life. Because I wanted to assess the relationship between trade and other facets of the life of women, I regularly attended those markets frequented by Awe women, and studied the activities of women who carried on their trade and manufacturing within the town or in the surrounding rural hamlets. In the markets I interviewed male and female traders from Awe and from other nearby towns and rural settlements.[1] Interviews with traders from communities other than Awe afforded a wider basis for generalization concerning the role of women in the trade network.

During the last five months of my stay in Nigeria, in addition to collecting field data, I spent time gathering materials on trade and markets from records in the offices of the Oyo Southern District Council (which then had jurisdiction over the town of Awe), the Ibadan City Council, and the Western Regional Ministry of Trade and Industry.

---

[1] In addition to brief conversations with many traders in Awe and in the markets which I often attended, I had more formal interviews with a number of traders:

Traders Interviewed

Location	Male	Female
Awe (incl. Awe traders interviewed in markets)	5	85
Aiyekale market	2	17
Ajagba "	3	4
Ajawa "	7	22
Akesan " (Oyo)		5
Apara "		1
Atan " (Oyo)		6
Emi-Abata "	5	4
Ife-Odan "	8	11
Iware "	2	15
Sakatu " (Oyo)	2	17
Tesan "	15	15
Total	49	202

Awe Female Producer-Traders Interviewed

Makers of Red Palm Oil	5
Makers of Palm Kernel Oil	10
Makers of Soap	18
Makers of Pottery	5
Total	38

I also interviewed a few traders at Igbeti market and talked to women in each of a number of rural periodic markets to which I paid only one visit. Since this study draws primarily on the data collected in Awe and environs, I have excluded from the above list the traders interviewed in Ibadan town markets.

Data on trade and family life and materials relating to community life in Awe were gathered from a number of men and women ("informants") many of whom, particularly men, are not accounted for in the above list of traders.

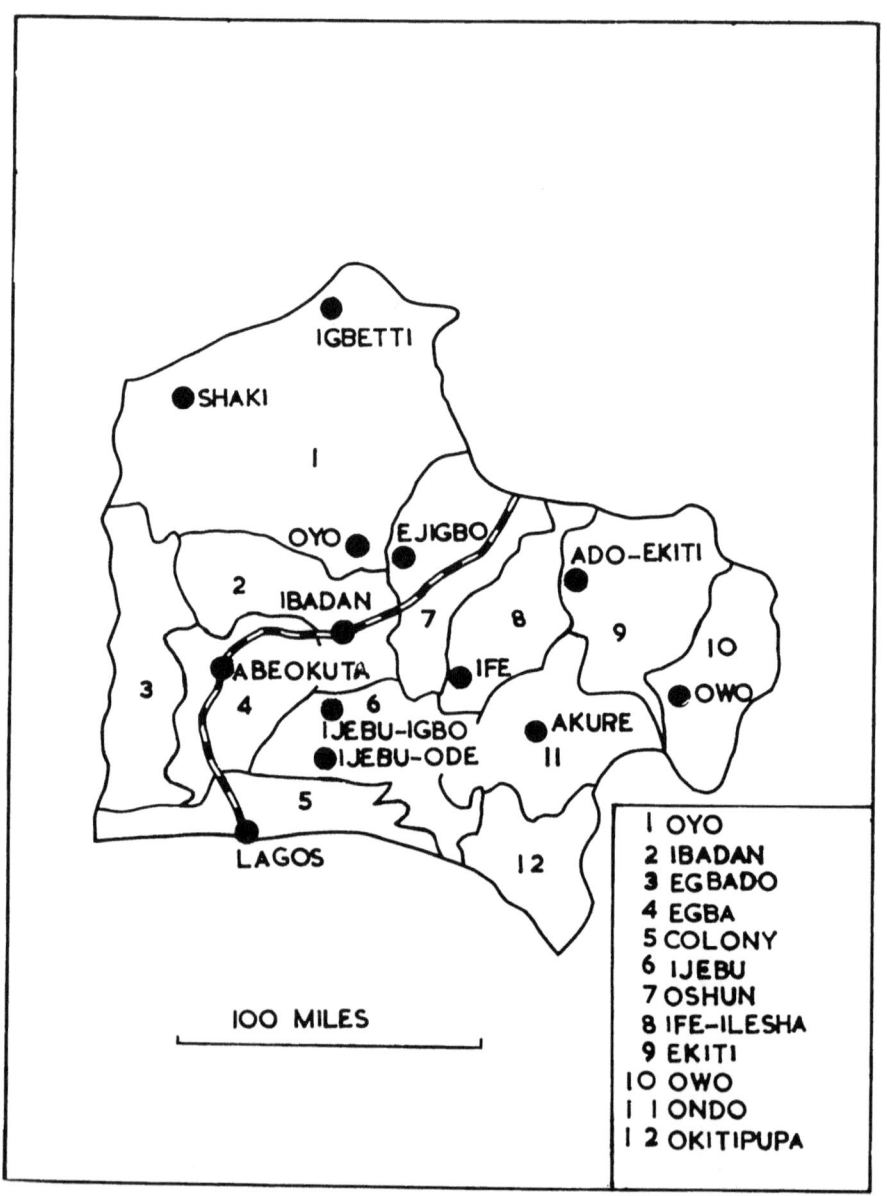

Fig. 2. Divisions and main towns of Western Nigeria, 1964.

I

THE SETTING: URBAN AND RURAL COMMUNITIES IN YORUBALAND

THE Western Region of the Federation of Nigeria is populated almost entirely by a people, numbering over four million, who are collectively known as the Yoruba.[1] There are various Yoruba subgroups, the majority of whose members occupy specifiable areas of the Region and speak their own dialects of the Yoruba language; but all Yoruba peoples acknowledge a common cultural history and share many common features of culture. Yoruba communities of varying age and size are located throughout the Northern, Eastern, and Mid-West Regions. The majority of the inhabitants of the Federal capital of Lagos, formerly a Yoruba town known as Eko, are Yoruba.[2]

YORUBA HISTORY

Yoruba oral traditions trace their history to Ile-Ife, a town in the central part of the Western Region of Nigeria, to which Oduduwa, the progenitor of all Yoruba peoples, migrated from "the east." The kingdoms of Oyo, Ketu, Ila, Owu, Sabe, and Popo and the kingdom of Benin were created by the grandchildren of Oduduwa (Johnson, 1921:3-14). According to some of the traditions set down by the Yoruba historian, Samuel Johnson (1921:15-25), the Egba, Ijebu, Ijesa, Ondo, and Ekiti kingdoms were not founded by sons or grandsons of Oduduwa. However, the oral traditions of each of these kingdoms trace their history directly to Ile-Ife and their ancestry to Oduduwa.

---

[1] Before the recent creation of the Mid-West Region, the southeastern part of the Western Region was populated by a number of other ethnic groups.

[2] The 1952 census reported the distribution of the Yoruba population as follows:

Western Region	4,302,401
Northern Region	536,109
Eastern Region	11,377
Lagos	195,974
Total	5,045,861

The Yoruba constituted 16.6 percent of the total population of the Federation and 95.7 percent of the population of Lagos. They were a little over 82 percent of the population of the Western Region, the other 18 percent consisting largely of peoples who now make up the Mid-West Region.

Most writers of recent years seem to accept the proposition, sanctioned in mythology and supported by some historical documents, that between A.D. 600 and A.D. 1000 the Yoruba migrated from the northeast of Africa into the savannah lands of what is now the northern part of the Western Region and the southern part of the Northern Region of Nigeria (Biobaku, 1955: 28-29; Mabogunje, 1962a:4; Crowder, 1962:46). Biobaku (1955:29) dates the earliest settlements at Ile-Ife to the tenth century A.D. The kingdom of Oyo is reckoned by Biobaku (1955:29)[3] to have been founded as early as the eleventh century and from that time onward, the Yoruba migrated, in a series of waves, from the savannah lands into the forest areas to the south. In some cases they established kingdoms in the lands of indigenous peoples whom they conquered.

During the early nineteenth century, the Fulani occupied the Yoruba town of Ilorin and subsequently invaded the kingdom of Oyo. The Yoruba of Oyo and surrounding towns pushed southward, many of them settling at the present site of Oyo where they established a new capital. A series of civil wars which had begun during the latter part of the eighteenth century (Biobaku, 1957:9), decades before the Fulani invasion, but which were intensified as a result of the population movements and political intrigues triggered by the invasion, were waged throughout most of the nineteenth century. These led to further population upheavals, culminating in the formation of the refugee towns of Abeokuta and Ibadan.

Traditional Yoruba Communities and Their Government

Despite the uncertainty surrounding their earliest history, it is known that traditionally the Yoruba were organized into a number of kingdoms (Johnson, 1921; Lloyd, 1954). Whether these kingdoms were ever effectively united under a single sovereign is open to dispute, but the *Alafin* of Oyo is acknowledged as the traditional sovereign over all the Yoruba[4] and even today at the time of the *Bere* festival, all the Yoruba *Obas* (kings) pay homage to the Alafin at Oyo.

The government of each Yoruba kingdom was centered in the hands of the Oba and his Chiefs-in-Council. The paramount ruler in a Yoruba kingdom was not only the political sovereign but a sacred king "upon whose ritual performances [was] thought to rest the well being of the people" (Lloyd,

---

[3] "Mr. Peter Morton-Williams in a paper read to the Historical Society of Nigeria suggests that Oyo was founded at the earliest in 1388 and at the latest 1438" (Crowder, 1962:48). Crowder does not cite the date of the paper.

[4] According to Johnson, during the reign of the Alafin Agboluaje, in the mid-eighteenth century, the Oyo kingdom reached its greatest extent, being "bounded by the river Niger on the north and a portion of the Tapa and Bariba countries, on the East by the Lower Niger, on the South by the seacoast, and on the West it includes the Popos and Dahomey. From all the provinces included within these boundaries, and by some including the Gas and Ashanti, tributes were paid to Oyo" (1921:179).

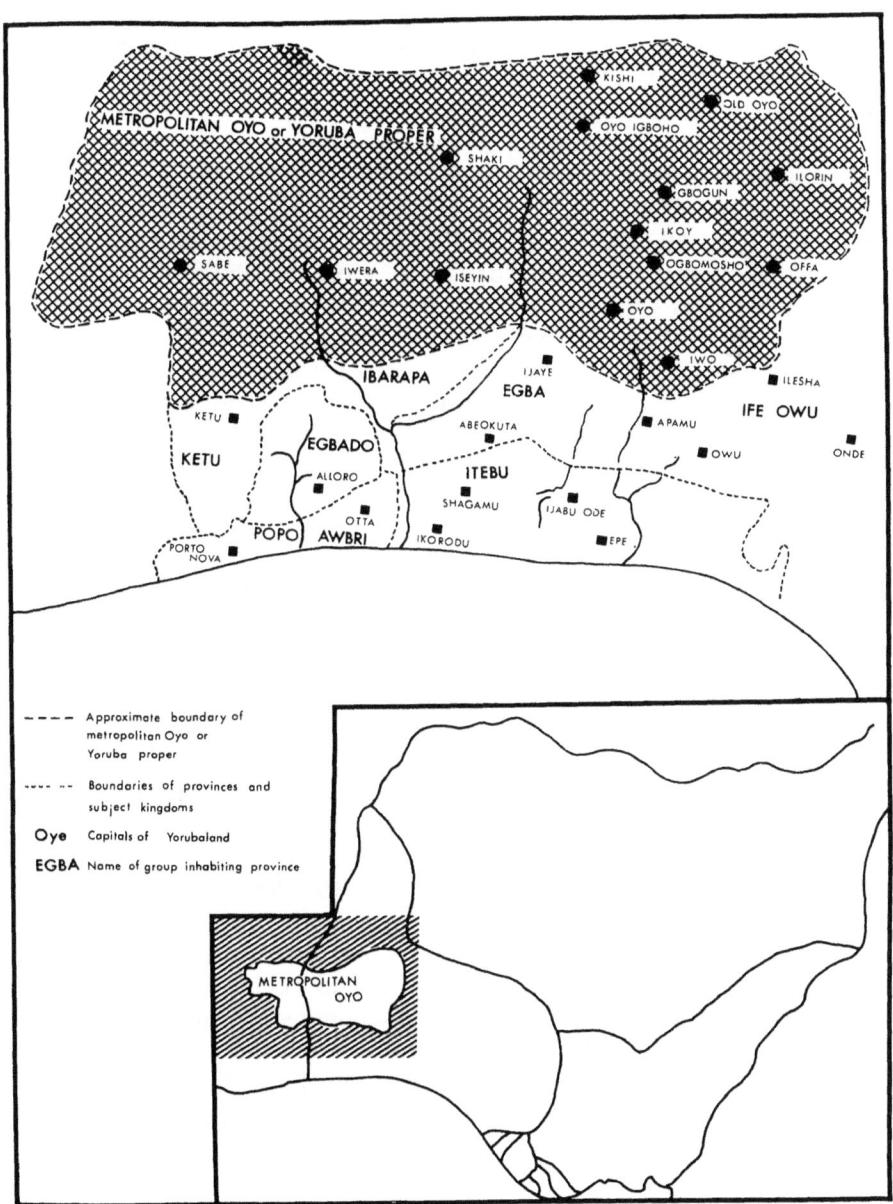

Fig. 3. Nineteenth Century Yorubaland (after Crowder, 1962:97).

1962:38). Ritual powers and prerogatives were also part of the offices of the chiefs on whom the Oba relied for counsel (Lloyd, 1960, 1962).

In the traditional system, in addition to being the political and administrative heads of the kingdom, the Oba and his chiefs constituted the highest judicial body. "There did not exist, therefore, any judiciary which was independent of the administration" (Lloyd, 1962:48).

To appreciate the nature of the political structure of Yorubaland, reference must be made to the territorial units over which the officials ruled. The most striking feature of Yoruba society is its high degree of urbanism (Bascom, 1955). All evidence indicates that the Yoruba lived in relatively large, densely populated communities[5] long before the advent of the British and the subsequent growth of many of the present-day Nigerian towns and cities. The size of the traditional Yoruba settlements; the fact that they were based on internal economic specialization, each having at least one market place where the exchange of goods took place; the existence in each community of a hierarchy of officials responsible for making and executing political decisions; and the fact that the population of each community was united by associational as well as kin ties have led scholars to designate them as urban areas (Bascom, 1955, 1962; Lloyd, 1953a, 1959; Mabogunje, 1962a).

The capital of each Yoruba kingdom was the urban center wherein were located the Oba's palace and the compounds of the Oba's chiefs. Each kingdom contained within it a number of subordinate towns whose governmental and administrative structure was modeled on that of the metropolitan town. The chief ruler of an outlying town bore the title of Bale (*Baba ile*, literally, father of the land); under the Bale was a full roster of chiefs who together with him were responsible for local affairs (Johnson, 1921; Lloyd, 1954).

Many of the subordinate towns grew up as offshoots of the metropolitan center and all of them were linked to the capital by ties of tribute. Each town within a kingdom paid periodic tribute to the Oba in return for military protection against enemies more powerful than itself. The Oba, being the "owner" of all the land within his kingdom, was the adjudicator of land controversies and other disputes between towns within his jurisdiction.

Both the metropolitan towns and the subordinate towns were, and are today, divided into a number of wards (*adugbo*), sometimes referred to as "quarters" since in some towns they number four. Each ward was made up of a number of compounds wherein resided a group of males, descended through the patriline from the founder of the compound, along with their wives, and their children.

---

[5]Population estimates are not available for earlier periods, but in the nineteenth century, there were at least 17 Yoruba towns whose populations were estimated to be over 20,000; there were three towns with a population of 60,000 or more, and many smaller towns whose populations numbered in the thousands (Bowen, 1857:218; Bascom, 1955:447).

Surrounding each town were its cultivated and uncleared farmlands and its hunting territories. These farmlands contained the dwellings (*aba*) where the farmers and some members of their families lived while on the farms. These settlements were not politically autonomous of the towns nor were they regarded as permanent residences by their occupants. Persons who lived in the farmlands looked upon themselves as townsmen and their family compounds were always located in the towns (Bascom, 1955).

It was over the urban complex and its surrounding farmlands that the government extended. The smallest administrative unit was the compound, whose head (the Bale), usually the oldest living male of the lineage of the founder of the compound, was responsible for running the affairs of the house. Each ward or quarter had a chief whose jurisdiction extended over the compounds in his area. At the top of the administrative hierarchy was the Oba or the Bale. The chain of command extended from the paramount ruler through the quarter chief to the Bale (*Baba ile*, lit. father of the house).[6]

In addition to the quarter chieftaincies, there were a number of other chieftaincy titles, most of which were open only to men who belonged to the "root" (*idi*) of particular houses (*ile*). Ideally this meant that these were lineage (*idile*) titles, open only to patrilineal descendants of the founder of the compound (*agbo ile* or ile).

In some Yoruba towns there was, in addition, a graded title system contained within an association, the lowest grade of which may have been open to all adult free men of the town. The *Ogboni* society was such an association. A man moved from one grade to the next by paying fees for various ceremonies and feasts. The highest grade was that of the six *Iwarefa* chiefs who were, in many respects, the most influential group of chiefs in the town (Lloyd, 1962:41; Morton-Williams, 1960).[7]

---

[6] A distinction should be noted between the terms ile (land) and ile (house), and consequently between the terms Bale ("father of the land") and Bale ("father of the house").

[7] Although a thorough discussion of the structure and process of the Yoruba political system cannot be undertaken here, I do not entirely accept Lloyd's interpretation of the political system for he implies that the government is embedded in rather than superimposed upon the system of lineages. For Lloyd (1953a, 1953b 1954, 1955, 1959, 1960, 1962), the Yoruba kinship structure forms the basis of the town and of the political system. From his own descriptive data, however, and from my field data, it seems clear that the Yoruba town is fundamentally a unit composed of smaller territorial units and that whereas corporate descent groups do exist and are very important insofar as the inheritance of land and movable properties is concerned, the government of the town is best understood in terms of territoriality, the compound rather than the lineage being the basic unit.

One example of the manner in which Lloyd's descriptive data contradict his theoretical position is seen in his discussion (1960, 1962) of the position of the Oba in Yoruba society. The Oba, we are told, is a member of the royal descent group but upon his accession to the throne, "he is lifted out of the royal descent group ... the constitutions of Yoruba towns are designed to remove him from the influence of members of the royal descent group lest this body usurps political power in the town" (Lloyd, 1962:46).

Although women were not participants in certain affairs of government, each Yoruba town had an *Iyalode* (mother of the town) who was the official head of all women of the town. There were a number of other titles held by females, and, in Oyo, certain important duties within the *Afin*, the residence of the Oba, were performed by women who held titled offices (Johnson, 1921:63-67).

The Growth of Rural Settlements

There were no permanent autonomous, rural settlements in pre-nineteenth century Yorubaland. All persons resident in the farmlands had permanent dwellings in the towns in which they exercised their political rights. Even if a hamlet of considerable size grew up around a farmer's dwelling or along one of the major trade routes, its members were still citizens of the towns in which their compounds were located and to which they regularly returned. However, as soon as a settlement attracted enough people of various specialties to make it potentially viable as an independent political and economic unit, its members would choose a Bale, perhaps the man or a lineal male descendant of the man who first settled in the area, and would apply to the Oba for recognition as a town (Johnson, 1921:90-93). Being granted independent status, the people chose the other chiefs from among the various houses, and a central market was officially established near the house of the Bale. Thus, whenever a settlement became permanent, it could not be considered "rural" for it had the characteristics by which traditional Yoruba urbanism is defined and it too would have its outlying farmlands and hamlets.

From the beginning of his reign, the Oba is a sacred person; he no longer lives in his natal compound, and in former times, his palace was inaccessible to most persons. He brings nothing to the throne; his properties would be cared for by his brothers and passed on to his children. The members of the royal descent group—Omo Oba—have no special privileges of access to the Oba even though some of them reside in a section of the palace allotted to them. The Oba is head of state, *not* head of the royal descent group; its head is "usually" its oldest member or a titled member whose offices include the duties of group head (1962:44).

The above description makes it obvious that the office of Oba is a political office, not in any way a kinship position. The fact that the Oba is chosen from among a certain group of men presumably related to each other by patrilineal descent from the founding Oba of the town *does not alter the fact* that the office is a political one, superimposed on the lineage system. (In societies where the polity is embedded in the kinship system, there are few or no political offices which are not also kinship positions. The kinship structure, in such societies, *is* the political structure.) The other Yoruba chieftaincies, like that of the Oba, are also political offices *qua* political offices. The installation of a chief, in effect, "lifts him out of" his kin group and makes him an official of the town.

The cause, it seems to me, of Lloyd's misinterpretation of some basic aspects of Yoruba society is the fact that when he undertook the analysis of the Yoruba data, he took as his theoretical framework one which had grown out of the investigations of "stateless" societies such as the Nuer and the Tallensi. While kin groups are important in Yoruba society, it is misleading to assign to the kin groups the complete multi-functionality which they have in some societies of "lower" levels of integration (Service, 1962:Ch. 5).

The nineteenth century civil wars resulted in considerable modification of the traditional territorial organization. Many of the small towns surrounding the metropolitan centers, and some of the old centers themselves, were destroyed. Their populations clustered in other existing towns or moved into the new refugee towns of Ibadan and Abeokuta (Johnson, 1921; Mabogunje, 1959, 1962a, 1962b).[8] During the middle and late nineteenth century, a new settlement pattern began to emerge around the towns of Abeokuta and Ibadan. A number of more permanent settlements were founded in the farmlands. These served as points from which the movement of hostile neighbors could be observed and from which some attempts to attack the town could be thwarted. Though they did not always have walls, these settlements were somewhat fortified by the forests and were only abandoned in times of severe attack or siege. The Egba, having concentrated at Abeokuta, and having lost between one-third and two-thirds of the land which constituted the old Federation, pushed out into the farmlands of their neighbors where they founded a number of small farming villages.

The need for more and more land forced the Egba, soon after they were established at Abeokuta, to start on a war of conquest and expansion at the expense of their weaker neighbours. To the east and south-east they were checked by the combined forces of Ijebu-Remo towns. To the west, their expansion began at first by a process of peaceful infiltration into the lands of friendly Egbado towns. In return, they offered the inhabitants of these towns (Ibara, Ishaga and Ilewo) safe refuge in Abeokuta during succeeding Dahomian invasions in the latter half of the nineteenth century. The rest of the Egbado people, as well as the Ibarapa to the north and the Awori to the south, were subdued by armed force and many of their towns were destroyed between 1832 and 1870.

Pushing out in all directions, the Egbas succeeded in creating for themselves a new living space, which has become the present-day Egba Division of Abeokuta Province. Behind the movements of the Egba armies followed their farmers, peacefully but effectively occupying the lands of their conquered neighbours, and spreading back as far as possible into their former territory. The hunter-group was in the vanguard of this radial movement from the base at Abeokuta, but was closely followed by tillers of the soil. As the distance from Abeokuta increased, it became more and more difficult for these people to return to the town at the end of each day's work. They therefore built fairly permanent structures to house themselves and their families in the new lands, and, unless there were rumours of war or when the important yearly festivals came round, they spent most of their time in their new rural settlements.

[8] The founding of the town of Ibadan is usually dated to c. 1813 when Lagelu, a soldier from Ile-Ife, and his followers moved into the area (Adediran, 1960; Akinyele, 1959). However, Biobaku writes that Ibadan was formerly an Egba town and that c. 1829, after the near complete destruction of all the Egba towns following the Owu war of 1821, Ibadan was populated by a large number of soldiers from the Ife, Oyo, and Ijebu kingdoms (Biobaku, 1957:14; Mabogunje, 1962b:56). Abeokuta was founded in 1830 as a town for the refugees from the vanquished towns of the old Egba federation (Biobaku, 1957).

Thus, from the chaos of the early nineteenth century a new Egba landscape emerged. It was not a landscape of small towns with extensive farmlands around them, but one made up of a single large town surrounded by a whole litter of small, insignificant villages and hamlets, with populations on the average of less than 200 each (Mabogunje, 1959:72).

With the cessation of warfare around the turn of the twentieth century, other developments led to the further establishment of permanent rural settlements in a number of Yoruba areas. Men, part of whose time had been consumed in wartime activities, were able to return to their crafts or to their farms. From the beginning of the century to the present day, the increased emphasis on export crop agriculture, the expansion of the internal market for agricultural products (the country of Nigeria rather than the Yoruba towns constituting the market), the decline in the importance of traditional crafts under the influx of imported and locally machine-manufactured goods, and the relative paucity of non-agricultural employment opportunities for unskilled workers, meant that most men looked to farming as their best or only means of securing a cash income. Whereas men had previously lived in the towns and worked the farms, many of them, spurred in part by colonial governmental pressure and the promise of increased economic gains, moved into the farmlands in order to devote more attention to the cultivation of the land.[9] They took with them some members of their families and settled in communities whose populations numbered in the hundreds.[10] In some cases, though not in all, the distance between the farmlands and town prompted the growth of these permanent rural communities.

> The term village is applied to these new or expanded settlements in order to distinguish them from the smaller, dispersed hamlets (Aba) which are occupied by farmers who still commute between the towns and the farms, and which have no political autonomy. Even villages are not entirely autonomous of the towns and many of the people in them still refer to themselves as members of the towns in which their original family compounds are located. But these are permanent communities whose members only return to their home towns for major religious festivals or other important events involving their families or close associates. A village has a headman, termed the *Olori* or the *Bale*, who may be ultimately responsible to a town chief but who, along with elders representing the various compounds which make up the village, is responsible for local affairs. However, villages do not have the full roster of administrative officials found in the small towns from which they are often physically indistinguishable; they do not have the economic diversification characteristic of towns, nor do they hold daily markets (Marshall, 1963).

---

[9] The farm villages under discussion here are not to be confused with the "farm settlements" established and financed by the Western Regional Government.

[10] The movement of men and their families into the farms has had interesting repercussions. Often a man will have only his Iyawo (the junior most wife) and her pre-school age children with him in the farm. The other wives and older children would reside in the town. Thus it is that some Yoruba towns, such as Iwo, have large populations but are composed mostly of women and children (Mabogunje, 1963).

PRESENT-DAY URBAN CENTERS

While some people have left the towns for the farmlands, others have moved from the less developed towns to those in which the opportunities associated with modernization are greatest. Young men from the small towns seek employment in Lagos, Ibadan, Abeokuta, and any other large town which promises more job opportunities than those available in their home towns. Young men from the erstwhile metropolitan centers such as Ọyọ and large towns such as Iwo seek employment and/or training in other towns which are being more rapidly developed.

As a result of the differential modernization of Yoruba towns it seems to be increasingly necessary to draw a distinction between those towns which were traditional urban centers and those which, in addition to being traditional towns, have become more Westernized urban areas. In the Western Region, Ibadan clearly stands out as a town in which the characteristics of modern urbanism are fast being added to traditional urban features. Side by side with those traditional crafts still being practiced are a number of modern crafts and small-scale industrial enterprises. The markets, while basically traditional in organization, are being modernized, and juxtaposed to them are the modern commercial firms. In Ibadan, more than in any other town in the Region, modern governmental machineries have replaced entirely or absorbed almost completely the traditional governmental organs: this has happened despite the fact that traditional chiefs remain very important in many spheres of life. Furthermore, alongside the traditional chieftaincies are numerous others, the creation of which reflects the general tendency to bestow titles on persons who do not hold traditional offices but who, because of their contributions to modern Nigeria, should be honored with the regalia and prerogatives of royalty.

For the most part, traditional Yoruba towns were ethnically homogeneous (Lloyd, 1953b). In a given town, not only were there few non-Yoruba in the population but there were also relatively small numbers of Yoruba who came from a sub-group other than the dominant one in the kingdom.[11] Today, some Yoruba towns have become cosmopolitan centers. Again, the most obvious example is Ibadan whose cosmopolitan character, it should be pointed out, cannot be accounted for simply in terms of its origin as a refugee town. In terms of ethnic composition, the old sections of the town contrast sharply with the sections which grew up during and after World War II (Adediran, 1960; Mabogunje, 1962b). Every dialect of the Yoruba language and virtually every other language spoken in Nigeria can be heard in the streets of Ibadan, their speakers having come to the city in search of the opportunities thought to lie in the governmental center and commercial hub of Western Nigeria.

---

[11] This latter statement would not apply to the refugee centers of the nineteenth century.

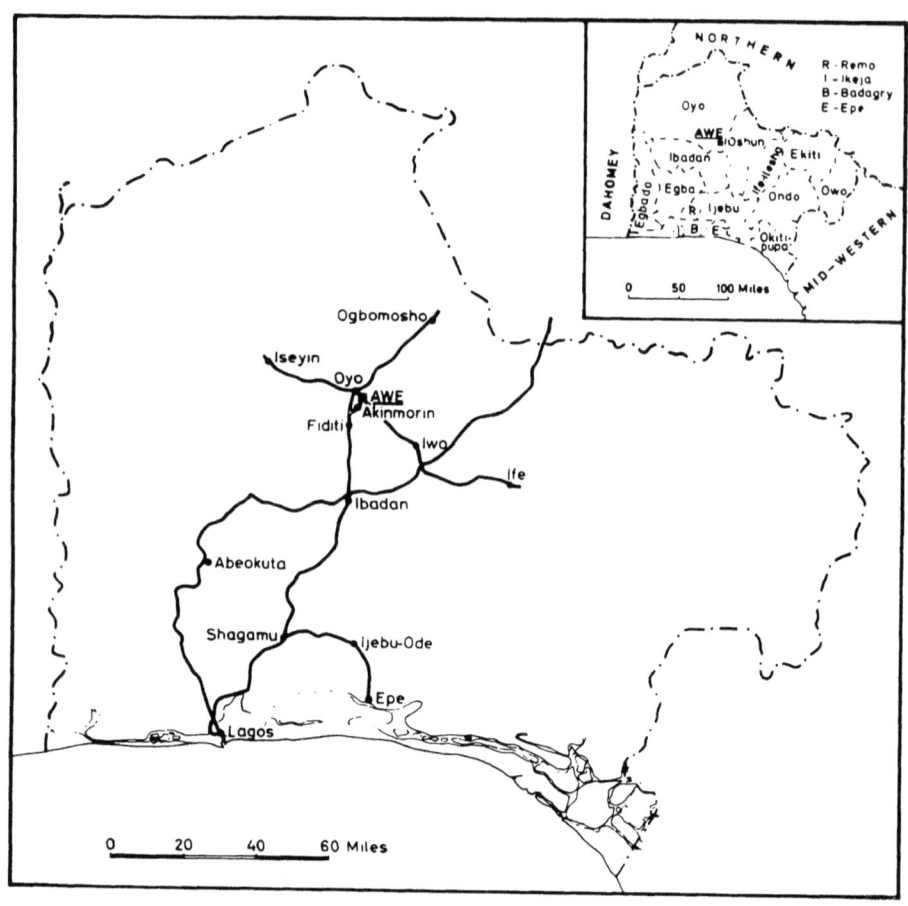

Fig. 4a. Map locating the town of Awe in Western Nigeria, 1964.

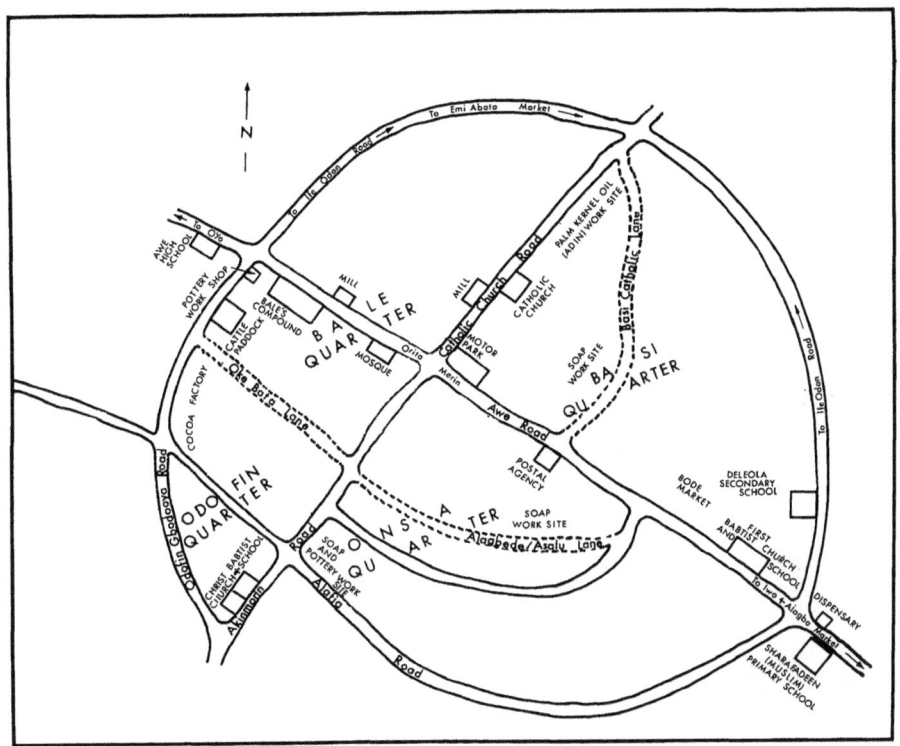

Fig. 4b. Outline map of the town of Awe (1968).

It may well be that students of Nigerian urbanism will find it appropriate to group Ibadan, a few other traditional Yoruba towns, and some large centers in the other regions, as the *cities* of Nigeria in recognition of the characteristically modern, more Western-type features which distinguish them from traditional Yoruba towns.

The Town of Awe

The town which served as a base from which my field work was conducted is situated about one and one-half miles east of Oyo, 20 miles west of Iwo, 33 miles north of Ibadan, and 36 miles south of Ogbomosho. It sits astride the major trunk road which links Oyo and Iwo.

There is no detailed history of Awe in print. However, there is a list of the Bales who have ruled the town and a few brief comments on the reigns of some of them contained in a history, written in Yoruba, of Oyo and some surrounding towns (S. Ojo). The brief comments contained in this "king list" are taken from oral tradition and they are substantially the same as those given me by residents of Awe.

Awe is said to have been founded by one Ladun who came from Ile-Ife. Ladun is reported to have settled first in the town of Olaromi, some three miles from the present site of Awe. When Ladun moved from Olaromi, he stopped first at the base of an Aruwewe tree, situated in what is now the Odofin quarter of Awe, around which tree the town grew and from which it takes it name. While he was at Olaromi, Ladun fathered a son whom he named Laro after the town in which the child was born. Laro is said to have succeeded his father as ruler of Awe.

It is not certain exactly when Awe was founded. According to the Rev. D. Olaopa, who has spent many years collecting the history of the town, Awe was one of the Egba Agura (Gbagura) towns founded, according to Biobaku (1957:3), in the thirteenth or fourteenth century A.D. Some writers (Crowder, 1962:48), it will be recalled, date the founding of the old kingdom of Oyo to this same period. The oral histories recorded by the Rev. Olaopa concur in the view that at the time the Oyo population was migrating from Ile-Ife, the people who settled at Awe were moving into the forest areas to the south (personal communication).

In any case, the names of the Bales who would have ruled Awe between the fourteenth and eighteenth centuries are not preserved in the oral history. The Bale mentioned after Ladun and Laro is Ladokun, the first Bale whose dates can be given with some degree of accuracy. Ladokun, though not regarded as the founder of the town, is sometimes said to be the first Bale since it was he who built the town wall circa 1781 (D. Olaopa, personal communication).

When the Fulani invaded Oyo Ile c. 1837, the Oyo population moved south into an area very near Awe and there they founded a new capital at Ago-Oja. The story as told in the Awe tradition runs thus:

During the reign of Ladokun, one Oja came with a group of followers to the town of Awe. The Bale of Awe proved very hospitable to his guests, going so far as to give Oja a farm next to his son. Afterwards, however, ill-feelings grew up between the two men because whenever there was a theft in the town, it was said that the "strangers" who came with Oja were guilty of the crime. Oja and his followers left the town and settled in a place they termed Ago-Oja. This land is said to have been part of that belonging to Awe.

During the reign of Mofile, Ladokun's successor, Atiba, son of the Alafin Abiodum, arrived at Ago-Oja and, against the advice of the Bale of Awe, was given permission by Oja to settle on this site. It was during the reign of Gbebi that Ago-Oja became the site of the Yoruba capital and its name changed to Oyo (S. Ojo). After the establishment of the Afin (palace of the Alafin) at Oyo, the former Ebga town of Awe, like other small towns surrounding the new capital, became in effect a vassal town of Oyo.[12]

TABLE I

RULERS OF AWE*

Ladun	?	Aiyeleru	1876-1881
Laro	?	Laniba I	1881-1908
Ladokun	c. 1781	Abiba	1908-1909
Mofile	1810-1821	Oyatolu	1909-1931
Bioku	1821-1824	Lawore	1931-1947
Akinoso	1824-1828	Adeoye	1948-1956
Gbebi	1828-1870	Laniba II	1956-
Lagbinyan	1870-1876		

*Supplied by the Rev. D. Olaopa and corroborated by the present Bale.

The town of Awe is divided into four quarters. Each quarter is headed by a chief from whose title the quarter takes its name. All chiefs of the town are ranked, the other three quarter chiefs being next to the Bale.

[12] There are two references to Awe in Johnson's *History of the Yorubas*. In discussing the final days of the reign of the Alafin Adelu (1858–1876), Johnson mentions that the Crown Prince, impatient to ascend the throne, was rumored to have poisoned his father: "... it was also said that his accomplice and agent was the King's favourite wife Alayoayo. Among all the denizens of the royal harem she was the only one who could be termed Queen, for she had the whole village of Awe and half the city of Oyo serving her ..." (1921:396).
Johnson, writing about conditions in the late nineteenth century, reports that "Oyo was connected with the village of Awe by a wall. This outer wall was called 'Odi Amola,' or by some, 'Odi Amonu.' The former term indicates 'The Wall of Safety,' used by those to whom it has proved a source of safety and the latter term, 'The Wall of Loss,' used by those to whom it has proved unavailing for security" (1921:455).

The Bale's quarter comprises the northwest section of the town and part of the southwest section. The Oyo-Iwo road divides the town roughly into two north-south halves and runs through the Bale's quarter. There are approximately 30 compounds in the quarter. The chief who ranks second to the Bale is the *Onsa*, whose quarter is in the southeast part of the town. There are about 30 compounds in this section. The third ranking chief is the *Basi*, head of the largest quarter in the town; nearly all of the northern part of the town comprises this quarter. It also contains about 30 compounds. The *Odofin*, head of that section of town in which Ladun first settled, is the fourth ranking chief in the town. Because this is the oldest quarter in the town, it has a semi-autonomous character unequalled by the other quarters. The list of chieftaincies within this section almost parallels those for the town itself; nonetheless, Oke Odofin is an integral part of Awe. There are about 20 compounds at Oke Odofin.

In addition to advising the Bale when any decisions concerning the town must be made, the quarter chiefs are responsible for government within their wards. If there is a minor dispute among the people of different compounds, it would be settled by the quarter chiefs in conjunction with other chiefs who live in their sections and with the heads (Bale) of the compounds concerned. If ever there is a community work project ot be undertaken, the quarter chiefs notify the Bales who are responsible for mobilizing all the able men of their compounds.

There are a number of titled officials resident in each quarter. Some of these are town chiefs, i.e., officials who are selected, presented directly to the Bale, and installed by him without his having to consult one of his quarter chiefs, and some are chiefs who are essentially officials of the quarter rather than of the town. Traditionally, each chief had stipulated duties to perform within the town or within the quarter but today many of these duties are no longer necessary to the running of the town. All the town chiefs, including the quarter chiefs, are members of the Awe Local Council, the organ which, in the modern Nigerian administrative network, is responsible for local government. Seven of the chiefs sit as judges in the Customary Court.

In all cases where a title rests within a particular compound (see Table 2), there are usually three "family lines," comprising the house, among which the title circulates (see Chapter V). Where the title is open to any compound within the town, it is filled by selection from among the candidates by the Bale and his chiefs. Today these "chiefs-at-large," as it were, are chosen from among men who have made important contributions to the town. Often the chiefs are wealthy merchants whose generosity to the town is rewarded with a title.

It should be noted that not all the chiefs need to be year-round residents of the town. At least three of the chiefs, the now-deceased *Balogun*, the *Ekerin*, and the *Aro*, resided part of the time in Lagos. They are, however,

TABLE 2

AWẸ TOWN CHIEFS

Title	Name	Compound (from which chosen)
Balẹ (Laniba II)	S. Afolabi	Ile Balẹ
Onṣa	K. O. Oyeremi	Ile Onṣa
Basi	O. Akimwumi	Ile Basi
Ọdọfin	S. Afoda	Ile Ọdọfin
Aṣipa	Okikiade Adeyele	Ile Bigun
Ekẹrin	S. Adebiyi	Ile Jẹgẹdẹloba*
Agba-Akin	J. Akinrinade	Ile Iyalọja
Bantun	Oni	Ile Lalemi
Seriki	D. Omosanya	Ile Alagba
Baraniṣe (Baniṣe)	S. Adejinle	Ile Komu
Jagun	Atoyebi	Ile Jagun
Jagun Ọdọfin	Idowu Odelana	Ile Jagun (Oke Ọdọfin)
Aṣaju	J. Ọjẹmuyiwa	Ile Basi
Ejẹmu	D. Ogunmọla	Ile Ejẹmu
Maiyedun	O. Oguniyi	Ile Alagbẹdẹ*
Aro	J. A. Ọdẹku	Ile Adunbiẹyẹ
Ọtun	D. Ọlaọpa	Ile Alaja*
Balogun	J. Ajao (deceased 1962)	Ile Fọkutu*

*Title not confined to a particular compound. The list of chieftaincies in the order of their rank was supplied by the Balẹ.

TABLE 3

CUSTOMARY COURT JUDGES

Balẹ (President of the Court)	Ọdọfin
Onṣa	Ekẹrin
Basi	Jagun

"sons of Awẹ" and their family compounds are located in the town. These men make regular visits to the town and they and their families exercise their political rights within the town.[13]

There is another point which must be made regarding the chieftaincies. Even though the official rank order of chiefs is the one given by the Balẹ, this does not necessarily represent the relative influence of a chief in town affairs.

---

[13] This pattern of residence outside of but maintenance of ties with the home town is widespread throughout the Western Region. It developed out of the fact, discussed earlier in this chapter, that educational, business, and employment opportunities are better in certain of the large cities and men, of necessity, turn to these for work.

The late Chief J. A. Ajao, Balogun of Awe̱ and *O̱tun* of Oyo, was said to be the most influential man of the town. Because he was a wealthy entrepreneur who was exceedingly generous to the town and its citizens (he not only donated money to most of the town projects but directly or indirectly provided employment for many of its sons and daughters), and who had considerable influence with the business men and politicians of the Region, it was to him that the chiefs turned for counsel on and support of any town project. Apparently, he himself did not often initiate policy but whenever the men whose opinions he respected decided on a course of action which would benefit the town, Chief Ajao was one of their staunchest supporters and benefactors. Chief S. A. Adebiyi, as Chairman of the Town Council, is also a man of considerable influence within the town. Another man of great authority is Mr. S. A. Akinabi who does not hold a traditional chieftaincy title but who is referred to as the *Alaga* or "Chairman" of the town. Mr. Akinabi was for years the head of the Awe̱ branch of the Action Group, the dominant political party in the Western Region. During the 1961 political "crisis" in the Western Region, he and many others gave their support to Chief Akintola, the Regional Premier, and they later left the Action Group for the United Peoples Party founded by the then-suspended Premier.

There are other chiefs, business men, and younger educated men of the town who are greatly respected by the people of Awe̱, and who share in the government of the town. Most of them are members of the Town Council and as such have a voice in town affairs.

In fact, the processes of decision-making and policy execution contain acknowledgment of multiple circles of influence and acceptance of zones of power. The high-ranking chiefs, on certain matters, defer to lower-ranking ones; and in some instances all the chiefs may defer to the younger, Western-educated men (some of whom are government employees, business men, or politicians). On the other hand, men without titles always give to the chiefs their due respect. In Awe̱, as in most Yoruba towns, the progress (*ilosiwaju*) of the town is foremost in the consideration of the officials. Men with ability, provided they are not arrogant, are always given the opportunity to make their maximum contribution to the governing of the town.

The population of Awe̱ as given in the 1952 census was 5,400. This figure is misleading in some respects and accurate in another. The number of people actually residing in Awe̱ town throughout the year would be about three or four thousand. However, a number of persons who regard themselves as Awe̱ residents spend much of the year in the hamlets (*aba*) surrounding the town. Some are resident in the village of Kiyeseni, an off-shoot of Awe̱ town. The largest group of persons who regard themselves as "Awe̱ residents" but who return to the town only for major holidays are the "sons abroad" found in Lagos, Ibadan, Ogbomosho, Ilorin, Kano, and other places throughout the country. During the April 1962 census, the results of which were subsequently declared invalid by the Federal Government, thousands of "sons abroad" returned to Awe for the count.[14]

Representatives from Awe communities in each major town where Awe people are found have seats on the Awe Town Council. They attend the meetings and they and their electors give financial support to the town's projects. Whenever there is a celebration, a major political rally, or a crisis, the "sons abroad" come in large numbers to the town.

Living in Awe, one often gets the impression that it is a town composed of women, young children, some unmarried young women, very few unmarried young men, a small number of married men (such as craftsmen and merchants) whose occupations keep them in the town, and old men who no longer work. The young men and some young women are away: in school or working in various jobs. The married men who are farmers are in the farms for days or weeks at a time. Other married men are in Lagos, Ibadan, or some other city, often times leaving their wives (or some of them) in Awe.

Over one-third of the people in Awe are Muslims; most of the others are at least nominal Christians. There are two Baptist churches, one Catholic church, and one mosque in the town. Awe has four primary schools: two Baptist, one Catholic, and one Muslim; two secondary modern schools,[15] one of which is Catholic; and one secondary school for boys (Awe High School). A maternity clinic and dispensary is located at the northeast edge of the town.

This then is a skeletal picture of the place in which much of the data on women's activities and Yoruba family life was gathered. The economic organization of the town, the roles of women within the market complex, and their positions within their kin groups will be discussed in succeeding chapters.

---

[14] Awe is not unique among Yoruba towns with respect to the problem of accurately assessing the size of its population. One of the major difficulties is in deciding who should be counted where. The return of "sons abroad" obviously distorts the population distribution for the country: small towns mushroom in size; the degree of population movement to cities is obscured by the fact that some people move out for the census; the growth of villages, while obvious from aerial photographs, is obscured because their populations are in the towns when the census-takers arrive.

[15] The curriculum of secondary modern schools differs from that of secondary grammar schools, the latter offering academic courses preparatory for the school certificate while the former offer a more general education for students who do not qualify for or who are financially unable to attend secondary school.

II

DIVISION OF LABOR BY SEX IN YORUBA SOCIETY

A GROSS statement of the division of labor by sex in small Yoruba towns would class men as agriculturalists and women as traders. This is roughly accurate even though some men are employed in various craft productions, in trade, as well as in other non-agricultural pursuits, and some women are wage earners outside the distributive sphere of the economy. It is a fact that a very high proportion of Yoruba men are independent farmers or engaged as laborers in some phase of agriculture. In the case of women, the general statement is even more accurate for virtually all women are traders or employed at some point in the distributive network.

Many writers have pointed out that traditionally most men were cultivators and most women were traders in Yorubaland. The general practice is to acknowledge this as a given fact and to go on to a discussion of the mechanics of one or more of the occupations engaged in by men or women (Johnson, 1921:117, 123-25; Talbot, 1936, Vol. III, 904; Forde, 1951:6-10). However, there has been at least one attempt to account for this division of labor. Writing concerning trade and markets in the present-day rural areas of Yorubaland, Hodder (1962:110), following Pedler (1955),[1] suggests that "this

---

[1] Taking note of the large number of women in the distributive sphere of the economy of Eastern Nigeria, Pedler states: "It is said that this is the legacy of conditions which obtained in that part of Nigeria until about fifty years ago, for the men were in danger if they strayed beyond the protection of their village comrades, but the custom of the country did not permit attacks upon women. Be that as it may, the female sex now does most of the marketing" (1955:139).

One wonders whether this is in fact what obtained in the East, for Ottenberg whose field work was conducted among one of the Ibo groups, says of women: "Before the establishment of the British Government Station in Afikpo in 1902, a woman was literally in a position of physical and economic dependence on her husband. She could go neither to farm nor to market without an armed escort, for slave-raiding and warfare between village groups made travel outside a person's own village perilous in the extreme. The men's crop, yams, comprised a larger proportion of the diet than now, and the economy was one of meager subsistence, with a small margin of surplus. Though markets existed, the scale of trade was small and restricted to the cluster of friendly villages which they served" (1962:214).

Apparently, neither women nor men were free from the danger of attacks outside their villages during the period of the slave trade; and, according to other statements by Ottenberg, it seems that the large number of Eastern Nigerian women engaged in present-day trade activities is attributable to the post-nineteenth century expansion of the exchange economy.

female predominance in rural marketing may date back to conditions of internal insecurity in which it was unsafe for men to move away from their farms, while women enjoyed relative immunity from attacks." Thus, Hodder proposes that the large-scale involvement of women in trade may, in part, be attributed to their relative ease of movement outside the areas in which they lived during the period of "internal insecurity."

The present chapter seeks to show that this interpretation cannot be supported by the facts of Yoruba history as it is known to date. Available evidence suggests that women have been involved in the distribution of goods for as long as the Yoruba have lived in urban areas, and that the historical precedent for present-day trade by women can be found in their participation in the markets *within the towns in which they resided*; for whereas some women did engage in inter-urban trade, by far the majority traded in their local town markets.

The conditions of insecurity which prevailed during the nineteenth century tended to intensify an already existing pattern of sexual division of labor. Agricultural production and defense against enemies were mainly carried on *outside* the town walls in actual or potential farming areas which were under periodic threat of attack. In a sense, farming *could not* be left to other than those who also had the responsibility of defending the society against attack by hostile groups. It is not surprising therefore that it was the males in Yoruba society who undertook both these tasks for, as Service (1962:34-50) and others before him have argued, owing to certain physiological facts, men are more suited to defense than are women.[2] Short of remaining safe within the town walls during the period of the civil wars, women were found in the relatively safe living areas in the farmlands. When they undertook trade expeditions, they did not usually travel in small numbers; rather they joined the caravans made up of *men and women*, for almost no one was "immune to attack" by marauders and kidnappers.

DIVISION OF LABOR IN YORUBALAND BEFORE THE CIVIL WARS

It has been pointed out that one of the most significant features of pre-civil war Yoruba society is that its basic settlements were urban com-

---

[2] No society has every left defensive arrangements entirely in the hands of women, though as in Dahomey, one may find female troops. Examination of instances where women did constitute a large part of the defense force of a particular society may well reveal that for some reason the number of available men had seriously declined. Slave raids and war which deplete the male population could lead to the militarization of women. Such may well have been the case in Dahomey. When women form a more or less permanent fighting force, it is to be expected that they would have to forfeit their right to bear and raise children for this would seriously impair their effectiveness as a defense unit. Of the female troops of Dahomey, it was said: "The Dahomy Amazons are said to have a perfect passion for the service, notwithstanding they are bound to perpetual celibacy and chastity, under the penalty of death" (Bowen, 1857:149)

munities, despite the fact that the Yoruba were an agricultural people. The picture of traditional Yoruba towns which emerges from the literature (Johnson, 1921:90-93, 117-125; Bascom, 1955) is one of more or less self-sufficient economic entities, each based on internal economic specialization. The population of each town consisted of farmers, food processors, craftsmen, and non-producing traders. Nonetheless, there were commercial links between the towns of each kingdom and certain frontier towns served as trade links between the different kingdoms.

Each town had at least one market place where goods were exchanged among the various producers.[3] These were daily markets held in the morning and again in the evening:

> ... the principal market of the town is always in the centre of the town and in front of the house of the chief ruler. This rule is without an exception and hence the term *Oloja* (one having a market) is used as a generic term or title of all chief rulers of towns be he a King or a Bale.

Minor chiefs also have markets in front of their houses. Market squares as a rule mark out the frontage of a chief or a distinguished man... The larger the town, the larger the principal market to which everyone resorts for morning and evening marketings and [which] is the general rendesvous of the town on every national or municipal occasion. It is planted all over with shady trees for sellers and loungers of an evening. The central market also contains the principal mosque of the town, and the fetish temple of the chief ruler, if he be a pagan (Johnson, 1921:91).

In addition to the daily markets, certain towns held periodic markets, referred to as "fairs" by Johnson, to which people from neighboring towns and farm hamlets came to trade. Apparently, Oyo-Ile, ancient center of the Yoruba kingdom, held a "five-day" market, for Richard Lander (1833:170) mentions that "twice a week" the main market at Oyo was "larger and better attended than on other days."[4] A number of frontier towns were famous centers whose periodic markets were attended by trade caravans from many parts of Yorubaland. Perhaps the best known of these is Apomu, a town in the Ife kingdom, where "the Oyos, Ifes, Owus, and Ijebus met for trade" (Johnson, 1921:188-89).

---

[3] In this context, "exchange" refers to the fact that goods "changed hands." Although there were market places in traditional Yorubaland, the evidence is not conclusive as to whether the *exchange principle* (Polanyi, et al., 1957) served as the integrative mechanism for the economy. It has been suggested by T. K. Hopkins (personal communication) that the establishment of market places near chiefs' residences and the existence of craftsmen associated with some chiefs' compounds could be an indication that additional data on the traditional economy would reveal that a mechanism other than *exchange* served to integrate the economy.

[4] Yoruba periodic markets are held "every fifth day" or "every ninth day." In reckoning the intervals at which markets are held, the counting includes both the day on which the market falls *and* the subsequent market day. Thus, if a five-day market is held on Monday, the subsequent market day is Friday. Therefore, in any eight-day period, there would be two five-day markets.

Richard and John Lander visited Oyo-Ile (referred to as Katunga) in May, 1830. Of the markets is written:

Most of the men in any Yoruba town were farmers. A large number of crafts (among them weaving, iron-smelting, smithing, tanning and leather-working, carving, drumming, and barbering) were practiced by men who did not engage in farming or for whom farming was only a part-time occupation. Much of the trade between towns was carried on by men (Johnson, 1921: 117). In the inland areas, hunting, and in the riverine areas, fishing, was also done by men.

Prior to the civil war period of the nineteenth century, war was not a profession as such among the Yoruba (Johnson, 1921:117). It was customary for the Alafin, upon ascendence to the throne, to "name his enemy" whereupon the *Kakanfo* (the "field marshall")[5] and a group of soldiers, selected from along all able-bodied men, marched out to battle. Thereafter, he and his men went out to fight every other year (Johnson, 1921:131-37).

> A market is held daily in different parts of Katunga, but twice a week it is much larger and better attended than on either of the other days. I visited one of the latter this morning, which is styled the 'Queen's market'; but as it is shifted to another place towards evening, it is then called the 'King's market.' The sellers were by far more numerous than the buyers; and, on the whole, the articles exposed for sale by no means realized the expectations we had formed of them. Among them we observed three or four different kinds of corn; beans, pease, and vegetables in abundance; the mi-cadania butter, Ground or Guinea-nuts; country cotton cloths, indigo, red clay, salt, and different varieties of pepper; besides trona, snuff and tobacco, knives, barbs, hooks, and needles, the latter of the rudest native manufacture. There were also finger-rings of tin and lead; and iron bracelets and armlets; old shells, old bones, and other venerable things, which European antiquaries would gaze on with rapture; besides native soap, little cakes of cheese and butter; an English common blue plate, a great variety of beads both of native and European manufacture; among the former of which we recognized the famous *Agra* bead, which at Cape Coast Castle, Accra, and other places, is sold for its weight in gold, and which has vainly been attempted to be imitated by the Italians and our own countrymen. Provisions also were offered for sale in abundance; and besides beef and mutton, which were made up into little round balls, weighing about an ounce and three-quarters each, and presented not the most delicate and tempting appearance, we observed an immense quantity of rats, mice, and lizards, dressed and undressed, all having their skins on, and arranged in rows.
> I met with and purchased a very curious and singular kind of stone in the market. The natives informed us that it was dug from the earth, in a country called *Iffie*, which is stated to be "four moons' journey from Katunga, where, according to their tradition their first parents were created, and from which all Africa has been peopled. . . . [the stone] consists of a variety of little transparent stones, white, green, and every shade of blue, all imbedded in a species of clayey earth, resembling rough mosaic work (1833, Vol. I:170-71).

In addition to this description, the Landers' journal contains descriptions of and references to markets in various other Yoruba towns (1833, Vol. I:86, 121, 124, 136-37, 142, 159-61, 185, 188).

On an exploratory archeological survey of parts of Oyo-Ile, Frank Willett visited the site of the King's market of which he reports: "The King's market is notable as being scarcely overgrown at all; merely a light grass cover is found. The deposits here have eroded extensively because it is very close to the foot of the hills and the rainwater rushing from the hills has eroded the upper deposits. A number of well shafts were dug in this area to discover whether there was any deposit of pottery; we found that the site was practically barren" (1960:68).

[5]"The title given in full is Are-Ona-Kakanfo. It is a title akin to a field marshal, and is conferred upon the greatest soldier and tactician of the day" (Johnson, 1921:74).

War, then, was for spoils and to keep their hands in, and not for captives; the victors rarely pursued the vanquished; those who concealed themselves behind heaps of rubbish, or in any hiding place in the town or in the fields were quite safe. When a town was taken the shade trees about the principal market . . . are cut down as a sign of conquest. Slave raiding and the traffic in human beings did not then exist. Long sieges were unknown, for whether victorious or defeated, the presence of the Kakanfo or his corpse was expected home within sixty days (Johnson, 1921:131).

It was the practice for each man to *return to his farm plot* after a warring expedition "and except on an occasion of importance, as when the King's messengers are to be received, even the Balẽ and the Balogun could not be found at home during the busy seasons" (Johnson, 1921:132).

Women in the Yoruba towns were engaged in craft productions, in the processing of foodstuffs, and in trade. Johnson notes:

It is specially the province of women advanced in age to seed cotton and spin thread. . . . These operations being an occupation of a sedentary nature, and more suitable for old women are performed by them leisurely all day. *Reels of spun thread are sold to dyers.*

Aged women who reside in the farms also employ their time in shelling the kernels from the palm nuts, and also tending poultry, goats, and sheep *for the market.*

Dyeing is done by women. *They buy a quantity of the yarn,* bleach and dye them in various colours, *and sell them to the weavers,* male and female. . . . *Women are equally with men engaged in trading and weaving...*

Palm oil making and nut oil making from the kernels of the palm nuts, as well as shea-butter from the shea fruit are exclusively female industires.

Beer-brewing from guinea corn or maize is also done by women. . . .

A large class is engaged in preparing articles of food. They are purveyors of cooked food, keepers of refreshment stalls and other branches of dietary for the market, especially to accomodate working men and caravans.

The manufacture of beads from the hard shells of palm nuts, or from the cocoa nut shells, is an important female industry. . . .

Pottery is also a female industry. Men may sometimes be seen assisting to dig up the clay and to perform some rough initial work, but as a rule the whole industry is in the hands of women. The drying, pulverising, sifting, mixing and moulding, are all done by women and girls.

Large pots for brewing beer, and for setting indigo dyes, and cooking Eko (the morning gruel) for sale are turned out with marvellous skill. Cooking utensils, dishes, water pots, etc., are also made for the markets...

Every woman whatever her trade may be, is expected to keep a few chickens and a goat or two from which she derives small income for housekeeping and general "pin money." The rearing of poultry then must be reckoned among female occupations.

Hair dressing may also be mentioned among female occupations. . . .

On the whole, the women seem to be far more industrious than the men, for whereas the men always contrive to have leisure hours and off days from work, the women seem to have none. Boys and young men certainly have more idle hours than the girls. The care of the children also devolves almost entirely upon their mother, an inevitable result of polygamy (Johnson, 1921:1235; all emphases mine.)

These brief references to the activities of men and women serve to support the claim that the traditional Yoruba settlement was one in which there was a high degree of specialization and one in which a continuous exchange of goods and services took place.[6] Most of the trade was carried on in the market places and cowry shells were the currency used in many of the transactions.

In order to understand the part played by women in the distribution of goods, it is necessary to say something about local and "long distance" trade in early Yoruba society. Local trade was carried on daily in the market places within the towns. Periodically traders came from various directions to exchange goods from their different areas among themselves as well as to sell to and buy from local people. At the time of such "fairs" (periodic markets), what were essentially two levels of trade activity would coalesce. That is, the "long distance" trade and the local trade would take place in the same town. It is likely that the local people at this time brought out their products in larger quantities than usual, hoping to sell to the incoming traders, although local trade would certainly be subservient to the other type of trade which was undoubtedly more lucrative than the day-to-day local exchange. Some persons who produced their items daily—for example women who sold cooked foods— would probably look forward to the periodic influx of traders as a time when the volume of their trade would be much increased.

At the outset of this chapter, it was proposed that the historical precedent for trade by women could be found in an examination of their role in *local* trade in traditional Yoruba society. A close examination of the list of female occupations set down by Johnson (1921) substantiates the claim that women were engaged in activities which brought them into the daily local markets. Although Johnson does not explicitly state that most of the traders in the local markets were women, he does imply that this was so. In referring to the upkeep of the towns, he notes: ". . . every compound looks after its own frontage and surroundings, in the market place every seller sweeps the space around *her* stall" (1921:92, emphasis mine).

While women did carry out most of their trade activities in the markets within the towns, there is evidence that they also went out into the farming areas to purchase farm products which they re-sold in their natural state or which they processed for sale in the towns. Furthermore, although most women spent their time in the towns, some of them did work at least part of the time in the hamlets outside the towns. According to Johnson (1921:103, 118) some women and children assisted in the harvesting of crops.

---

[6] Bascom (1955:450) has noted that: "Trade was based on specialization within the city rather than the city being based upon trade growing out of extensive regional or tribal specialization."

Some women as well as men were engaged in inter-urban trade. A number of visitors to Yorubaland during the nineteenth century reported that women were among the caravans which traded between towns, and there is no reason to suppose that this was not a well-established practice.[7] Many women probably traded in the periodic markets of a nearby major town, and a smaller percentage of them travelled with the caravans that undertook longer expeditions.

To point out that women had as one of their roles that of distributor is not to account for the nature of the sexual division of labor in Yoruba society. The question as to why the division of labor took the form it did can be posed in two ways: we can ask why the distributive tasks were mostly in the hands of women or why the job of cultivating fell to men.

Given the Yoruba pattern of settlement in compact, walled towns[8] with outlying farmlands, it is not surprising that men were the cultivators. The farming areas were located from three to 15 miles outside the town walls whereas the permanent dwellings were situated inside the town walls. Once the pattern of walled towns with surrounding farmlands came into general existence, it would seem that women, whose job it is in all societies to see after certain household chores and to care for their children, could not easily attend to these tasks and work on the farms which were usually miles away from the main dwelling. Furthermore, towns are walled for defensive purposes, and it may be assumed that even before the war years of the nineteenth century, the greater threat to safety lay outside the towns.[9] Since the

---

[7] Before the war years, roads leading from one town to another were kept in good repair to allow ease of movement at times of important festivals as well as on other occasions, and caravan routes transversed the country, allowing the movement of trade expeditions (Johnson 1921:90, 93).

[8] "Every town is walled, deep trenches are dug all around it outside, the more exposed to attack the more substantial the wall and for the greater security of smaller towns a bush or thicket called Igbo Ile (home forest) is kept, about half to one mile from the walls right around the town. This forms a security against a sudden cavalry attack, a safe ambush for defence, as well as hiding places in a defeat or sudden hostile eruption. The tall trees in them are sometimes used as a watch tower to observe the movements of the enemy: except in times of profound peace, it is penal to cut trees in the home forest. Highways are made through them straight to the town gate, and are always kept in excellent repair.

"Towns in the plain that are greatly exposed to sudden attacks or those that have had to stand long sieges have a second or outer wall enclosing a large area which is used for farming during a siege. This wall is called "Odi Amọla" (wall of safety), sometimes it is called "Odi Amọnu" (wall of ruin) as the wall has been to them the means of safety, or has been unavailing for its purpose" (Johnson, 1921:91).

The above statement notwithstanding, Johnson gives evidence that prior to the nineteenth century, some towns, for example Ilorin (Johnson, 1921:195), were not walled. Apparently all the metropolitan capitals were walled while some of the outlying towns were not. However, whether walled or not, all towns were compact clusters of dwellings with farmlands stretching for miles around.

[9] During the reign of the Alafin Kori, who ruled during the late fifteenth or early sixteenth century (S. Ojo), it was reported that the Ijẹsas were "proving very troublesome to their neighbors by kidnapping them in their farms, and molesting caravans to and from

distance between the farms and the towns was a matter of miles rather than a few hundred yards, women would not be exposed to the possible risks involved in farming but would be employed in the safer living areas. In times of relative peace, some women would be found in the farmlands along with their husbands, but in times of war they would be sheltered within the towns.

THE CIVIL WAR PERIOD

The beginning of the decline of the Yoruba kingdom centered at Ọyọ-Ile may be dated to the eighteenth century when the Dahomeans and the Egba declared their independence, but the disintegration of the kingdom was signalled by the rebellion of a few provincial chiefs, led by one Afọnja of Ilorin, during the reign of the Alafin Aole (c. 1805–1811). By 1820 the Fulani, with the active support of Hausa warriors who were ex-slaves and with the tacit support of Yoruba Muslims led by one Ṣolagberu, had defeated their former leader Afọnja, the Kakanfo of Yorubaland, and had established an Emirate at Ilorin. The Owu war, begun in 1821, was the first of a series of civil wars, triggered by events at Ilorin, that were waged intermittently throughout the greater part of the nineteenth century (Johnson, 1921; Biobaku, 1957; S. Ojo, n.d.; Ajayi, n.d.).

The division of labor in Yorubaland cannot be viewed as a social organizational response to the internal unrest which prevailed during the civil wars; however, the events of this period did serve to intensify the existing pattern. Ajayi (n.d.) has argued effectively that the civil wars had their origin in power politics and cannot be said to have been motivated by the slave trade. He also disclaims the assertion that there was a "general holocaust" throughout Yorubaland during the nineteenth century. It is true, nonetheless, that because of the traffic in African captives, unarmed persons did not usually risk travelling alone in hostile areas outside the towns, and that in any area under attack or threatened by attack, people were only relatively safe if they remained within the town walls.

It is important for our purposes to point out that many of the wars were fought in the farmland areas surrounding the towns. The besiegers often moved into the areas around the town while the besieged fought from stations along the town wall (Johnson, 1921:206-10, 240-41, 242-44, 266-68, 298-99, 336-54; Ajayi, n.d.:28, 30, 36, 46, 47). There are numerous instances of a town being conquered not so much by the military prowess of the enemy but by the fact that many in the population were starved to death, lacking access to cultivable land. During the Owu war (c. 1821–1826), for example, the

Apomu a frontier town where a large fair is periodically held for the exchange of goods with the Ijẹbus, and also getting frequently embroiled with the king of Ido their neighbour...." To arrest this marauding, the Alafin sent out a hunter, noted for his "deadly arrows," who stationed himself at Ẹde and "established himself as a kinglet with the title of Timi" (Johnson, 1921:156).

population was forced to retreat behind the town walls without provisions except those supplied by a small Egba town nearby. The Owu people were forced to eat a type of bean hitherto considered unfit for food. Famine raged within the walls and ultimately the town fell to the combined forces of the Ijẹbu and Ife soldiers (Johnson, 1921:206-09). Of one period during the Ijaye war (1860–1865) Johnson writes:

> ... all the farms being in the hands of the Ibadans, the distress, starvation and consequent mortality at Ijaye were indescribable. Hundreds nay thousands died in the streets from starvation, whole families perished without anyone to bury them. All the livestock had been consumed, the garden, the streets, and the yards were all planted with corn, the cornstalks were devoured when they could not wait for the corn to develop. The herb Gbọrọ, a common creeper in the streets was planted in every available place and used for food (1921:344).

The farmlands were not only pillaged and captured in order that the routers could grow food during their campaigns, they were also areas in which kidnapping took place. While the Ibadan soldiers fought at Ijaye, "the unfriendly Ijẹbus of Ode and Igbo were daily raiding the Ibadan farms. Flying columns had to be organized to protect the farmers and chase away the Ijẹbus" (Johnson, 1921:342; See Mabogunje, 1961a:260). Prior to the "Sixteen Years War" which began as a conflict between the Ekiti and Ibadan peoples c. 1878, but which came to involve nearly all the Yoruba sub-groups, the Ibadan chiefs had been engaged in a series of raids on the Egba farmlands, the main purposes being to kidnap, "to destroy foodstuffs, fire the barns, cut down standing corn, [and to] chop in pieces yam and other tuberous foodstuffs" (Johnson, 1921:416, 420-23). The Ekiti, noting the entanglements of Ibadan with its neighbors to the south, seized the opportunity to rebel against Ibadan. When the Ibadan army had left their town to fight the rebels:

> ... the Ijẹbu and Ẹgba kidnappers were not inactive at home, raiding the Ibadan farms, sometimes successfully, but sometimes repulsed, but making farming risky and unsafe until a scheme was evolved of a complete organization for home defence.
>
> There are three main points from which the attacks may be expected (a) the farms contiguous to those of the Ẹgbas; (b) the route leading to Ijẹbu Igbo; and (c) that leading to Ijẹbu Ode. Arrangements were perfected by building forts in the central point in each of these main routes, for the better protection of the farmers. Whilst the hunters were in the forests, hunting for game and on the look-out for kidnappers, the farmers could work in their farms with composure and confidence. They were instructed to hasten to the forts with their women and children at a given signal by the hunters. The men went to their farms well armed, and were ready for any emergency.
>
> The fort in the direction of the Ẹgbas was left in charge of some hunters, and a few old warriors left at home. But the Ẹgbas once surprised the fort at Itosi and carried away [many] people; some of them, however, were rescued by hunters who pursued after the kidnappers (Johnson, 1921:450).

These references to some of the civil wars are by way of impressing upon the reader the fact that during any campaign it was only within the town walls or within fortified areas of the farmlands that citizens could feel a degree of security. The arming of farmers was not an unusual practice. As one man from Awe said to me, "if you went to the farms in those days, you went prepared as if you were going to war." Given the fact that much of the warfare, kidnapping, and pillaging that took place was carried out in the farmlands, it is not surprising that those were the province of men rather than of women.

During the civil war period, most of the men in Yorubaland were engaged as soldiers or in activities associated with warfare (some were hunters whose duties included policing the farms, some were warrior-marauders), in crafts, in trade, and in farming. It should be pointed out that although farming was exclusively a male occupation,[10] in some places it was not regarded as a "noble profession" befitting a free man. During the war years, most Ibadan youth were trained to be soldiers while slaves and prisoners of war were left to cultivate the farms (Ajayi, n.d.:9-10). Johnson writes concerning the slaves taken to Ibadan:

The able-bodied men are kept and trained as soldiers, and it has become the law and custom that soldier-slaves are never sold under any circumstances; they are to remain permanently as members of the house. The fair young women are added to the harems by the great, and young men save themselves the expenses of a dowry by making wives of any that come into their hands. Any slave-woman taken as a wife becomes *ipso facto* a free woman. All the rest are sent into the farms, each to be employed in his or her own line of work. The chiefs had large farms and farm houses containing from a hundred to over a thousand souls. The men are engaged in clearing the bush, cultivating the soil, cutting palm nuts and doing other male work; the women in making palm oil, nut oil, soap, weaving mats, rearing poultry and the smaller cattle, cultivating kitchen vegetables of all kinds for the weekly markets and the fairs; older women in preparing and spinning cotton, shelling palm nuts, etc. All are engaged as "hands" in time of harvest (1921:324-25).

Apparently, in other parts of Yorubaland, the men, except for the Oba and highest ranking chiefs, worked their own farms while most of the women worked in the towns (Bowen, 1857; 1858; Mabogunje, 1959: 1961a). Around Ibadan and Abeokuta where there were fairly large farmland settlements which provided the produce to sustain the large urban populations, men worked the fields while women carried on duties which kept them in the comparatively safer living areas of the farms. In times of severe attack or siege the farmland settlements were abandoned, the populus moved to safety within the town walls.

---

[10] "For the most part, men and women have their own occupations, and it is worthy of particular remark that women never cultivate the soil as they do in Guinea" (Bowen, 1857:308).

Inside the towns, the world of the market was largely a woman's world. Nearly every type of commodity offered for sale was handled by women (Bowen, 1857:296-97; 1858:46-57). When a town was under attack, the women were busy securing the provisions that sustained the men fighting at the walls (Johnson, 1921:315); in some cases they even organized the supply of food to troops fighting miles away from home (Ajayi, n.d.:28).

As they had in the past,[11] some women undertook journeys to trade in distant towns. Men and women who engaged in long distance trade always travelled in caravans, since small groups were subject to attack and seizure. Any argument that women were the principal traders *because* they enjoyed relative freedom of movement cannot be supported by the facts. Trade caravans, whether they included women or not, were under danger of attack when travelling through hostile territories and in fact often had to have armed escort to get them safely from one place to another (Johnson, 1921:245, 248, 332, 342-44, 351, 577-83; Bowen, 1857:189-90; Ajayi, n.d.:74). One of the major results, as well as a major perpetrator of inter-group fighting, was the harrassing and closing of trade routes. Thus, it was not "relative immunity" from attack that accounted for the involvement of women in trade. Women engaged in local and long distance trade because the degree of specialization necessitated the exchange of goods and because most of the men of the society were otherwise engaged in farming and in warfare activities. It might be said that some women had to endure the risks of long distance trade because most men were experiencing the even greater risks involved in farming and warfare.

[11] The earliest travellers to Yorubaland encountered wives of the Alafin (the "King of Katunga") trading in various parts of Yorubaland. According to Lander (1833, Vol. I:122, 182) the wives of the Alafin, more than any other group of women, could afford to travel about the kingdom because they were exempt from the taxes levied on other traders and because they could reside in the chief's compound in any town in which they stopped. Hugh Clapperton in 1825 is said to have found wives of the Alafin trading at "Duffo," south of Shaki, and to have noted that "like women of the common class they carried large loads on their heads from town to town" (Mabogunje, 1961b:15). In 1830, Richard and John Lander met wives of the Alafin trading in Jadoo, a town not more than 50 miles north of Badagry. "The yard wherein we reside is perfectly round, and walled with huts, all tenanted by the late chief's widows, who employ their time and earn their livelihood by spinning and weaving. Not less than a hundred of the King of Katunga's ladies are lodging in the yard with them. They have all passed the bloom of life, and arrived here lately with loads of trona and country cloth, which they barter for salt, and various articles of European manufacture, particularly beads; with these they return home, and expose them for sale in the market, and afterward the profits are taken to their husbands. These royal ladies are distinguished from their countrywomen only by a peculiar species of cloth, which is wrapped round their goods, and which no one dares to imitate, on pain of perpetual slavery. This severe punishment is often inflicted; for, as the king's wives pay no tribute or turnpike dues whatever, and must besides be entertained by the chiefs of every town through which they pass, strong inducements are offered for others to attempt to deceive by using the forbidden cloth, and hence examples are necessary" (Lander, 1833, Vol. I:122).

SUMMARY: DIVISION OF LABOR IN TRADITIONAL YORUBA SOCIETY

The argument throughout this chapter has been that the task of cultivating the soil was the province of men owing (1) to the nature of the Yoruba settlement pattern in which farmlands stretched for miles outside the towns in which the permanent dwellings were built and, related to this, (2) to the risks involved in this enterprise, especially during the nineteenth century civil war period, because the farmlands were the natural targets for warriors and kidnappers. In the nineteenth century, farmlands were more unsafe than they had been in earlier periods when threats to safety came primarily from rival ethnic groups rather than from the various Yoruba sub-groups themselves. Women were found primarily in the towns where they undertook many occupations including the rearing of children and the processing of farm produce. They also constituted the vast majority of the traders in the local town markets, and some of them, along with men, engaged in long distance trade.

DIVISION OF LABOR IN PRESENT DAY YORUBA SOCIETY

Subsequent to the establishment of British colonial government in Yorubaland and throughout the area that became Nigeria, two major factors served to perpetuate the Yoruba pattern of division of labor into male agriculturalists and female traders.

One of these was the promotion of cocoa and oil palm kernels as cash crops and the increase in their importance on the world market. Inasmuch as men had been the cultivators in the traditional society, the promotion of crops which promised substantial monetary remuneration served as incentive to keep them employed in agriculture. The possibility of exporting crops other than cocoa and palm kernels, the expansion of the internal market for farm products, the increase in the number of persons who were not involved in agricultural pursuits and who had to purchase all their food supplies on the market, and the relative lack of alternative employment opportunities, kept the majority of unskilled men on the farms.

A concomitant development within the distributive sphere of the economy also helped to perpetuate the traditional division of labor. European firms moved into the West African countries, including Nigeria, as importers and exporters. These companies monopolized trade on a large scale. They, in conjunction with "Levantine" traders from the Middle East, controlled the higher levels of the distributive sphere of the Nigerian economy. The existence of small-scale traders, most of whom were female, served the needs of the large firms, for consumers demanded goods in quantities too small to make it economical for the expatriate companies to enter the lower levels of the distributive chain. The necessary tasks of bulk-breaking fell to indigenous traders who could buy and sell in progressively smaller quantities until finally the goods reach the consuming public (Bauer, 1954).[12]

The existence of small scale traders can also be related to the nature of the productive activities within the country. In the case of agricultural production as well as craft production, activities are on a small scale. Particularly in the case of farming where a variety of crops are planted on small plots, is it necessary to have a number of persons who perform the task of bulking for the markets and subsequent bulk-breaking for consumers.

Even though most Yoruba men are farmers and most women are traders, both sexes engage in a number of other occupations. A number of traditional crafts such as leather-working, carving, weaving, etc., are still carried on by Yoruba men. In addition, they are engaged in crafts which were more recently introduced into the country (Lloyd, 1953*b*). Some women are likewise employed in crafts—such as weaving, dyeing, hairdressing—which were practiced by members of their sex in the traditional society.

Occupations created by twentieth century innovations such as railroads, building industries, factories, etc., are filled mostly by men. They are also involved in the distributive sector of the economy. Indigenous importers or merchants who deal on a large scale with European firms are mostly men, and, as would be expected, such enterpreneurs have businesses in the large cities, many of them in Lagos or Ibadan. However, some male traders can also be found in all large towns and in small towns and villages. A number of men and women are professionals: teachers, lawyers, doctors, engineers, or have clerical and administrative jobs with various branches of the government; in industries owned by the government (e.g., radio and television), or with private businesses.

In summary, it must be re-stated that the increasing opportunities for other types of employment notwithstanding, most Yoruba women today are traders. For the most part they operate within the internal marketing system of Nigeria, and although their employment in trade pre-dates the colonial era, the twentieth century expansion of the market economy has led to an expansion in the range and scale of their activities.

---

[12] As will be shown in a later chapter, the distributive process does not involve the degree of vertical specialization implied in this statement. That is, there are very few intermediaries who sell *only* to other intermediaries or who sell *only* to consumers. At nearly every level, those persons dealing in imported items sell to resellers as well as to consumers (see Bauer, 1954:Ch. I).

III

YORUBA MARKETS: CENTERS OF WOMEN'S TRADE ACTIVITIES

THE markets in which women carry on their trade activities are located in or near every type of settlement in Western Nigeria. The basic type of settlement in Western Nigeria is still a large town surrounded by settlements of smaller size and subordinate political status. The large towns have been termed "metropolitan towns" by Lloyd and "metropolitan centres" by Mabogunje. Surrounding each of the metropolitan centers are a number of smaller towns which were administratively linked to those centers in pre-colonial times and which, in most cases today, are under the jurisdiction of District Councils whose headquarters are located in the metropolitan centers.

In what are essentially the farmlands for these two types of towns are located villages and dispersed hamlets (*aba*). It is significant that although a distinction is here drawn between villages and hamlets, the former being a more autonomous and more permanent type of settlement, Yoruba speakers sometimes use the term "aba" to refer to both types of settlements.[1]

There are, then, two types of locations in which markets are found: in towns and in farmland areas. Specifically, markets are located (1) in metropolitan centers, (2) in small towns which surround these centers, (3) in villages which are essentially large compact settlements in the farmlands,[2] and (4) in uninhabited farmland in the neighborhood of hamlets and villages.

If the urban-rural distinction is to be applied to Yoruba markets, all markets located in outlying towns should be classed along with those in the larger towns as urban markets. The term "rural" should be applied only to those markets situated in villages and to those which are open plots surrounded by cultivated and fallow farmland, hamlets, and villages. This point must be stressed because persons who use models taken from other societies to

---

[1] In actuality, this terminology is not altogether inaccurate for the difference between villages and hamlets is a matter of degree whereas the difference between these farmland settlements and towns is one of kind. Villages are essentially agglomerations of hamlets: they lack the autonomy and internal political and economic role differentiation characteristic of towns.

[2] This is true notwithstanding the fact that certain villages are located along major roads. One has only to leave the road to realize that these villages are in fact settlements in farming territory.

discriminate urban areas from rural areas might characterize the small Yoruba towns as rural areas, reserving the term "urban" for the metropolitan centers or for those of these centers which have certain features of Western urbanism.[3]

Yoruba markets of the present day are still held daily or periodically. Yoruba speakers refer to the periodic markets as "five-day" markets or "nine-day" markets. They are held at intervals of four days and eight days respectively, however, in reckoning market days, Yoruba speakers calculate from the day on which the market is held up to and including the subsequent market day. Thus, when a five-day market is held on Monday, the subsequent market falls on Friday which is reckoned to be the fifth day following. If a nine-day market meets on Monday, the next market day would be Tuesday of

---

[3] The classification of settlements outside the major towns as rural or urban can present a real problem. As pointed out in Chapter I, traditional Yoruba settlements are classed as urban on the basis of their size, their internal economic specialization, their possession of a daily market, their having a full roster of political and administrative officials, and their populations being united by associational as well as kin ties.

Without a study of the structure of some present-day communities, it is difficult to say if they have the characteristics of traditional towns although it is obvious that they do not possess the features of the westernized towns. On the face of it, one can hardly distinguish a large village from a small town. As a rule of thumb, one might class all those "marginal communities" which hold periodic markets but do not hold daily markets as villages rather than as small towns. It was probably on this basis that Hodder (1961; 1962) termed Iware and Ijaye (see Fig. 7) as villages and referred to their markets as *rural* periodic markets. However, Iware, Ife-Odan, Ijaye, and Ajawa (see Fig. 7) are settlements whose populations number in the thousands; they have a number of local officials, and seem to have just as much internal economic role diversification as is found in a place like Awẹ which is a small town. Although they do not hold daily markets, some trading does take place on a daily basis in the small shops in these settlements and in the compounds in which people live. It may be that historical research and a detailed study of their community organization would lead to their classification as towns. Certainly Ijaye is the remnant of what was a major nineteenth century Yoruba town.

The problem of classification is further complicated by the fact that the possession of a prosperous periodic market is one means by which a rural settlement attracts permanent settlers and with expanding size becomes increasingly more independent, resembling the small towns (Marshall, 1963). Whether the settlements referred to above were large hamlets which expanded mainly because of the success of their markets can only be determined by a study of the historical processes of their growth.

Whether these communities are towns or villages, vis-a-vis the large towns, they are the geographical and functional equivalents of present-day villages. They are situated well into the farmlands, each more than 10 miles from the major town with which it has administrative and economic links. They are so situated that they are pivotal links between the large towns and the farms, and given the economic changes which led to the proliferation of periodic markets in the farmland areas, it is not surprising that these communities would hold periodic markets.

Generally speaking, even though many Yoruba settlements would be classed as "urban" using the criteria by which traditional Yoruba urbanism is defined, as the differences between small towns and large centers become increasingly a matter of *kind* rather than *degree*, it may be necessary to class small towns along with villages and hamlets as rural settlements. In fact, in an earlier paper (1962) I referred to small town markets as "rural markets" because at that time it seemed that small towns and villages should be termed rural areas in contrast to large towns like Ibadan.

the following week which is the ninth day hence. Even though the timing of Yoruba periodic markets conforms to a pattern widespread in West Africa, the Yoruba do not appear to have had the five-day (i.e., four-day) week in which the name of each day corresponded to the name of the market held on that day (see Bowen, 1857:282).

In classifying their markets, three sets of distinctions are used by Yoruba speakers. The first distinction is made between daily markets and non-daily markets. Yoruba speakers do not use a general term such as "periodic" to refer to the non-daily markets since, with respect to any particular market, it is always necessary to state whether it is a five-day market or a nine-day market. Thus, they speak of markets which are held every day (*l'ojojumo*), every fifth day (*ijo karun, karun*) or every ninth day (*ijo kesan, kesan*). The second distinction is made between day markets and night markets. With respect to any market, Yoruba speakers state whether it commences in the morning (*l'aro*), as do all of the day markets, or in the evening (*l'ale*), as do the night markets. The third distinction is drawn between markets located in urban settlements and those in the rural areas. The Yoruba refer to markets as being located inside a town (*nigboro*) or in the farmlands (*l'oko*).

Using these three sets of criteria, there are eight *possible* types of markets in Yorubaland. In fact, not all these types exist in the areas in which my field work was carried out. There are three main types of markets in these areas: (1) the urban daily market, (2) the urban nightly market, and (3) the rural periodic day market. The urban daily market is more common than the urban nightly market. However, where the latter type is found it is usually an important social center and fulfills the same economic functions as would a daily market. The other types of markets which exist but which are less common are: (1) the urban periodic day market, (2) the urban periodic night market, and (3) the rural periodic night market.[4]

---

[4] Hodder (1961; 1962) sets forth five main types of markets found in the area in which he worked, which is also a part of the area where my field work was carried out. The types he lists are:

"i. the urban daily market, characteristic only of the larger towns, like Ibadan;
ii. the urban nightly market, commencing at dusk and continuing to about 10 p.m.;
iii. the rural daily market, which is often only for fresh meat;
iv. the rural periodic night market; and
v. the rural periodic day market" (Hodder, 1961:149).

In a later publication, types four and five are termed "the rural night market," and "the rural market," respectively (1962:104). A comparison between the types given by the two of us shows that he did not include in his list *urban periodic markets of the day or night variety*, whereas I do not include *rural daily markets* among the main types. The discrepancies in our lists stem from two factors: (a) an apparent oversight on the part of Hodder and (b) an apparent difference of interpretation as to what constitutes a "rural" community in Yorubaland.

First of all, it is not clear why Hodder did not include among his types the *urban periodic day market* since there are two such markets in Ibadan which was the major center from which he worked. Many other Yoruba towns also hold periodic day

THE URBAN MARKETS

In present-day Western Nigeria, as in Yorubaland of the past, there are in the urban areas both daily and periodic markets of the day and night varieties. It will be recalled that in the traditional system, most of the local trade took place in the daily markets in both the metropolitan towns and in the small towns surrounding them. Inter-urban trade was carried on in the periodic markets held in some frontier towns and in a number of the major towns.

The trend in twentieth century Western Nigeria seems to have been toward daily markets in the large urban centers and periodic markets in the farmland areas. This is not surprising since the rationale for periodic markets lies in the fact that it takes time for traders to collect and transport items which they would sell in the market, or to dispose of items which they buy in the market. The periodic markets of the past served as a means whereby traders could replenish the supply of goods which they sold in the local daily markets. With the increasing efficiency in the distribution network between large towns, the daily markets are replacing periodic markets as centers for inter-area trade while remaining the important centers for local trade. It is significant that where urban periodic markets still exist, they are usually

---

markets. It is easier to see why he did not include the *urban periodic night market* since this type is common in the northerly Yoruba areas. The largest market of this type known to me is at Igbeti, a town near the border of the Northern Region.

With respect to the types of markets which exist in rural areas, there is more of a problem. If one accepts that what were traditionally small towns are to be classed as urban rather than rural communities, then there is no question but that *daily markets* of the day or night variety are characteristic of large and small *urban* communities, not of *rural* settlements. Even though this is generally true, some problems arise when one looks at specific communities. As has been said, it is often difficult to distinguish small towns from large villages without a detailed study of the structure of the community. On the face of it, Moniya, which Hodder terms a rural community with a daily market, appears to me to be a small town similar to Awẹ or Fiditi. Neither Hodder nor myself has studied the structure of the community at Moniya so the problem remains as to whether it is a village or a town. Another point must be raised concerning large villages. When such villages are located along major roads, one of the first characteristics of a town which they assume is the daily trading site. This is particularly true if the settlement is the point of convergence for unpaved roads connecting the interior settlements with the major roads. Passengers who live in the interior would come to this place to board lorries; traders would come to join lorries which would take them to the various markets which they attend. Wherever there is an important lorry stop, sellers of various items will display their wares or hawk them near the lorry park. Villages which become important stops between towns may become increasingly populous and autonomous until they become towns in their own right; or they may remain villages while retaining their trading site. Moniya is an important motor transport station on the Ọyọ-Ibadan road, and at times one sees various kinds of trade activity near the lorry stop. Since it is a large settlement, it is not surprising that it can sustain a daily market which, contrary to Hodder's report, contains more than just fresh meat. *If* Moniya is a village rather than a small town, one would expect to find that the market is not an officially established one with an official head and other officers but rather that it has simply grown up unofficially, owing to the strategic location of the community.

specialized markets for trade in indigenous manufactured commodities which take a relatively long time to produce or for agricultural products for which the process of bulking and transporting from the farms is still a relatively slow one. The urban periodic markets, like their rural counterparts, are *primarily* places where *traders* purchase items which they resell to other traders or to consumers.

One such urban periodic market is Oje, a nine-day market, at Ibadan. It is alternately a "cloth market" and a "soap market." On one market day traders from Oyo, Iseyin, Shaki, Ilorin, and other northerly Yoruba towns bring locally woven cloth (primarily the type known as *aso oke* or *aso ofi*) which is mostly sold to Ibadan traders. Many of the traders from these northerly towns are men; some of them are weavers who sell their own cloth or that made by other men in their compound or in their trade association. On the same market day, women from Abeokuta and environs sell the dyed *adire* cloth for which their area is famous. In addition to these cloths, there are many other types available at Oje. Most of the buyers in the market are women. The subsequent market day is devoted largely to the sale of indigenously manufactured soap, particularly *ose dudu* made from a mixture of the ashes of the cocoa fruit from which the beans have been removed and *adin*, a type of oil extracted from palm kernels. Women traders who come mainly from towns and villages north of Ibadan sell this soap to Ibadan women who resell it in various places in the town. During the intervals between market days, the producers prepare more goods which they subsequently take to Oje or sell to traders who take them to the market.

The five-day market at Igbeti, a town about 80 miles north of Oyo, is representative of the urban periodic markets which specialize in agricultural items.[5] In many respects, Igbeti seems similar to the old "market towns" described by Johnson and referred to earlier. The town itself is noted primarily for its periodic market which is attended by traders from many towns in the Western Region and from nearby towns and villages in the Northern Region. Traders from Ilesha, Ilorin, Ogbomosho, Oyo, Ibadan, Lagos, and smaller towns come to Igbeti by lorry on market days. People from villages and small towns nearby come to Igbeti by foot, by cycle, as well as by lorry. On the eve of the market, which is held *at night*, dozens of lorries crowd the motor park.

Igbeti is an enlarged version of the rural periodic markets. It is particularly noted for yams and maize although it usually contains large quantities of pepper, *gari* (cassava meal), and *elubo* (dried slices of yams which are gound into flour) as well. In fact, every type of produce grown in the areas around Igbeti can be bought in the market. In addition to farm products, there are for sale in the market various types of smoked and dried meat, eggs, cooked

---

[5] Ibuko market in Ibadan is also representative of this type of market.

foods, packaged foods and household items, cloth, ready-to-wear clothing, locally-made and imported sandals and shoes, jewelry, hardware, enamelware, glassware, cutlery, locally-made pots, mats, baskets, calabashes, soaps, oils, etc.

Many of these items are sold to consumers and to local traders but the bulk of the farm produce is sold to women traders who come from towns near and far. These women buy in bulk—by the hundred-weight bag or by the basket—and resell to traders and consumers in their home towns. Some women from Lagos and other cities buy yams by the "gauge"[6] and resell in smaller quantities to traders at home. Some women from towns outside Igbeti, including one woman from Awe, have taken up residence in this market town and during the main harvest season, they take lorry-loads of yams to sell in Lagos or Ibadan (Marshall, 1962).

On the eve of the Igbeti market, traders start to flow into the marketplace and preliminary bargaining and scouting take place. Trading in earnest beings after nightfall; by 9 or 10 P.M., the market is at its fullest and the sound of voices can be heard for over a mile. Some female buyers from out of town do not sleep the entire night, but remain in the market area, packing their loads and arranging for men to transport the heavier ones to the lorries. From the early morning hours until 7 or 8 A.M., lorries head toward the various towns from which they came.

Every Yoruba town has at least one *daily* market. In all large towns, there are usually more than three such markets. In Ibadan, there are nine daily markets: Oja'ba (held nightly), Dugbe, Gege, Mokola, Oke-Ado, Oranyan, Ayeye, Orita Merin, and Gbagi. The latter three "markets" might better be referred to as "trading areas" rather than as markets. In any case, these are all indigenous trading sites where the sellers have shops, stalls, or "verandahs" from which they carry on their daily trade.

Daily markets in the large towns fall into two categories: they are primarily places for local trade or they function as markets where local and inter-area trade activities coalesce. In the former case, they are mainly consumers' markets whereas in the latter case they serve both traders and consumers. It must be emphasized that this last statement is true only in a relative sense for *all* markets serve traders of one type or another as well as consumers. Since some women buy very small quantities which they resell in even more minute measures, they might buy in a "consumers' market" as easily as in the other type. A woman who sells matches by the bundle or cigarettes by the stick could buy a single box or pack anywhere, for the price would be the same for her as it would be for a consumer.

---

[6] Lorry space is often measured in terms of "gauges." A "gauge" (called *gaji* in Yoruba) is the amount of space from ceiling to floor which would be vacant if a specified number of passenger benches are removed. Sometimes one-bench space equals one gauge; sometimes two-bench spaces equal one gauge. This seems to vary with the size of the lorry. A "gauge" may be a space approximately eight feet long, five feet high, and two feet wide.

Dugbe market at Ibadan is illustrative of the "all purpose market" (Adediran, 1960). There is virtually no commodity or service which cannot be purchased in the area of the market. It functions as a supply center for Ibadan traders and for traders from outlying towns and villages, and it serves as a shopping center for consumers. Many of the items which come by rail from the Northern Region (for example, ground-nut oil, onions, beans, rice, dried meat, pepper, and eggs) flow into Dugbe market which is located near the railroad station. Men and women traders at Dugbe usually have "suppliers" (many of whom are Yoruba women residents in the Northern towns) who send them periodic shipments of goods. These are then resold to traders, most of them women, who sell in Dugbe and other Ibadan markets or who sell in other towns or villages. Women from outlying towns, including some from Awe, buy beans or rice at Dugbe and resell in small town daily markets or in rural periodic markets. Dugbe also supplies a large area with imported items such as enamelware and packaged or canned foods. In each of the rural markets which I attended (some of which were over 50 miles from Ibadan), in the Oyo town markets, and in Awe, the women who sold enamelware either bought it at Dugbe from Ibadan market women or bought it from women who had themselves been supplied at Dugbe. There are numerous other items which are purchased in this market by Ibadan women who resell in the town or, in some cases, who travel out to nearby rural markets.

Orita Merin is a "specialized" daily market in which inter-area trade takes place. Women from the Yoruba areas north of Ibadan and some from the "middle-belt" area of the Northern Region (which includes Nupe settlements) bring various types of farm produce—yams, maize, peppers, gari (cassava meal), elubo (dried slices of yams), *lafun* (dried pieces of cassava), rice, etc.—to Orita Merin to be sold to traders in Ibadan. Some consumers—particularly those who grew up in Ibadan and who know the "specialities" of the different markets—buy certain of their foodstuffs at Orita Merin where they are likely to be cheaper than most other town markets.

Most of the cloth sold by women in outlying towns (in large ones such as Oyo, Iwo, and Ogbomosho and in small ones such as Awe or Fiditi) and villages is bought from women traders (occasionally from men) at Gbagi in Ibadan.[7] Traders at Gbagi purchase their supplies from importers at Lagos or Ibadan or from wealthy Nigerian traders who buy directly from the large firms. They sell to local consumers and to traders from Ibadan and from out of town.

With the possible exception of Ayeye, the other daily markets in Ibadan seem more oriented toward local trade than are the markets mentioned above. This is not to say that goods from other parts of Nigeria or from abroad do not flow through these markets. On the contrary, they all contain imported

---

[7] It has been pointed out that Gbagi (like Amunigun, an area where provisions and hardware are sold) might properly be called a "shopping area" rather than a market.

goods and, in fact, Ọja'ba, the large night market, is as much an "all purpose market" as in Dugbẹ. The point is that the traders in these markets are residents of Ibadan; most traders from out of town buy (and, in some instances, sell) in the markets mentioned and in the Amunigun-Agbẹni shopping area.

There are eight daily markets in Ọyọ: the two major markets, Akẹsan and Aṣipa, as well as Agunpopo are held at night but, as is usually the case, some trading goes on in the marketplaces during the daytime. Atan, Sakatu, Tengba, Iṣokun, Iṣekẹ, and Idiṣango are small markets which are held during the day. The daily markets in Ọyọ appear to function like the daily markets of traditional Yorubaland. All the morning markets serve the local population: women from Ọyọ town sell to consumers and to other local traders. For example, women who buy onions by the hundred weight bag would sell to consumers in piles of three or four each; they sell to other traders in piles of 40 each. Some women who attend these morning markets come from the farm hamlets around Ọyọ. They bring firewood, leaves, and a few foodstuffs (particularly gari or maize) for sale to women of the town.

Very few men can be found in most of the morning markets at Ọyọ although a few men who sold dried fish from the Ijẹbu or Nupe areas did attend Sakatu market. Even so, of the 200 or more traders who regularly attended Sakatu, only three were men. The only morning market attended by a number of men is Akẹsan which is primarily a night market but which also meets between 7A.M. and 1 or 2 P.M. Nearly all the fresh beef sold in the town is sold at Akẹsan in the mornings. The principal fresh meat sellers are men, many of them Hausa who live at Sabo at the northern end of the town. Ọyọ women who sell at Akẹsan in the mornings sell the cheaper parts of the cow (especially livers, kidneys, and other internal parts) or they sell foodstuffs in consumable quantities. In Akẹsan, as in all these morning markets, the range of goods available in quite extensive—including a variety of vegetables and staples, packaged foods ("provisions"), cooked foods, cloth, various types of dried fish, enamelware, and local medicines—but the amount of goods displayed by any trader is likely to be small.

It is the night market at Akẹsan which is the large all-purpose market as well as the social center of the town. All types of goods available in Ọyọ can be purchased at Akẹsan in the evenings. Both consumers and local traders *buy* in this market. The women traders who *sell* there buy from Ibadan, from the rural markets, from Aṣipa (the evening market at which farm products predominate), from craftsmen in the town or in other northerly towns, etc. Most of the men selling at Akẹsan in the evenings deal in live goats, mats which are made in the Ijẹbu areas or in the Northern Region, or in a combination of hardware, men's underwear, and other clothing items for men, women, and children. These latter items they purchase at Amunigun in Ibadan.

Akẹsan is not a center for inter-area trade as is Dugbẹ in Ibadan. Nonetheless, a few women traders from nearby towns do purchase their supplies at Akẹsan or at Asipa. Occasionally Awẹ women who sell cooked foods made from beans which come from the Northern Region buy at Akẹsan. These are women who cannot afford to purchase beans by the hundred-weight bag, hence they purchase by the pan-ful from women who buy in large quantities. Most of the time, these cooked-food sellers are supplied by Ọyọ women who hawk about Awẹ but when necessary, they walk to Ọyọ to buy the beans.

Each small town, like the large ones, holds at least one daily market. At Awẹ, a market is held in the morning and in the evening. The morning market at Bode is much like the morning markets in Ọyọ. The main articles on sale are: farm products and various kinds of fried meat and fish, all displayed in small piles or measures which could be bought by consumers; imported food items such as canned goods; firewood and leaves (used for wrapping foods); and cooked-foods such as *ewa* (beans), *igbalọ*, and *akara* (both made from beans). Most of the items offered for sale are bought by consumers but some traders, especially cooked-food sellers, buy produce at Bode market. The market commences about 6:30 or 7 A.M. and by 8:30 A.M., most of the produce brought in by farm women, and most of the firewood and leaves would have been sold. By 9 A.M. some women (e.g., some stockfish sellers) leave the market to hawk about the town. Trading in consumers goods (provisions, vegetables, bread, etc.) goes on until late in the morning after which time most women return to their compounds. By noon, there are only a handful of women in the market and in the afternoon only two or three women display their wares under the shade trees.

The daily markets in most small towns have declined in importance with the growth of rural periodic markets. Whereas farmers and women who live in the hamlets used to sell their produce in markets like the one at Bode in Awẹ, they now sell in the rural markets. The activities of most rural women and of many small town women center in the rural periodic markets rather than in the small town daily markets with the result that small town markets have relatively few people in attendance. There are virtually no men to be seen in these markets. Many of the women who trade at Bode are old women or women who, for various reasons, cannot or choose not to trade in the rural markets. For example, women who deal in farm produce may not have sufficient capital to warrant regular trips to the rural markets so they buy from women who attend these markets or from farm women who bring produce to Bode in the mornings.

The daily markets are also undermined by the existence of small shops and stalls throughout the town. Major centers like Ibadan can sustain numerous shops, large stores, and daily markets, but in small towns such as Awẹ the markets have tended to decline with the growth of small stores which, because of their dispersal throughout the town, make shopping more convenient. Competition between the small town markets and shops is somewhat minimized by the fact that shops handle mostly packaged foods and beverages, household supplies, and various imported goods while the markets mostly contain the agricultural products. Even so instead of being *the* central shopping area, the market is now just one of many places in which goods are bought and sold.[8]

Whereas there is usually a central site in which the small town morning market is held, the night market may, as in Awẹ, consist of a number of traders lining part of the main street which runs through the town. This seems to be true of Fiditi and other small towns which straddle the Ọyọ-Ibadan road. The roadside is lighted by small oil lamps set out by traders who exhibit their wares on mats or on small wooden tables. Most of the items displayed are put out in small measures since the buyers are mostly consumers. The night market, unlike that held in the morning, is always a social center which attracts both sexes and nearly all ages of people, but the majority of the sellers are women.

THE RURAL MARKETS

Permanent rural settlements and rural markets are comparatively recent features on the Yoruba landscape. In those parts of Yorubaland where, during the middle and late nineteenth century, villages replaced small towns as the predominant type of settlement surrounding the metropolitan center, rural markets grew up to "serve the needs of the highly dispersed agricultural population" (Mabogunje, 1959). Most of the rural markets are of more recent origin, the oldest of them dating back to the first two decades of the twentieth century while the majority of them were founded even later.[9] The increase in the number of these markets and the growth of the settlements within which or in the vicinity of which they are located appear to be directly related to the increased demand for agricultural products in Yoruba towns, in other parts of Nigeria, and in countries abroad.

[8] Interestingly, the "dispersal of the market" in Yorubaland seems to have begun more than a century ago. Bowen (1858:46) noted: "In the old towns... a large open space is always reserved for the market; but in the more modern towns, the market is often a long line of open shops, or sheds, built against the backs of houses."

[9] Hodder (1962) reports that Ojo, the oldest market in the "Akinyele Ring," was established about 1905. According to the chief ruler at Iware (referred to by the people of Iware as the *Oniware* but termed the Balẹ by some people in Ọyọ), the market, which is the largest in the "Akinyele Ring," was founded "about forty years ago" using the "English system of reckoning" (Interview November 4, 1961). Records at the Ọyọ Southern District Council Office and the Ibadan City Council Office show that many of the rural markets which surround Ọyọ and Ibadan were founded in the 1930's and 1940's. According to women traders and lorry drivers from Awẹ, most of the rural markets in the triangle formed by Ibadan, Ọyọ, and Iwo were founded within the past 25 years. The two markets attended by the majority of Awẹ women were founded less than 15 years ago.

The rural markets are periodic markets which meet every five days or every nine days. Throughout the farmland areas, they are within three to 10 miles of each other and operate in what has been termed "market rings" (Galletti, et al., 1956:58; Hodder, 1961:1962). As Hodder points out, "these rings are by no means self-contained; for each rural market ring impinges upon and is itself impinged upon by adjacent market rings" (1962:107). In any given locality, the residents will list a number of neighborhood markets which together may be said to constitute a "ring." However, the number of markets which an *investigator* includes in any given ring, and in fact *the particular markets* which he includes in a ring would depend on the locality he chooses as a starting point and, in some cases, on the persons whom he interviews concerning the constitution of the ring. A study of the timing and location of markets over a wide area could yield a number of ideal rings but these would not necessarily correspond to those which would be obtained by interviewing people in various parts of the area concerned. In any case, when two markets fall on the same day, investigation would probably reveal that the founders of the newer market do not regard the older market as part of the group of markets which constitute their ring. The exceptions to this are two: a five-day market may share every other market day with a nine-day market in the same ring, and rival villages or groups of hamlets may deliberately hold their markets on the same day.

The fact that rural market rings are relative entities rather than absolute ones can be illustrated by reference to the Akinyele ring described by Hodder (1961; 1962). The locations of markets which comprise this ring are shown in Figure 5. Excepting Ijaye (also spelled Ijaiye), which is held every five days, these markets meet every nine days.[10] Hodder lists Akinyele as the "first" market in the ring but, in actuality, any market can be taken as the starting point for any ring in which it falls. The following calendar shows the manner in which the ring operates.

Sunday	Monday	Tuesday	Wednesday	Thursday	Friday	Saturday
Akinyele	Ojo	Iware	Elekuru	Olorisa Oko	Arulogun	Onidundun
Ijaye				Ijaye		
	Akinyele	Ojo	Iware	Elekuru	Olorisa Oko	Arulogun
	Ijaye				Ijaye	
Onidundun		Akin-yele	Ojo	Iware	Elekuru	Olorisa Oko
		Ijaye				Ijaye

[10] The problem of distinguishing large villages from small towns has been referred to in two earlier footnotes. Until further research is conducted, I shall follow Hodder and include Ijaye and Iware in the "rural" market circuit although, as indicated earlier, I think these communities are small towns of rather great antiquity.

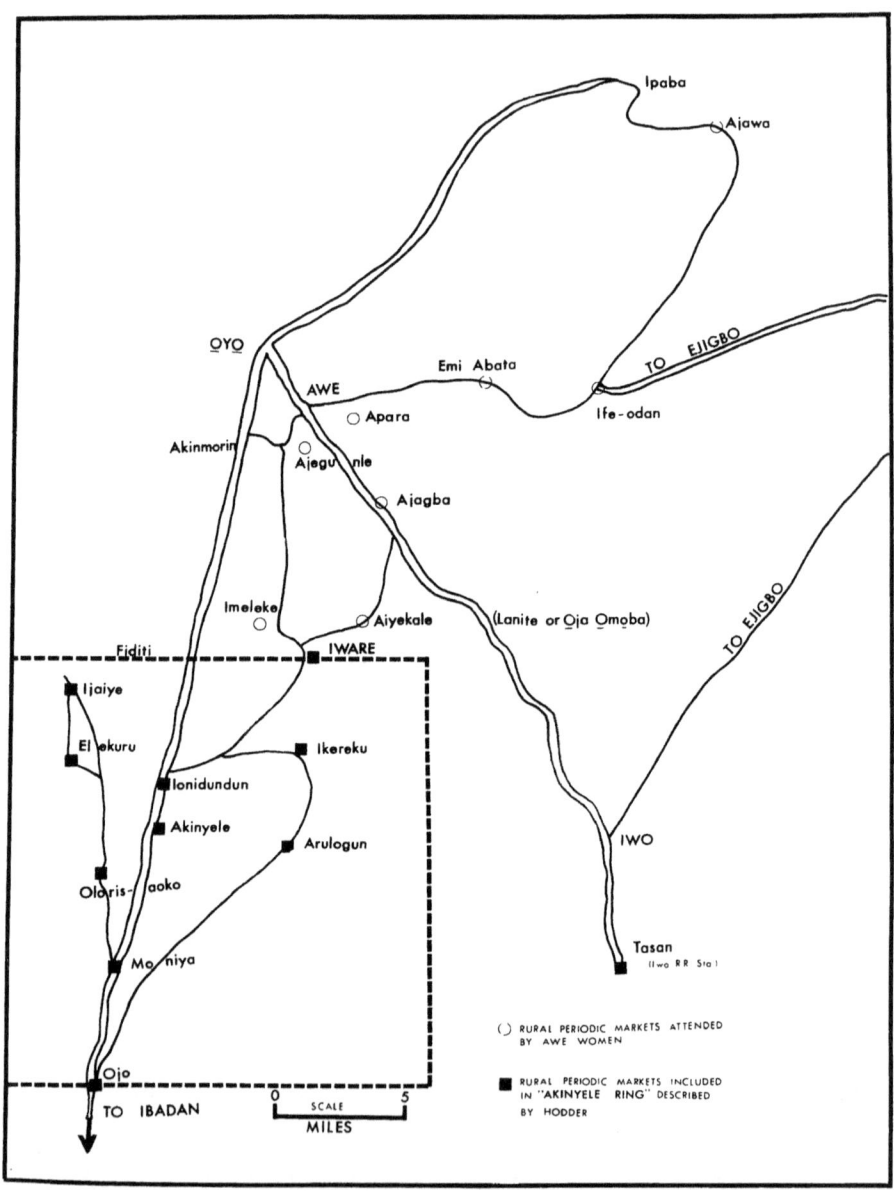

Fig. 5. Some rural periodic markets around Awe.

Iware market falls into another ring which includes Aiyekale, Imeleke (see Fig. 5) and some other markets which are not shown on Figure 5. Aiyekale is a five-day market which is held on the same day as Ijaye, and Imeleke is a nine-day market whose days coincide with those for Onidundun.

The point to be stressed concerning rural markets is that they function primarily as "feeder markets" for the towns. Although various kinds of trade take place in these markets, they are primarily centers for the sale of agricultural products which are bulked and redistributed in the towns (see Hodder, 1961; 1962). Women who live in the villages and hamlets buy from the farmers and they themselves, along with some of the farmers, sell foodstuffs to other women who later resell in the small towns or in the larger urban centers (Marshall, 1962).

Every type of produce grown in the areas surrounding the markets can be found in a natural state or in a processed state (see Table 2). For example, yams are sold as they come from the ground, or in the form of elubo, i.e., in slices which have been pre-cooked and dried in the sun. The dried yam slices are used to make flour which is also termed elubo. Cassava is seldom sold in its natural state since it must be processed before it is eaten; it is sold as gari (cassava meal) or in the form of lafun, i.e., small dried pieces which are gound into flour. Figure 6 illustrates the arrangement of the market at Ajagba.

Rural markets also serve as places where the people who live in villages and hamlets can buy some of the non-agricultural items which they need. Goods from various parts of Nigeria and from abroad are sold by male and female traders, most of whom live in nearby towns and purchase their stock in Ibadan. Sometimes traders from Ibadan come to sell in the rural markets, but the farther the market is from Ibadan, the fewer the full-time Ibadan residents who come to *sell* there. Also in the markets are people who render various services (such as tailors, barbers, and hair dressers), and numerous cooked-food sellers who cater to the culinary tastes of the marketers.

Only a small percentage of those attending the rural markets are men. Some of the services offered in the markets are performed by men; and a certain combination of goods (hardware, ready-made clothing for children and men, sandals and shoes, school supplies) is always handled by male traders. Men who buy palm kernels and cocoa for sale to the Marketing Board (see Chapter IV) have weighing scales in all the rural markets which I attended and on market days as on other days they buy from the farmers or their wives. Young men from the Eastern Region sell second-hand clothes; in some markets, Hausa men sell dried fish and buy kola for shipment to the Northern Region. By far the largest group of men to be found in rural markets are farmers who bring their own produce for sale. Lorry drivers and their attendants must also be numbered among the men in the markets.

Thus, most of the *sellers* in these markets and virtually all of the foodstuffs buyers are women. The lorries which converge on these markets

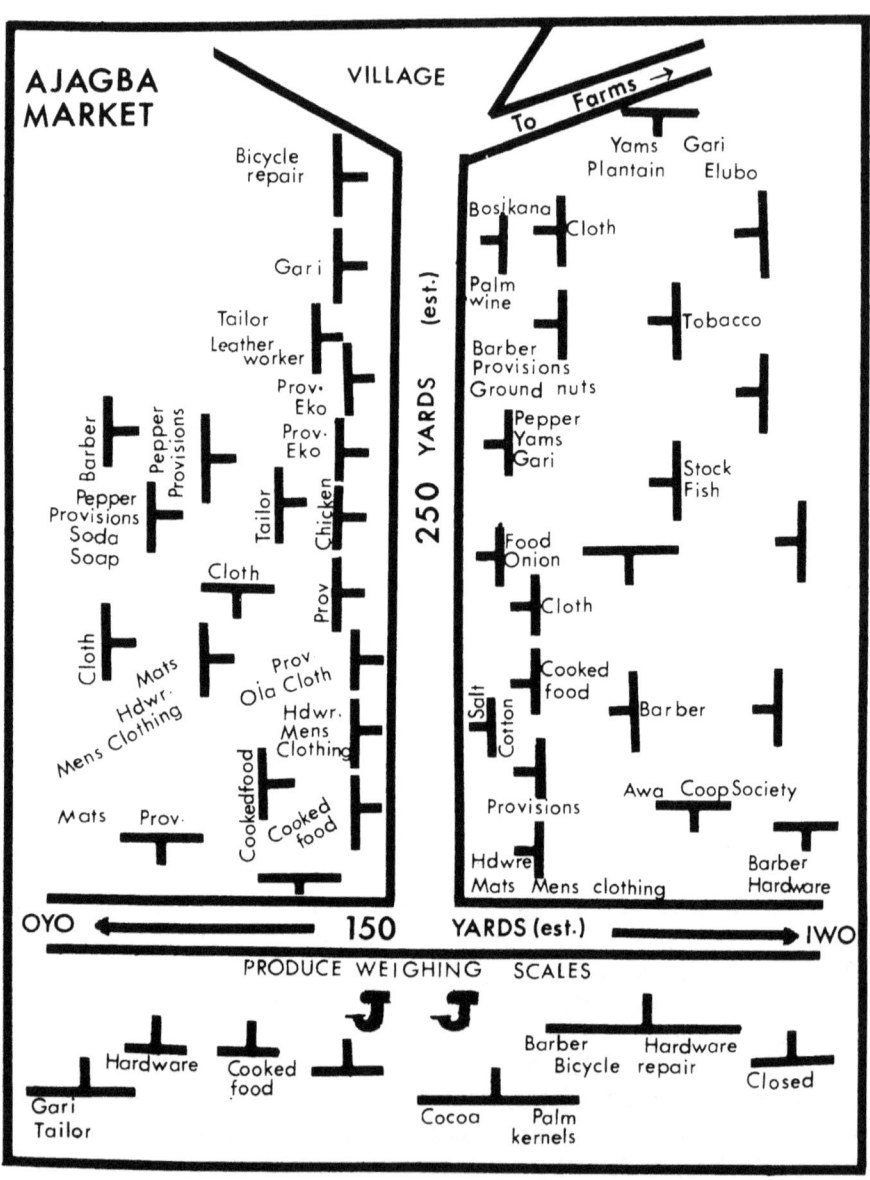

Fig. 6. Ajagba market, showing arrangement of seller's huts.

YORUBA MARKETS

TABLE 2

COMMODITIES SOLD IN RURAL MARKETS

Markets and dates of census Number of sellers	Emi-Abata 30 March 62 M		Ajagba 3 April 62 M	F	Ife-Odan 4 April 62 M	F	Iware 5 April 62 M	F	Ajawa 7 April 62 M	F
Farm Produce										
Yams	37	38	13	14	4	8	18	23		17
Elubo	30	35	7	4	1	34	1	10	5	16
Cassava (unprocessed)										
Gari		35		11		20		25		13
Lafun		15		5		15	5	37		11
Pepper	1	29	3	10		19		31		15
Maize	1	9	2	6		4		15	4	11
Millet	1	3		4				4		5
Plantain	1	8		3		5		4		5
Bananas		7		2		2				
Tomatoes										5
Groundnuts	5	4		2		1		3		1
Oranges										
Kola		3		3		9	7	136		8
Orogbo		1				2		5		3
Grapefruit										
Efo, Eyo & Ewedu (Greens)		6		3		8		10		22
Egusı		5		8		7		7		4
Onions		12		5		10		18		8
Beans		7		2		4		10		4
Tobacco		5	3	4		8		6		8
Rice		2						6		
Coco Yams										3
Palm Kernels*	(5)*13	23		(2)*8		(1)*5		10		(6)*10
Cocoa		5								
Iru (Locust Beans)		10		4		10		10		15
Okra				1		3		3		8
Coconuts		5		1				1		
Sugar cane				1				17		3
Cotton										
Kaun		3		2		3		6		10
Osan Agbalumo ("White Star Apple")						3		4		6
Apon (Fruit of the "Wild Mango")				2						
Farm Produce on 1d. Scale		5		3		3		10		5
CLOTH:										
Adire								4		
Oja		3	1	1	2	1		2		3
Ankara, "Brocade," etc.		6		9		9		14	1	16
Aso Oke						1		2		
SECOND-HAND CLOTHES	1		3	1	3		7	2	2	
OILS:										
Epo Pupa (Red Palm Oil)		6		3		6		8		5
Adin (Palm Kernel Oil)						3		2		
Ororo Egusi (Egusi oil)		3		1		2		2		3
Ororo Epa (Groundnut oil)		3		2		3		4		2
Adin Agbon (coconut oil)		2		3				4		1
Ori (Shea butter)						1		5		8
PROVISIONS		27		19		22		30		11
HARDWARE, ETC.	10		6		6		9		4	
ENAMELWARE		6		1		4		6		5
LOCAL POTS						1		4		
LOCAL BROOMS		2						1		
LOCAL SPONGES		8		4		3		6		4
CHEWING STICKS		2		1		2		5		
MEAT & FISH:										
Stockfish		10		5		5		31		4
Kundi		3				5		3		3
Fresh Meat	1	1	1			2	5	6	4	4
"Bush" Meat								1		
Dried Fish (Northern Region)		2	1			6	2	13	1	2
Dried Fish (Ijebu area)	3	1			2	1		1	1	1
COOKED FOODS		15		22		24		41		36
MILLET BEER										
PALM WINE		2		4		3		3		2
HONEY										1
BREAD		4		2		2		6		5
WARA (cheese)		2								3

54 WHERE WOMEN WORK

Markets and dates of census Number of sellers	Emi-Abata 30 March 62		Ajagba 3 April 62		Ife-Odan 4 April 62		Iware 5 April 62		Ajawa 7 April 62	
	M	F	M	F	M	F	M	F	M	F

TABLE 2 Continued

	M	F	M	F	M	F	M	F	M	F
SALT		10		4		7		11		13
GOATS		9				7		5		
CHICKENS		18	1	7		10		31		13
GOURDS		4				4		20		4
FUELS										
Kerosene		5		2		3		4		7
Iha								5		
LOCAL MEDICINES		2		1		3	1	7		3
LEAVES		5		5						13
ROPE								1		
CAPS (See also: Hardware, etc.)								5		
SANDALS (ditto)					2	1	2			
TOYS							2	1		1
JEWELRY		1		2		4		8		2
ELU (dye)				2				3		2
FLOUR SACKS				1						
SHEETS OF BROWN PAPER		3		1				2		
COW DUNG		5								
EMPTY BOTTLES, TINS				1				3		
HOES (see also: Hardware, etc.)			1							
MATS	5	2	2	3		3	6	9	2	1
BASKETS										
CHICKEN BASKETS				3						
PLAITED SACKS (saka)				3		1		4	6	3		1
SERVICES:										
Barbers	7		5		3		4			3
Tailors	8		4		7		8			8
Blacksmiths	1				1		2		1	
Goldsmiths							1			
Bicycle Repairmen			4		1					
Seamstresses						2				2
Shoe repairmen			2		1		5		3	
Hairdressers		1				2		4		
Tatooers				1			1			
GRINDING MACHINE OPERATORS	1					2		2		1
SOAP (Local):										
Ose Dudu		5		1		3		13		5
Ose Soda		5		5		6		18		4
Total (sellers)	126	464	60	222	35	341	107	764	29	569

*Numbers in parentheses refer to *buyers* of palm kernels and/or cocoa.

from various towns almost never have more than one or two male passengers. The men who do attend the rural markets walk from their farms or cycle from nearby towns. Sometimes Hausa men who buy kola will come by lorry to the rural markets. But often they are men who live in the rural areas for weeks at a time and they, like the other men, walk to the markets. They usually send their purchases by lorry to the town in which the kola would be packed for shipment to the North. Table 2 gives approximate numbers of men and women *sellers* present on one market day in five of the markets in which I worked. The female *buyers* in all these markets outnumbered the men by a ratio of more than 10 to one.

During the main harvest season from September to December, the markets are usually in full swing by 8:30 A.M. Women who buy foodstuffs arrive by 7 or 7:30 A.M. because the farmers and farm women start to reach the market about this time. The female buyers try to get to the market as early as possible in order to strike early bargains. Some of them try to meet the farm people along the roads leading to the market so as to start the bargaining as soon as the farmers or farm women unload the goods from their heads. These are not the "forestallers" mentioned by Hodder (1961:154) who station themselves along farm paths and buy from people who then return to the farms, leaving the "forestaller" to take the produce to the market. Rather, these are women who try to waylay sellers just as they approach the market. Such traders even assist the farm people in unloading the produce and try to get the sellers to agree to give them preference in the bargaining which follows. That is, since many female buyers surround a newcomer, the seller who meets him on the way tries to stake out a claim as the first "customer"—but there is no commitment on the part of the buyer or seller. If the two are not able to agree on a selling price, the trader moves on to buy from someone else and other women start to bargain for the produce.

By 9:30 A.M. most of the farm products are sold. Yams, plantain, bananas are piled in heaps; elubọ, gari, and lafun are packed in crocus sacks; tomatoes, okra, and ẹfọ (greens) are packed in large baskets. These and other items are ready to be loaded onto lorries and taken to their destinations. By 11 or 12 A.M. there is a decided lull in the market. Last minute bargains may be transacted but for the most part, buyers have completed most of their packing and a good number have loaded their wares onto the lorries. They now have time to make purchases for themselves and to eat; rarely do they rest as such, although they stand around or sit in groups waiting to be transported home.

It must be emphasized that the pace of market activity is set by buyers of farm produce and the brisk trade takes place within the first two hours after the produce arrives from the farms. Trade in other items is always more leisurely and goes on at a more steady pace throughout the morning and into the early afternoon.

From my observations it appears that at about 9:30 or 10 A.M. the market population is at its highest for the day; all sellers would have arrived and the first loads of foodstuffs buyers would just be preparing to leave the market (this is contrary to Hodder's observation that the peak hour is around mid-day). By mid-day, many of these buyers have left the market. Between 7 A.M. and 10:30 A.M. lorries from nearby towns make two or three trips to the market, and from about 10:30 A.M. onward, people start returning to their residences. Very few people arrive at the market on foot after 9:30 A.M. and all lorries which come back to the markets from the towns after 10:30 A.M. are empty except for the attendants.

The attendance at markets is decidedly higher during the months of October, November, and December than at any other time of the year. The markets whose populations were given for March and April (Table 2) would have one-half again as many people during the main harvest season.[11] There are many more traders in non-agricultural produce than there would be at other times of the year. There is a notable increase in the number of cloth sellers and stockfish sellers. Women who sell canned goods and other provisions have replenished and enlarged their stock. Men who sell ready-to-wear clothes and hardware and the young men from around Port Harcourt, Calabar, and Aba who deal in second-hand clothing have a wider variety and greater quantity of goods than during the rest of the year. Tailors, barbers, hairdressers, and others who sell their services in the markets are in greater demand than at other times. Part of the market land and many stalls which fall into disuse during other months are utilized at the peak of the trading season. In some cases, new stalls are erected on vacant land. This physical expansion of the markets was particularly noticable at Aiyekale, Ajagba, and Emi-Abata between late August and early October.

During the months between February and June, the market populations decrease in size, and markets tend to start later in the mornings. Markets which have hundreds of people by 8 A.M. during the main harvest season may have only a few dozen traders by 8 A.M. in the early months of the rainy season.

Immediately before the major Muslim and Christian holidays, many people living in the hamlets and villages return to their home towns for the festivities that always take place at these times. Women who usually go out to the periodic markets confine their trading activities to their compounds or to markets within the towns for a week or two. For the most part, the women are busy preparing food for the weddings, naming ceremonies, house warmings, and funeral celebrations that are held during the major holiday seasons.

The increase in size of the rural markets coincides, then, with the main cocoa harvesting season which is also the time of year when maize and yams are being harvested in the largest quantities. Decrease in size of the rural markets occurs during the main growing season and at occasions when many of the traders and farmers spend much of their time in the towns from which they originally came.

---

[11] My observations at Ojo market and other markets in the Akinyele ring, as well as of the other markets included in Figure 5 lead me to conclude that Hodder's estimate of 5,000 in attendance at Ojo or any other rural periodic market is perhaps too high. Iware, the largest market in the Akinyele ring, would have 2,000 to 3,000 people in attendance at the peak of the season.

THE ESTABLISHMENT AND ADMINISTRATION OF MARKETS

During the pre-colonial period in Yorubaland it was the chief ruler who established or authorized the establishment of the markets in his town. Thus, in the case of a metropolitan town, the creation of a market was the prerogative of the Ọba; in outlying subordinate towns, it was the prerogative of the Balẹ. According to the present Alafin of Ọyọ, when a market was to be established in an outlying town, it was customary for the Balẹ to notify the Ọba of whose domain the town was a part. This signified acknowledgment of the Ọba's suzerainty over the territory.

I know of no recorded description of the opening of a Yoruba market during the period before the colonization of Nigeria, but the ceremonies probably included sacrifices to the ancestors, propitiation of various orisa (gods), erection of an Ẹsu shrine,[12] and the planting of shade trees by the Ọba's representatives and by other important personages.

The administration of the central market was primarily in the hands of three officials appointed by the Ọba or the Balẹ. It may be presumed that markets other than the principal one were managed by persons appointed by the chiefs in whose honor these markets had been created. Referring to town officials of the Old Ọyọ Kingdom, Johnson reports:

> The Ẹni-Ọja [Iyaloja] is at the head of all the devil worshippers [Ẹsu worshippers] in the town. She also has charge of the King's market, and enjoys the perquisites accruing therefrom. She wears a gown like a man, on her arms the King leans on the day he goes to worship at the market, i.e., to propitiate the deity that presides over the markets. She has under her (1) the Olosi who has joint responsibility with her for the market. and (2) the Aroja or market keeper, and officer whose duty it is to keep order, and arrange the management of the market, and who actually resides there (1921:66).

During the period of "Indirect Rule" by the British, the establishment and maintenance of markets was brought under the purview of the authorities responsible for governing Western Nigeria. The Market Ordinance made the Divisional Native Authorities responsible for regulating market affairs and conferred upon each Native Authority the power to draft by-laws governing the markets in their jurisdiction. An illustration of the type of laws adopted is supplied by the 1949 Market Rules of the Ibadan Division Native Authority. These laws: (1) prohibited the creation of markets except by approval of the Resident for Ọyọ Province of which Ibadan Division was a part, and listed in

---

[12] Joan Wescott writes: "... the activities and characteristics of Eshu cause him to be associated with the market, the cult officials have ... a special responsibility for market affairs, and every Yoruba market includes a shrine to Eshu.... He [Eshu Elegba] is also described as a homeless wandering spirit, and as one who inhabits the market-place, the crossroads, and thresholds of houses.... In a town's central Eshu shrine, and in a sanctuary in every market-place, a laterite pillar or mound of mud is erected as a symbol of this god.... On behalf of the entire town the cult officials of the market shrine pour daily offerings of palm oil over this pillar.... his mud pillar symbol is placed wherever trouble may break out—in the market where crowds and money transactions excite men's anger...." (1962:337, 338, 345).

an attached schedule the established markets in the Division; (2) stipulated the hours within which a market could be held; (3) provided for the inspection of the market by Health Officers and any other persons appointed by the Authority; (4) stipulated that traders desiring the use of market stalls erected by the Divisional Authority or by a subordinate District Authority should make application to the Authority concerned; (5) stipulated in an attached schedule the rents to be charged for stalls and selling plots; (6) prohibited cyclists and motorists from using the market; (7) prohibited hawkers within 200 yards of any market in which stall fees were collected; (8) prohibited the use of weighing scales in places other than established markets, stores occupied by exporting firms or their agents, and stores occupied by cooperative societies. This latter provision was obviously an attempt to regulate the purchase of cocoa, palm kernels, and coffee, which are the Region's chief export crops.

The finances of most Authorities did not enable them to erect stalls in more than one or two markets or to engage personnel to adequately oversee the markets, hence *de facto* control of most of the markets remained in the hands of those who had administered them before the laws came into effect. However, steps were taken to bring at least one or two principal markets of the major town within a Division under the supervision of the Native Authorities, and certain measures of control, such as periodic inspection, were begun in all town markets. In almost all cases, the urban markets within any Authority's jurisdiction had been established before the laws came into effect. Hence, the work of the Authorities was not so much to establish as to renovate and, in some cases, to relocate the urban markets that were already in existence. The rural markets, nearly all of which were established in this century, were left almost entirely in the hands of local traditional authorities.

The basic administrative bodies in present day Western Nigeria are the territorially defined Councils which in 1954 replaced the Native Authorities. The Region consists of Divisions which are sub-divided into Districts. Towns, large and small, have local or town councils which are under the authority of the District Councils. At least one large center (Ibadan) has a city council, independent of its District Council, which was established by instrument under the Western Regional Laws.

The present laws of Western Nigeria give the District Councils and the independent City Councils created by instrument the power to "make provision by by-law" for governing markets within their territorial jurisdiction. Town Councils within any District are responsible for administering their markets in accordance with these by-laws. These by-laws have replaced all rules made by a Native Authority or Local Authority under the Market Ordinance. Rather than write their own rules, most Councils have voted to accept the Market Adoptive Bye-Laws (1956 and 1959) issued by order of the Minister of Local Government. Generally the Councils are empowered to:

(1) stipulate market days and the hours during which a market is to be held; (2) erect or authorize the erection of stalls; (3) allot specific areas within the market for the sale of the various items; (4) authorize persons who may sell in the market; (5) prohibit the intrusion in the market by specified persons or vehicles; (6) levy and collect fees from stall-holders; (7) levy and collect tolls from commercial vehicles authorized to use the market; (8) make provisions for maintaining standards of sanitation in the market and for its general upkeep and (9) employ or appoint various officials to see that the laws are upheld. Persons guilty of certain offenses which are stipulated in the by-laws are subject to arrest and may be fined upon conviction by the courts.

Although these Adoptive Bye-laws provide for the administration of markets by the Councils, they do not include a section stating that permission or approval of the Council must be obtained *before* a market can be established. Thus, Councils which operate under the Adoptive Bye-Laws are in the awkward position of being able to control, for example, the days on which a market may be held but are not able to legally control the establishment of markets. Of course, provision is made in the Local Government Law for a Council to be able to draw up its own Market Bye-Laws, and I know of one Council, the Ibadan City Council, that was in the process of doing so while I was in Nigeria. The Council had drafted Bye-Laws which included the stipulation that "it shall be unlawful for any person to use or allow to be used any premises in his possession as a market." If these Bye-Laws are approved by the Ministry of Local Government and adopted by the Council, only the Council will be able to establish a market.

In any case, this omission in the law does not present a serious problem in the towns where it would be difficult to establish a market without the authority of modern governmental organs. However, this omission does create problems in the rural areas. Some people who want to establish a market in the rural areas and who know of the Councils' administrative prerogatives assume that their Council's consent must be given before the market is established (Councils often propagate this "fact") and write for permission to start the market. But markets are sometimes started without the consent of the District Council for the area and may go unnoticed unless they are involved in some dispute which is brought to the attention of the Council. If the Council orders a market closed it cannot, if challenged, point to any law which says it has the right to authorize the creation of a market. Usually, however, if the Council charges that the market was created without its permission, the people responsible do not challenge the Council's authority. Rather, they maintain that in fact there was no *new* market created but that theirs is an "old established" market which for some reason had fallen into disuse and is now re-opened in order to bring added prosperity to the area.

I had the opportunity to study the records pertaining to markets and to interview some of those persons responsible for market affairs in the offices of the Ibadan City Council and the Oyọ Southern District Council. The latter Council had within its jurisdiction a number of towns and villages, including the towns of Oyọ and Awẹ. The materials gathered in these offices show clearly that despite the attempt to place the responsibility for the administration of markets in the hands of the modern Councils, many present-day Yoruba markets remain under the *de facto* control of local personages who are not directly linked to the Councils.

All markets in Ibadan are legally under the control of the City Council but at the present time, owing to limited financial resources, only three (Dugbẹ, Mọkọla, and Gẹgẹ) of the 11 markets and "trading areas" are actually run by the Council. Permission to occupy stalls in these three markets must be obtained from the Council's Market Committee, and monthly rents are paid into the Council's treasury. The official heads of the markets are the Market Masters employed by the Council. They, along with local policemen, are responsible for maintaining order. Periodic inspection of these three markets and all other town markets is carried out under the auspices of the Health Officer. All of the persons officially responsible for governing the markets are men.

Beneath the governmental superstructure are the female heads of the women traders. These women and their organizations contribute to the management of the markets through their representatives on the Council's Market Committee, through the petitions which they send to the Council office, and through the influence they have over the comportment of their members. In Ibadan, most of the female trade associations are market-based;[13] women selling the same commodity or commodities form "societies," each of which has an official head. At Dugbẹ and Mọkọla, where there are a number of non-Yoruba traders, associations based on ethnic group affiliation cross-cut those based on commodity line, or they constitute subdivisions of those based on commodity line. At Dugbẹ market, there is also an Iyalọja who is the head of all the women traders.

The Oyọ Southern District Council offers a revealing contrast to the Ibadan City Council with respect to its role in market administration. In the first place, responsibility for markets in small towns and rural areas outside Ibadan rests with the Ibadan District Council whereas all markets in Oyọ Southern District,[14] whether they be in the metropolitan town or in the outlying areas, come under the control of a single Council. Secondly, the funds for market development at the disposal of the Ibadan City Council,

---

[13] There was an attempt made by Madam R. A. Obisesan to organize all Ibadan market women into one association (the *Orẹdẹgbẹ* Market Women's Association) but apparently this attempt has not proven successful.

[14] Since I left Nigeria in the fall of 1962, Awẹ and a number of small towns in the Oyọ Southern District have been granted permission to form the Afijio District Council. Presumably many of the outlying markets which were in the Oyọ Southern District will come under the jurisdiction of the new Council.

though they are not adequate for the renovation and administration of all that city's markets, are nonetheless much greater than those in Oyo.

At present, the markets in Oyo town are not run by the Council.[15] There are no formal administrators for the morning markets in Oyo. No one collects fees from the sellers. There are no police in the market; when disputes arise, a number of traders intercede, enjoining the parties concerned to settle their differences calmly. These markets have no female heads of various sections because there are no formalized "societies" of traders dealing in the same line. However, some of the townswomen who trade in them may belong to associations which have their base in the night market at Akesan. The principal market (Akesan) is the King's market; traditionally the Alafin's representatives collected goods from sellers in the market. I was told that this is still done at the will of the Oba; however, it is definitely not a regular practice. In some instances, women who deal in the same commodities have a "society" with a recognized head and these women are in charge of their sections of the market. Generally speaking, they might be called in to settle any differences which arise between women selling in their sections but they may or may not become involved in disputes between buyer and seller. Major disturbances in the market are handled by the local police whose station, incidentally, is situated in the market area.

Whereas the Oyo Southern District Council has not been directly involved in the administration of town markets, it has been concerned with the supervision of the system of rural markets in many parts of its area of jurisdiction. Many of the rural markets have submitted disputes to the Council for settlement. The Council has attempted to adjudicate disputes arising when neighboring settlements hold their markets on the same day or on succeeding days. However, the Council's success is settling conflicts over market days has been limited by the unwillingness of one or both parties to abide by its decision. In such cases, it appears that the economics of location, rather than the Councils, operates as the final arbiter, with many of the conflicting markets dying off. When the Council has been involved in disputes concerning ownership of land on which rural markets are located, it has often had to submit the controversies to higher Regional Authorities for settlement.[16]

---

[15] The Council has plans to assume control over the principal town market as well as to re-establish a now-defunct market at Owode in the southeastern part of the the town.

[16] The question of ownership of land on which a market is established is a complex one. Markets within the *towns* are located on "public land"; rights over this land are vested in town authorities (Galletti, et al., 1956:111). Nowadays if a District or Town Council wants to acquire land for the establishment of a market in a town, the land must be legally transferred from the owners to the Council.

In the *rural areas* around Oyo and Awe, I noted several different types of market land ownership. In one instance, the Chief of Agunpopo Quarter in Oyo town had given permission for some persons in his quarter to settle on and cultivate lands over which he had ownerships rights. He subsequently gave permission for the establishment on his land of the Emi-Abata market (founded in the late 1940's). Chief Agunpopo is said to be the

Although the Council has attempted to deal with the problems created by the *system* of rural markets, it has left the day-to-day administration of rural markets in the hands of local authorities. In this respect, the Council seems to be following a common practice throughout the Region.

When a market is located in a village, it is the *Olori* or the Bale who is the local head of the market. Generally speaking, however, on market days the affairs of rural markets are attended to by about a half-dozen men who are referred to as "market elders." It must be emphasized that this system of market elders represents an administrative device quite distinct from, though modelled after, the traditional system of market chiefs who functioned in the urban context and who were integrated into the total governmental complex of the towns.

It is the duty of the elders to put down any disturbances which occur and to settle disputes which arise among traders in the market. They also see to it that sellers use the areas allotted to their commodity lines. These men have a right to collect produce from farmers and farm women as remuneration in kind for the use of the market. Sometimes there is a nominal fee levied against those traders who deal in non-agricultural commodities. Usually a man termed the *Areja* goes about the market collecting the payments in kind or in cash. At Emi-Abata and Ajagba, the items collected are then sold to women traders and the money is divided among the elders or used by them to purchase refreshments for themselves.

Elders can declare that a market will not be held on a particular market day if serious disputes break out or if for some other reason they deem it necessary. In one instance, the women traders from Oyo protested a rise in

official owner of the market although it is administered on market days by Elders from the surrounding hamlets. Aiyekale market (also called Ojaomoba) is said to have been established by a previous Alafin on Oyo farmland which was not under cultivation and which had not been vested in any lineage. The market is regarded by *Oyo people* as belonging to the town authorities in Oyo. A market near Igbori, a village north of Oyo, was established by a farmer on land belonging to himself. He is regarded as the owner of the market. When Apara market (founded 1962) was to be established, the farmers who owned the land submitted a notarized statement of conveyance to the Oyo Southern District Council and the land, in effect, became "public land." This market, like all others located on cleared plots of farmland, would be run by Elders from nearby hamlets.

Once a market is established, the question of land ownership becomes important only when there are conflicting authorities who claim the right to collect revenues in the market. Where markets are not directly controlled by the Councils, the right to administer a market is vested in those who established it, hence it becomes necessary to ascertain *who* established the market and whether the land on which it was established rightfully belonged to or had been handed over to the founders.

When markets in the farmlands are situated near the boundaries which demarcate the area of jurisdiction for different District Councils, disputes as to their ownership are often part of much more elaborate disputes over the extent of the Councils' areas of administration. So many of these cases exist that the Western Regional Ministry of Local Government has deemed it necessary to establish a Commission which would adjudicate boundary disputes.

lorry fares which the lorry owners claimed was necessitated by an increase in motor vehicle licensing costs. The elders at Emi-Abata decided that there would be no market until the lorry owners lowered the fares. The fare from Oyọ to Emi-Abata had been raised from 9d to 1s, 6d, but after the closing of the market, the fare was reduced to 1s.

Elders do not control prices in the market. Occasionally I saw an elder intercede between a buyer and a seller, but at most he would appeal to the seller to break bulk for a buyer who could not afford to purchase in the quantity set out by the seller. If the seller refuses to accede to the entreaties of the elder, the matter is dropped; the buyer must look elsewhere for his produce.

There is no official Iyalọja in the rural markets for the circumstances which make her a necessary official in town markets are absent from the rural situation. One factor which makes the Iyalọja an important personage in town markets is the relative permanence of the market personnel. Women who sell in these daily markets have regular stalls and attend the same market each day. Furthermore, they have multiple ties with each other and with persons in other institutions that make up the town. The Iyalọja would function not only within the market, but would represent the interests of the market women vis-a-vis other groups. The urban situation affords a definite contrast to the rural one. Even though women tend to frequent the same group of rural markets, they can buy or sell in any market, and they do not necessarily attend the same market every five days or every nine days. The ties established among women in the rural markets are largely economic ones and have but superficial social and political dimensions. Moreover, most of the women trading in the rural markets come from towns where there are formal and informal associations of women traders and it is with these "societies" that the women affiliate. If there is an Iyalọja or any female head of a trade association to whom they acknowledge allegiance, she would be in their respective towns.

SOCIAL LIFE OF THE MARKET

In the small towns and in the major towns, the night markets are more important social centers than are the daytime markets. The night markets are places where people celebrating important occasions bring their entourage and drummers. At Akẹsan market in Oyọ, hardly a night goes by without the appearance of a group of dancers in the market place. People celebrating weddings, funerals, and other occasions dance to the market on one of the nights during which the celebrations take place. Night markets are also accepted places of rendezvous for unattached males and females.

The morning markets are business affairs. Of course, they are places where one hears the town gossip, and buyers and sellers, being mostly women, exchange news of their children, households, churches, mosques, and the like. As in all markets, however, much of the talk centers on trade and financial affairs. Yoruba traders greet each other with salutations concerning trade: *Ṣe e nta?* (I hope you're selling well?; lit: are you selling?), *Ẹ ku tita* (I greet you in the act of selling); *Ẹ ku ọrọ aje* (I greet you for persevering in the struggle to make money). Buyers and sellers "pray" that each will prosper in their trade or financial endeavors.

The rural periodic market which is almost always held in the daytime is a social as well as an economic center. When the market is "resting" toward mid-day, people have time to chat about affairs in their respective towns and villages. Often people who live in the farms look forward to the arrival of traders from their home towns for this is one way in which they are kept abreast of town news. The older men gather about the stalls of tailors, barbers, and blacksmiths, and discuss affairs relating to their farms or towns. Young men stroll about the market hoping to make the acquaintance of single girls who are trading in the market. These young girls are well aware of the fact that young men are "scouting" the market; they wear eye make-up (*tiro*) to the market and, though they may be working very hard, they are careful about their appearance. When there are men in the market who paint "tatoos" on the arms, legs, or face, many young women have various designs painted on themselves during the mid-day hours when there is a lull in the market. Young brides come to the market wearing gold jewelry and expensive outfits as an indication of their new status.

Much has been said in the existing literature on Yoruba markets about the role of markets in the social life of the Yoruba, and some writers have maintained that women attend markets primarily for social rather than economic reasons. It should be stressed that attendance at market is first of all an economic activity, the social importance of the marketplace notwithstanding.

IV

AWẸ WOMEN AS TRADERS AND PRODUCERS

HAVING surveyed the world of markets in which Yoruba women operate, let us examine by reference to the activities of women in the small Yoruba town of Awẹ some specific ways in which women enter into the distributive system. It must be emphasized that the economic activities of Awẹ women cannot be said to represent all the types of trade undertaken by Yoruba women. In the first place, the scale of most Awẹ women's trade operations is very small. Those women dealing in imported goods, unlike some women in Ibadan and other towns, do not have the capital to buy in gross quantities from European importers. In fact many of them buy from other Yoruba women. The women who buy farm produce for resale in Awẹ or in other towns do not buy in quantities as large as those purchased by other women whom I interviewed during my field work. Secondly, the range of goods handled by Awẹ women is not as extensive as that carried by women in the larger towns. The limited range of goods reflects the smaller amount of trading capital available to these women and the nature of consumer demand in small towns: for example, many women traders in Ọyọ, and an even larger number in Ibadan, deal in various types of cloth; only a few Awẹ women sell cloth and those who do so have a very limited selection of goods. Having a small amount of capital, they cannot buy many pieces of cloth; those which they do stock are the cheaper varieties of imported cottons which most consumers can afford. Thus, while the activities of women in Awẹ provide insight into the nature of trade in Yorubaland, and in many respects are typical of operations carried on by women in small towns and rural areas, they do not reveal many of the equally important patterns of trade encourntered in the activities of city market women and wealthy women traders.

WOMEN TRADERS IN AWẸ

Nearly all women in Awẹ are engaged in some type of work for which they receive cash remuneration and which takes them outside the home for much of the day. But being "outside the home" means very different things, depending on the nature of the employment in which a woman is engaged. Most women are traders of one type or another but while some of them operate in the daily markets situated inside the town, the activities of others involve travel to periodic markets, most of which are located within 10 miles of the town and a few of which are farther away. Other women move between nearby periodic markets and daily markets in Ibadan, some 33 miles away, or Lagos, about 123 miles away. Some women who do not trade in the markets hawk their goods about the town or in the neighboring towns of Oyo and Akinmorin. Still others have shops or stalls located in various parts of the town and carry on their trade in these locations. As will be shown, a single trader may combine more than one of these modes of operation in order to maximize the returns on her investment.

The trading orbit of any woman depends primarily on the type of goods which she handles and the amount of capital at her disposal for investment in these lines.[1] For example, the pattern of movement for a woman dealing in imported cloth differs in detail from that of a woman dealing in locally grown foodstuffs. On the other hand, the trading orbit of women dealing in locally grown foodstuffs depends on the size of their trading capital. A trader in farm produce may buy in the rural markets for resale in the town; she may buy in the rural markets for resale in Ibadan or Lagos; or she may *buy* and *sell* in the town, her suppliers being women who have bought the foodstuffs in rural markets. *In general*, women who buy farm produce in the rural markets for resale in Lagos or Ibadan have greater amounts of trading capital than those who resell only in the town and these latter women in turn have more working capital than those who *buy and sell* farm produce in the town.

The trade orbit is also affected by a number of sociological factors such as age, point in the domestic cycle, number of children and/or co-wives, and other considerations which will be taken up at a later point.

Whether their trade activities are carried on mainly within the town or outside the town, most women in Awe deal in agricultural products. Either the women buy and sell these foodstuffs in their natural state or they trade in processed items such as gari (cassava meal), lafun (dried pieces of cassava), or elubo (dried slices of yams). Others buy foodstuffs which they cook and sell to the general public. There are no agricultural products destined for the internal Nigerian market that are not handled by women.

As a rule, however, women do not figure prominently in the marketing of export crops. The marketing of cocoa and palm kernels, the two most important export crops grown in the areas studied,[2] is carried on by men. The Western Region Marketing Board, which is the final buyer for all export crops grown in the Region, issues licenses to firms who act as its buying agents. One

---

[1] A woman's choice of commodity line is determined by a number of considerations, but the size of trading capital is a major factor. A trader with £5 to invest may carry on a lucrative trade in gari and certain other farm products but she could hardly think of trading in cloth.

[2] Some coffee and ground-nuts are also grown in the area, however, the amount of coffee grown is very small and most of the ground-nuts are consumed locally.

of the firms, the Association of Nigerian Co-operative Exporters, purchases its crops through the various cooperative societies affiliated with it. Other Nigerian, European, and Levantine firms licensed by the board purchase the crops through buyers referred to as "commission agents" or "middlemen traders." The buyers may have working for them men who are known as "scalers" because they have weighing machines in various markets and settlements throughout the buyer's district. These "scalers" in turn sometimes "make use of assistants known as 'runners' and 'pan buyers,'" the latter term referring to the fact that these assistants purchase by volume rather than by weight. Runners or pan buyers have the task of collecting small quantities in remote areas not equipped with cocoa weighing scales (Galletti, et al., 1956:Ch. 4).

Galletti and his associates report that women in the Owo and Akoko areas act as sub-buyers. In the markets around Awe, there were no women sub-buyers although some women did bring to market the cocoa grown by their husbands or other male relatives. I knew one woman who was a cocoa farmer in her own right, having inherited the trees from her father; she belonged to the Awe Cooperative Society and sold her crop through that organization.

The virtual exclusion of women from the marketing of export crops may be due to the nature of the system by which the crops are collected for shipment abroad. At the beginning of each season, the licensed agents for the Marketing Board make advances to their buyers for the purchase of export crops. These licensed firms guard against default on the debt by taking security from the buyer to cover part of the advance. The terms of security accepted are "deposit of cash, deposit of deeds, of buildings, and guarantees by sureties" (Galletti, et al., 1956:43). Even though women earn money and own property, it is the men who own and control most of the real property in Yorubaland and who have been able to accumulate the greatest cash and surety reserves. Therefore, men have been in a better economic position to take advantage of the trade niches created by the necessity to decentralize the process of collecting export crops. Then too, because the men cultivated the crops, it was they who received information from the government and other sources concerning the procedures by which the crops were to be marketed and hence some of the farmers themselves negotiated for jobs as buyers (commission agents or middlemen traders) with the firms licensed by the Marketing Board.

Whereas cocoa is grown almost entirely for export, palm kernels are grown for the internal market as well. Almost all the internal trade in palm kernels is carried on by women. The black oil (*adin*) which is extracted from the kernels is used primarily in the manufacture of a type of soap referred to as *ose dudu* (black soap). Makers of adin are supplied with palm kernels (ekuro) by women traders who buy in the rural markets.

Whereas the export crops handled by men do not flow through the entire system of indigenous markets, the non-export crops bought and sold by women are traded in every type of market in Yorubaland. There are three general patterns of movement for Awẹ women who deal in agricultural products:

1. Some of them buy in the periodic markets, in farm hamlets, or at places along the roads leading to the farms, for sale in their compounds or in the daily markets within the town;
2. Others buy in the rural markets, in the farmlands, and along roadsides for sale in Ibadan or Lagos;
3. Some women buy produce in the town from Ọyọ women or from other Awẹ women and they sell in small measures in the town.

From the three general patterns of movement outlined above, it can be seen that women who buy outside the town purchase their supplies in one or more of three locations: markets, "roadside buying stations," and farm hamlets. The most important supply centers are the rural periodic markets, including a few markets located in settlements which might properly be termed small towns (see Chapter III).

Most Awẹ women buy produce at Ajagba and Emi-Abata markets. Ajagba is located five miles east of Awẹ on the Ọyọ-Iwo road, and Emi-Abata is seven miles northeast of Awẹ on the road to Ejigbo (see Figure 5 for the location of these and other markets attended by Awẹ traders). According to the Yoruba calculation, these are both nine-day markets whose timing is such that one of the two meets every fifth day (see Table 3 for the calendar of market days). When Ajagba is held on Sunday, Emi-Abata falls on Thursday of the same week. Ajagba is held again on Monday of the following week and Emi-Abata meets on Friday of that week. Although both markets are within walking distance of the town, the women usually travel to them by lorries which depart from Awẹ and from Ọyọ. Some women walk home from Ajagba but very few walk to Awẹ from Emi-Abata.

A number of Awẹ women, especially those who spend much of the year in the farm hamlets, attend Aiyekale market which, by the most commonly used motor roads, is 12 miles southeast of Awẹ. To reach the market by motor transport, one travels seven miles east along the Ọyọ-Iwo road, turns south, and travels five miles along an unpaved road. Most of the Awẹ women, however, like the Ọyọ and Iwo women who also attend this market, come by foot from the surrounding farm hamlets in which they live. A few lorries transport women from Ọyọ and Awẹ to the market, but because the unpaved road leading to the market is virtually impassable during much of the rainy season, women from the town do not regularly attend this market. In any case, Aiyekale is a five-day market whose days coincide with those of Ajagba and Emi-Abata so that any woman who regularly attends the other two markets could not attend Aiyekale.

WOMEN AS TRADERS AND PRODUCERS

The market at Ajawa, some 20 miles northeast of Awe, is also attended by a few Awe women, but the only one among them who goes to the market each time it meets was born and bred in Ajawa. The lorries which take Awe and Oyo women to Ajawa travel 16 miles north along the Oyo-Ogbomosho road to Ipeba and four miles east along an unpaved road leading to this small town. Ajawa market is held every fifth day; its market days are the same as those of Aiyekale, hence, women who attend this market do not attend Aiyekale, Ajagba, or Emi-Abata.

TABLE 3

CALENDAR OF MARKET DAYS*

Sunday	Monday	Tuesday	Wednesday	Thursday	Friday	Saturday
Ajagba Aiyekale Ajawa	Ife-Odan Ajegunle Igbeti	Iware		Emi-Abata Aiyekale Ajawa	Ife-Odan Igbeti	Apara
	Ajagba Aiyekale Ajawa	Ife-Odan Ajegunle Igbeti	Iware		Emi-Abata Aiyekale Ajawa	Ife-Odan Igbeti
Apara		Ajagba Aiyekale Ajawa	Ife-Odan Ajegunle Igbeti	Iware		Emi-Abata Aiyekale Ajawa

*The markets in this calendar do not constitute a ring. They are periodic markets in which Awe women buy produce for resale in other locations. Each woman frequents two or sometimes three of these markets. The following combinations were reported: (a) Ajagba, Emi-Abata; (b) Ajagba, Emi-Abata, Ajegunle; (c) Ajagba, Emi-Abata, Ife-Odan; (d) Ajagba, Aiyekale; (e) Aiyekale, Iware; (f) Ajawa, Ife-Odan; (g) Ajawa, Igbeti.

Since nearly all these markets enter into more than one ring, there are a number of partial rings in this group. *Some* of them would be constituted as follows:
  (1) Ajagba, Emi-Abata, Aiyekale, Ajegunle, Apara;
  (2) Ajawa, Ife-Odan (plus Iwoate, Idewure, Lagbedu and other markets near Ife-Odan);
  (3) Ajawa (plus Awereke, Ijawaya, Idiya, Olo and other markets on or near the Oyo-Ogbomosho Road);
  (4) Ife-Odan (plus Sagbe, Tesan, Ogbagba, Oyedeji and other markets between Iwo and Ibadan);
  (5) Aiyekale, Iware (plus Imeleke, Agberire, Elesu and other markets near Iware);
  (6) Iware (plus other markets in "Akinyele Ring" described by Hodder).

Most of the markets in parentheses are not shown on any map in this book and not all of them were visited by the writer. Nonetheless, their locations and timings were given by traders interviewed in various markets, and most of the settlements in which they are located appear on maps of Oyo Division, Oshun Division, or Ibadan Division prepared by the Surveyor-General of Western Nigeria. From the interviews conducted, it appears that traders who reside in the same community tend to frequent the same markets. In each market, I found that traders who came from the same place, irrespective of the commodities in which they dealt, would list the same two or three markets as the ones in which they traded. One or two of these traders might attend one or more markets in addition to the most frequently mentioned ones.

A few women buy produce in the market at Ife-Odan, some 12 miles east of Awe on the road to Ejigbo. The market is only five miles east of Emi-Abata but the part of the road from Awe to Emi-Abata is considerably better than that from Emi-Abata to Ife-Odan.[3] This latter portion of the road is sometimes not negotiable during the heavy rains and it is a difficult passage at any time of the year. The lorries at Ife-Odan market are usually not Oyo lorries but those that have come from Ibadan via another route or from Mosifa near Ejigbo. Ife-Odan is a five-day market which falls on the day after Aiyekale, Ajawa, Emi-Abata, and Ajagba.

Occasionally, some Awe women buy foodstuffs at Iware, the largest of the periodic markets in the Awe-Oyo area. The distance from Awe to Iware is 12 miles via the unpaved road through Akinmorin; however, the lorries which transport most Oyo and Awe women travel via the Oyo-Ibadan road to Fiditi, then east along an unpaved road, a total distance of about 16 miles. The market at Iware is held every nine days; its market day falls on the second day *after* Ajagba. When Ajagba is held on Sunday, Iware is held on Tuesday.

In January of 1962, a new market was opened at Abowu-Apara, a site about three and one-half miles east of Awe in the farmlands. The market is held every ninth day, and its market day is two days after that of Emi-Abata. When Emi-Abata falls on Thursday, Apara is held on Saturday. Almost all of the Awe women who trade in Emi-Abata and Ajagba attended Apara for a while after it had opened. However, by March, there were complaints that the Oyo women who lived in the surrounding farm hamlets and who sold produce in the market had been hostile toward the buyers from Awe and the Awe women decided to boycott the market.[4]

There are a few other markets that are occasionally attended by Awe women, or that are frequented by one or two women. Ajegunle, a small market located about one and one-half miles south of the town on land belonging to an Awe farmer, is attended by a small number of Awe women. Apparently, this market has not been very successful because if is held on the day after the older market at Ajagba. Most farmers and women from the

---

[3] Women from Ife-Odan who attend Emi-Abata go by foot.

[4] The hostility of the Oyo women may have been due to the fact that the Awe people had opposed the opening of the market (the town Council had even protested to the Ministry of Local Government) on the grounds that the farmland on which the market was to be established was part of Awe farmland. During this time, there was pending an inquiry into the legitimacy of the claim by Awe and some other small towns that they should be allowed to secede from the Oyo Southern District Council to form the Afijio District Council. Awe leaders argued that should the decision be made in their favor, many of the lands under Oyo's jurisdiction, including those at Abowu-Apara, would belong to Awe. Furthermore Awe people claimed that these and other lands were rightfully theirs but that from the 1830's onward they had been progressively encroached upon by Oyo people. It will be recalled that Oyo people moved into this area after the Fulani invasion of the old capital to the north. Awe, which had formerly been a town in the Egba Agura kingdom, subsequently became a vassal town under Oyo.

hamlets would have sold their foodstuffs at Ajagba on the day previous to Ajegunle, hence, they would have little or nothing to sell at Ajegunle. Aiyekale is also held on the day before Ajegunle so that people in the farmlands lying south of Ajegunle would also have sold their produce before this market meets.

Two women reported that they buy foodstuffs in the *daily* market at Iseyin, a large town some 20 miles northwest of Oyo, and four women said that they occasionally purchased pepper at Soku, a periodic market near Iseyin. One woman regularly buys a number of farm products at the periodic night market at Igbeti, a town about 80 miles north of Oyo.

Women who buy produce in the periodic markets usually attend two or three markets which fall on different days so that the morning and early afternoon of two or three days of each week would be spent in the market. Most Awe women attend the same markets each time they meet, and have established "customer" relationships with some of the farmers and farm women who bring produce for sale. If women receive reports that a market other than the ones they attend is a good place to buy, they might try this market for one or two times and if they are able to establish good relationships with the sellers, they may continue to trade there. That women like to "know" new markets is illustrated by the fact that when it became known that I attended a number of markets in addition to those frequented by Awe traders, some of the women asked to go along with me to those markets. On different occasions I took women to Ife-Odan which, of course, was known to them but which, as I said, is not easily accessible from Awe. On one occasion I took a woman to Teṣan (from the English, "station") market located in the village which has grown up around the Iwo railroad station. In some cases, women volunteered to introduce me to markets in which they did not trade but which were known to them. In no case, however, would a woman accompany me to a "new" market which fell on the same day as the one she regularly attended. For example, even though I often discussed Ajawa market with a number of women, none of those who attended Emi-Abata or Ajagba would accompany me to Ajawa which falls on the same day as both the other markets. Having established trading ties with people at Emi-Abata and Ajagba, these women preferred not to risk attending Ajawa where they might be less successful in buying produce. Similarly, a woman from Ajawa who had lived in Awe during the eight years of her marriage did not attend Emi-Abata nor Ajagba but preferred to buy in Ajawa where she had trade and kinship ties.

In addition to the periodic markets, there are certain generally known points along various of the roads and paths leading to the farmlands at which women who live in the town buy foodstuffs from the Awe and Oyo women who live in the farm hamlets. There is one place, referred to simply as Ona (literally, road or roadside), at which Awe women have been buying produce for over 25 years. This "roadside station" is just outside the north edge of the town, about one mile from the point where the Awẹ-Ejigbo road branches from the Ọyọ-Iwo road. Some women who attend Ajagba and Emi-Abata also buy at Ọna on days when the periodic markets are not being held. About a dozen women, most of them over 60, do not attend any periodic market but they buy farm products at Ọna each morning.

On non-market days, some women go out to certain of the hamlets to buy gari from the farm women who process this meal from cassava. Those women of the town who trade in gari usually do not buy in the periodic markets at all; rather they go out to the farm hamlets or to certain roadside points to buy from their regular suppliers.

Women who trade in agricultural produce usually deal in more than one commodity, the exceptions being that many women trade *only* in gari and some of them trade only in different varieties of pepper. The most common items handled are: yams, elubọ (dried yam slices), gari, lafun (dried pieces of cassava), maize, pepper, egusi (melon seeds), millet, beans, ẹfọ (greens of different varieties), plantain, bananas, okra, tomatoes, oranges, groundnuts, kola nuts, orogbo nuts, and palm kernels. One trader usually handles at least three of these items and many of them deal in six or eight different ones.

Women who buy produce in the markets and at the roadsides, and in the farm hamlets *for sale in the town* have three main outlets for their goods: they sell to cooked-food sellers and to manufacturers of adin (palm kernel oil); to women who break bulk and sell to consumers; and to consumers. I will illustrate these patterns of trade by reference to the activities of a few women.

A woman from Ile Alagbẹdẹ Akinye (literally: The Compound or House of Alagbẹdẹ Akinye) buys yams, elubọ, three varieties of pepper, plantain, oranges, groundnuts, lafun, gari, and egusi at Ajagba and Emi-Abata. Occasionally she buys at Ajegunle, and while I was in Awẹ, she accompanied me to Tẹsan and to Ife-Ọdan where she bought some of the items in which she trades. This trader sells nearly all the elubọ, lafun, gari, and peppers to a cooked-food seller at Ile Asalu. When she comes from the markets, she notifies this customer that there is a certain amount of produce on hand, and the customer buys these items on credit or with cash, depending on her financial position at the time. Plantain and egusi (used to make oil and in cooking a type of stew) are sold to the women who prepare the meals for the boys at Awẹ High School. Some plantain is purchased by another woman who sells dodo (fried plantain) at one point along the main road in the town. Most of the groundnuts are bought by a woman from Ile Komu who is a seller of roasted groundnuts. Oranges are sold to women who peel them and sell them in the streets to passers-by who "drink" them for refreshment.

The trader who is a native of Ajawa and who is married into Ile Akoroewe at Awẹ, buys maize, elubọ, gari, yams, and pepper at Ajawa and Igbẹti. Occasionally, she buys in the daily market at Iseyin and at Ife-Ọdan.

She has a shop in the Bale's Quarter (see Chapter I) where she sells on those days when she does not go to market. The maize which she buys by the hundred weight bag is sold by the bag and by the *denge*, which is the name given to one type of pan used in measuring a number of foodstuffs. When women are planning a celebration in their compound, they may buy one or two bags of maize at a time. On one occasion when I was in the shop, three women came to buy two bags of maize. When they had negotiated the price, they asked the seller to hold the bags until later in the week when they would be able to pay for them. The seller agreed to hold the maize but said that if they did not come at the appointed time, she would send the maize by lorry to be sold by her sister who lives in Ife-Odan because she did not want to keep too many bags on hand at Awe. Later in the week, the women came to pay for one bag and were given the other bag on credit, they having promised to pay in another week's time. This trader regularly sells maize by the denge to women who prepare ogi and eko (two types of cooked foods) for sale in the town. Gari is sold by the denge directly to the consumers. The pepper is sold to resellers by the denge and to consumers in small piles costing from 1d. to 6d. Yams are sold separately or by the ile (three yams = one ile) and elubo by the calabash to consumers.

A woman who lives at Ile Lalemi buys pepper, (and occasionally) tomatoes, and okra at Ajawa and at another periodic market near Iseyin. These items are sold by the denge to women who resell in the morning market at Awe or in various places throughout the town. Many of the resellers who buy from this trader are old women with very little trading capital. They sell tomatoes or peppers in small piles costing from 1d. to 3d. The okra they cut crosswise into thin, round slices which are allowed to dry and are sold in little piles costing a half-penny or a penny each. The trader herself also sells pepper in her compound and, in the mornings, on the porch of a compound near Bode market. Most of the women who buy from her in these places are consumers.

The women who buy only at Ona trade mostly in lafun and elubo but whenever other items are brought to the roadside by women from the farms, they are purchased by the two or three women who buy a variety of foodstuffs in the periodic markets and who also buy at Ona. The elubo and lafun are resold to women who prepare oka amala, a type of cooked food, for sale in town. Sometimes the farm women have ekuro (palm kernels) for sale; these are bought by a few traders who resell to the makers of adin.

The gari sellers who buy at various roadsides sell to consumers in the town. There are many gari sellers in Awe; one can hardly find a compound in which there is not at least one woman dealing in this important staple. It is bought from the makers by the denge and resold by the denge or in smaller measures. A gari trader who resells by the denge makes her profit in the following manner. When she buys from the maker, she is allowed to extend the volume of the pan by putting one arm around its rim as she measures the meal into it. When the gari is resold, customers are not allowed to "put their arms around the pan" but are simply given a heaping panful (no measure is considered full if its contents are level with the brim); the small extra amount of gari (worth two or three pennies) obtained from the makers by "putting the arms around the pan" constitutes the trader's gain on the transaction.

Another group of women buy foodstuffs for resale in Ibadan and Lagos. At the time that I was in Awe, there were only two women who regularly sold their purchases in Ibadan. One woman from Ile Sogbo bought lafun, gari, elubo, yams, maize, and peppers at Ajagba, Emi-Abata, and Ona and sold them at Orita Merin, as she had done for the past 25 years. During the months from September to December, she travelled to Ibadan about twice a week, but throughout the year, she went to Orita Merin once a week or once every two weeks. For the trip to Ibadan, each item, except yams, is packed into hundred weight bags. At Orita Merin, she sells mostly to Ibadan women who resell in various parts of the city; all items except yams are sold by the panful (denge) or by the bag, depending on the quantity on hand and on the nature of the market in Ibadan. Yams are sold by piles of three, i.e., by the ile. Like all women who sell at Orita Merin, the trader pays to the person on whose "porch" she displays her goods one shilling for each bag of foodstuffs brought from Awe. In the case of yams, it is the *buyer* who pays the fees charged by the people at Orita Merin. The buyer pays 1d on every shilling she spends for yams so that the fee for 5/- worth of yams is 5d. The trader from Awe sometimes spent the night in Ibadan; when she did so, she slept free of charge in the compound of one "Raji" whom she described as the "head" of the traders at Orita Merin.

A trader who lives at Ile Olode buys gari, lafun, elubo, maize, yams, peppers, and plantain at Ajagba, Emi-Abata, and Ajegunle. On non-market days, she buys gari in the hamlets around Awe. Three or four times a month, she takes gari to Ibadan to be sold at Ayeye; the other items are sold in her compound at Awe. The procedure for selling at Ayeye is the same as that at Orita Merin, the trader paying 1s on each bag of gari sold in the market. This woman usually stayed in Ibadan for two or three days at a time, spending the evenings with relatives in that city.

Several Awe women sell produce in Lagos; one of them is a woman from Ile Bale. In addition to the usual variety of foodstuffs, she takes chickens, and a type of locally-grown beans to Lagos at the end of each month. All the foodstuffs and many of the chickens are bought at Ajagba, Emi-Abata, and Ona. During the time that she is collecting the items for her trip, she sells to consumers and traders in Awe. In fact all of the plantain and much of the gari which she buys during the month are sold at Awe. Generally, the trader does not sell yams in Awe because she can get a higher price for them at Lagos. In the city, she sells mainly to other women traders; she sets out her commodities in front of one of the shops belonging to the Ajao Bros. There are no set fees for trading at the shop; however, each of the women who sell there give a small donation to a man whom the property owners designated as their collector. Women who go from Awe to Lagos stay with relatives there for a period of about one week. They do not pay for their lodgings but they always take foodstuffs as presents for those with whom they live and for other relatives and friends.

It was said earlier in this chapter that whereas most women are engaged in work that takes them outside their homes, the actual time spent away from their residences and the distances travelled in any given period vary considerably depending on the line of work in which a woman is engaged. Generally speaking, trade in foodstuffs can be an almost sedentary occupation, it can involve movement over short distances, or it can entail more mobility than any other occupation engaged in by Yoruba women. The various degrees of mobility are illustrated by the activities of the women described above.

At the one extreme are old women who buy small quantities of produce from traders in the town. Often these women buy from others who live in the same compound or in compounds nearby. They resell very near their places of residence; at most, they walk to the main street in their quarter or to the main street in the town where they display their commodities on mats or calabashes placed on the ground, or on the porch of a compound. These women come out early in the morning and by mid-morning most of them have returned to their compounds where they remain for most of the day. Of course, their relative immobility is in part a function of age but some women of the same age are engaged in more active occupations. The point is that if women have very little capital and if they invest this in foodstuffs, theirs will be a relatively sedentary existence. There is little point in hawking these bits of foodstuffs about the town since there are many women selling the same items in every part of Awe.

A more mobile group are the women who buy outside the town for resale in the town, but here again degrees of mobility can be distinguished. Women who buy gari and other foodstuffs from the farm hamlets or roadside stations spend most of their time in the town. Gari sellers usually buy their stock two or three mornings a week. They walk about a mile or two to places where they meet the women who make the cassava meal, buy as many panfuls as they can afford, and return to their compounds by 10 or 11 A.M. Many of them are back home by 9 A.M. Only a few gari sellers trade outside their compounds; those who do so walk two miles to Oyo, hawk about the town and return to Awe before noon. Women who buy lafun or elubo at Ona follow a pattern similar to that of the gari buyers. They walk to the roadside (about one and one-half miles away) in the mornings, and make their purchases, load them on their heads, and return home before noon.

Traders who buy in the periodic markets for resale in the town are in the markets two or three days a week. They leave town in the early morning and return by mid-afternoon or earlier. On non-market days, these traders spend their mornings in places where their customers come to buy from them: most of them sell in their compounds, one among them has a shop.

The most mobile of the traders in agricultural products are those who buy primarily for resale in the city markets. They are seldom at home on *any* morning: they are buying in the markets, at the roadsides, or in the farm hamlets. On market days they are away buying foodstuffs until about 2 P.M. The traders who sell in Ibadan travel to that city at least once or twice in each two-week period. The older woman who sells in Ibadan buys red palm oil, beans and, occasionally, rice for sale on her return to Awe. Much of the time when she is not buying in the farmlands or selling in Ibadan, she is out collecting money from women who buy the oil, beans, or rice on credit. The women who sell in Lagos are away from the town only once a month but they are usually away for five to seven days at a time.

One point must be stressed. The women who *regularly* trade *farm products* between Awe and Lagos or Ibadan do not number more than a dozen. There are hundreds who trade between the nearby farmlands (including markets) and the town. About a dozen women regularly buy in markets farther away. Only one woman buys regularly in Igbeti, some 80 miles away (although there is another Awe woman who lives at Igbeti, takes yams to Lagos, and makes periodic trips to Awe where she sells non-agricultural commodities). Thus, by far the largest number of foodstuffs sellers move within areas near the town.

There are many women in Awe who trade in "provisions." The term *wosiwosi* (which is translated in one dictionary as "petty trading") denotes a certain variety of goods, most of them packaged and many of them imported, and English-speaking traders translated it by the term "provisions." Thus, women who trade in these packaged commodities, regardless of the scale of their operations, will say: "Wosiwosi ni no nta" or "I trade in provisions."

Women who sell provisions handle a variety of canned and packaged foods (milk, tomatoes and tomato products, various types of fish, corned beef, coffee, tea, ovaltine and other chocolate drinks, sugar, bread, crackers, candies, cookies, etc.), cigarettes, matches, imported soap, detergents, cosmetics, hair pomades, patented medicines, and other commodities. Some women also carry sewing articles, trinkets, a few school supplies, and small items of hardware such as padlocks. Women with provisions shops also stock beer, stout, and soft drinks. There is a striking contrast between the stalls and shops of females who deal in provisions and those of men who also describe themselves as traders in "wosiwosi." Generally, these men handle a combination of hardware (cutlasses, lanterns and lamps, rat traps, bicycle parts, nails, hinges, locks, clocks, etc.), men's underwear, caps and belts, ready-to-wear clothes for young children, sandals and shoes, various items made of plastic ("carry-all" bags, women's purses, etc.), and school supplies (exercise books, rulers, pencils, readers, etc.). Some men also carry canned milk but no other food items.

There are many provisions shops in Awe. There are eight shops located along the main road of the town, one or two shops inside each Quarter, and a large number of small stalls scattered throughout the town. A number of provisions sellers stack their most common items (especially cigarettes, matches milk and cube sugar) on calabashes that are displayed at any convenient spot in the town. There is one large store (Ajao Bros.) which sells provisions to traders rather than to consumers.

About a half-dozen of the provisions sellers who have shops or stalls in the town also regularly sell at Emi-Abata and Ajagba. A few of them attended Apara market when it first opened. Women take to the markets only two or three of each item which they handle; sometimes they do not take their entire range of goods, but only those things that are usually bought by people in the rural areas. From October to December, provisions sellers expand the range and increase the quantity of items which they take to the rural markets, because the demand for their stock is greater during the main harvest season. These provisions sellers are patronized by traders as well as by consumers. Some women who live in the farm hamlets buy cigarettes, matches, milk, and a few other items for resale in the settlements in which they live.

Those provisions sellers who have shops or large stalls buy their stock at Amunigun in Ibadan or at the Ajao Bros. store in Oyo. At Amunigun, Awe women buy from other Yoruba women, some of whom buy directly from the importing firms, others of whom have themselves bought from women traders. Those items which sell relatively quickly such as cigarettes and canned milk are often bought from the Ajao Bros. store in Awe. One woman reported that she patronized the United Africa Company store at Oyo. While I was in Awe, many women bought canned milk from a company that had recently introduced a new brand (Mello) into Nigeria, and that sent its supply truck to Awe and other small towns.[5] Women who buy at Ibadan, or from Ajao Bros. and other companies, purchase their stock in parcels or by the dozen. In the latter case, a price is quoted for the dozen and a woman may buy the entire dozen or she may buy one-half, one-third, or one-fourth at the dozen rate. For example, a woman may buy one dozen jars of Ovaltine for 19/-[6] and she may

---

[5] Whereas nearly every provisions seller in Awe (like those in Oyo and in all the periodic markets visted) had stocked the Peak, Brooke Bond, or Duck brands of evaporated milk, most of the Awe women began to stock Mello which cost the same as the other brands.

[6] The Nigerian pound (£), like other sterling currencies, is divided into 20 shillings (written as 20/- or 20s.); each shilling is divided into twelve pence (written as 12d.). In 1961 and 1962, the Nigerian pound (£) was equivalent to approximately $2.80 in U.S. Currency.

buy three jars (one-fourth) for 4/9 (i.e., 1/7 each), but two jars would cost 1/9 each.

Many of the Awe women who sell provisions on a small scale (such as those whose entire stock consists of items carried on one or two trays) buy from Awe women who have shops or large stalls. A woman with a shop buys a parcel (12 cartons) of matches for £1.1, £1.1.6, or £1.2, depending on the source of her supply. She sells one carton (10 boxes) to resellers at 1/9, 1/11, or 2/-, according to the price which she paid for the parcel. Five boxes would cost a reseller one-half the price of a carton. Both the woman who bought by the parcel and the one who bought by the carton would sell each box of matches for 3d. Still other traders buy one box (72 to 76 matches) at 3d. and sell a bundle of eight matches for ½d., making a total of 4½d. for the box. I have even known a trader who sold 12 matches to the bundle, her only gain being the few extra matches that were sometimes left over in the box.

Some of the women buy matches by the parcel (12 cartons) and compete with their trader-customers at every level of distribution: they sell by the carton (10 boxes), by the half-carton, by the box (72-76 matches), and by the bundle (eight matches). Similarly some of those who buy by the carton sell by the box and by the bundle.

Women who buy by the box can only realize a gain by reselling in loose bundles because no one would pay more than 3d. for a box of matches. Women who buy their stock at Amunigun in Ibadan purchase their stock about once a month. During the main harvest season, they may go to Ibadan every two weeks. Unless they have other business in the city, they usually return to Awe on the same day. Those who buy at Oyo and Awe do not have any fixed intervals at which they replenish their stock. They buy as they sell, each time purchasing only those items which have been sold from the shop. Women who carry small stocks sometimes purchase items just at the time there is a demand for them. For example, the petty traders in Awe usually stock one brand of cigarettes, namely Galleon which is the cheapest of the Nigerian-made brands. If a person asks one of these women for Bicycle, a more expensive brand, and if there is a child around, the woman would send the child to buy the cigarettes from another trader; she might even buy only one pack. The seller charges the reseller 2/2 or 2/3 for the pack which is the same price that consumers pay in some places, but in small towns such as Awe where the turnover on these expensive cigarettes is very slow, many traders, regardless of the quantity in which they buy, charge the consumer 2/6 which amounts to 1½d. per cigarette. In the present case, the consumer is almost sure to pay 2/6; however, if the reseller knows him very well and if she bought the pack for 2/2, she might sell it for 2/3.

Generally speaking, trade in provisions is a relatively sedentary occupation, carried on near the places where the women live. Many women have their shops in their compound area. A few provisions sellers have set up stalls in the area of Bode market and they sell there on the mornings when they do not attend Ajagba or Emi-Abata. Provisions sellers with shops spend most of the day from about 7 A.M. until sundown in these places. Those with stalls in or near their compounds might also spend most of the day in them, but those who come out to Bode market in the mornings usually return to their compounds before 1 P.M., and may or may not return to the stalls in the afternoon. Those of their neighbors who need anything would buy from them in the house.

Another type of trader to whom reference has been made is the cooked-food seller. The involvement of women in economic activities outside the home has led many women to specialize in the sale of prepared foods, at once providing themselves with a livelihood and supplying a service to other women who cannot do all their own cooking.[7]

In Awe, the morning meal for nearly everyone—men, women, and children—is purchased from cooked-food sellers. The most common breakfast foods are made from beans or corn. Ogi and eko, two foods made from maize, are the most common breakfast foods. Eko, a solid food, is most often eaten with akara (fried cakes made from ground beans and condiments). Both these foods are prepared by cooked-food sellers, but the women who make one do not make the other. Amala, made from elubo (yam flour), is also bought in the morning but it seems that adults and older children, more than young children, eat this as a breakfast food. When eaten in the mornings, amala is usually supplemented with a stew (obe gbegiri) made from beans. Other common foods sold in the morning are: igbalo (made from ground melon seeds, ground beans, ground pepper and onions) and ewa (beans cooked with oil, onions, and salt).

Women often prepare their own afternoon meals after they have returned from their morning's work. Those who buy produce in the periodic markets are sometimes too tired after a day in the market to cook for

---

[7] The sale in cooked foods appears to be as old as the occupational specialization which gave rise to it and of which it is evidence. The nineteenth century writers referred to cooked foods as "provisions" and remarked on cooked food sellers in the various towns (see Lander, 1833, Vol. 1:170; Bowen 1857:297; 1858:12-13; 35).

It can be proposed that the sale of prepared foods is also related to the nature of the domestic units in Yorubaland. As will be seen in Chapter VI, women's economic activities often require that children be left in their compounds while the mother goes to work. Mabogunje has stated that polygyny sometimes leads to a jealousy among wives with respect to their children and "most mothers would be afraid to have their children fed by other women" (Odu:no. 5:29). Thus, it seems a tenable hypothesis that the system of "restauranteering" is a complement of a situation where women cannot assume full responsibility for their children and where they have reason to be anxious about leaving them to be tempted to take food from women who might want to do them harm. The cooked-food sellers, who prepare food for the general public, can be trusted to provide food for the children. (It should be noted also that women usually buy prepared foods from women whom they know well and have been patronizing for a long time. If they leave their children to buy their own foods, they usually give instructions as to whom they should patronize.)

themselves and their children and may buy their afternoon meals; on non-market days, they too usually prepare the afternoon meal. Amala, iyan (pounded yams), isu sise (boiled yams) and eba (gari prepared in hot water) are the most common afternoon meals. These are eaten with various kinds of stews. Only occasionally would a woman buy eba from a cooked-food seller for it is a very easy food to prepare, but men who buy their meals and women who are away from their compounds do buy eba as much as any other food. Women take great pride in making amala and iyan, hence whenever time permits, they prepare these foods themselves. However, precisely because they are favorite foods, and because many women do not always have time to make them, any woman who sells well-prepared amala (an Okoka) or iyan would have many customers during the day.

In the evenings, cold eko is the most commonly eaten food. Eko is almost always bought from cooked-food sellers because to make it is a time-consuming process. The evening portion is eaten in the compound, with a stew which the woman herself has prepared in the afternoon.

Women who sell prepared foods have stalls or shops near their residences or they cook in large pots situated under a shade tree somewhere in the town. In the morning, cooked-food sellers are found all along the main street of the town, especially at Orita Merin (literally, crossroad) and at Bode market. In the early afternoons a number of women sell fried plantain (dodo), fried yams (dundun), oranges, roasted groundnuts, and other foods to school children and to people who pass along the streets.

One Oloka (seller of oka amala and other foods) has a shop at Ile Asalu where she resides. This Oloka sells amala, eba, and three types of stews: obe gbegiri (made from beans), obe ata (made from pepper), and obe ewedu (made with a type of green vegetable). During Ramadan, she also sells akara in the evenings.

She buys elubo, lafun, pepper, and gari from a woman who buys foodstuffs in the periodic markets. The ingredients for the stews (salt, beans, iru [locust beans], onions, and tomatoes) are bought from women who bring them to her shop. The fresh beef cooked in the pepper stew is supplied by one of the men who sell meat about the town.[8] The firewood used in cooking and the leaves used for wrapping the foods taken out by people who do not bring their own pans are bought from farm women who bring these items into town in the mornings. The woman who supplies elubo also supplies palm oil bought by the four-gallon tin (garawa) in the rural markets. In this instance,

---

[8] In Awe, Oyo, and in the surrounding rural markets, nearly all the sellers of fresh beef were men. When women in the Awe-Oyo area dealt in meat, they usually sold the less expensive parts of the animal, especially the internal parts (liver, kidneys, etc.) and cuts taken from the head and neck. In other Yoruba towns, however, many more women sell fresh meat. At Gege market in Ibadan and at the main market in Ilorin, there are hundreds of female meat sellers. At Dugbe and Mokola markets in Ibadan, women, although outnumbered by men, also sell fresh meat.

the supplier makes no gain on the oil, but simply collects the cost price plus the cost of transporting the oil from the market.

The Oloka opens her shop by 6 A.M. and by 7 A.M., she has prepared the amala and stews for the morning. Between 7:30 A.M. and 8 A.M., school children come in to buy their breakfast. They sit and eat on the benches that line the walls of the shop. Between 8 A.M. and 11 A.M., adults—women who hawk about the town, men who work in the town, etc.—stop by the shop for breakfast. By noon, all of the food which she prepared in the morning has been sold. Between noon and 1:30 P.M., she and the girl employed by her begin to prepare the afternoon meal of eba and stews. She does not prepare amala again until the following morning. In the early evening, about 6:30 P.M. or 7 P.M., she prepares another small batch of eba which she sells in the shop until about 9 P.M. Each day, except Friday when she goes to the mosque, this woman works in her shop.

One of the women who sell akara lives and works at Ile Elewetu. The akara is fried in a large enamel pan over an open fire in front of the compound. The beans used to make akara are bought by the hundred-weight bag at Dugbe or Orita Merin in Ibadan. A lorry dirver from Awe usually purchases the bag for her and charges 2/- for transporting it to Awe. Pepper and onions are bought in Awe from women who hawk about the town. Palm oil is brought from Ibadan by the trader who sells foodstuffs at Orita Merin. Throughout the day, the Alakara makes and fries the bean cakes which are bought by people of all ages but which are a special favorite of children.

There are probably close to a hundred women who sell eko in Awe. During the late afternoon and evening, women prepare the supply which they sell on the following day. The Eleko sell in their compounds and hawk about the streets. By 7 A.M. they start hawking about the town or leave for Oyo where they also hawk about the streets. Those who go to Oyo start back toward Awe by 10:30 A.M., by which time most of the women who hawk in the town have finished their sales. After their morning sales, women collect the maize which had been left at the grinder, return to their compounds, and begin to prepare for the evening's cooking. They sift the maize, separating out the chaff which is sold as food for goats. At about 4 P.M., they begin to boil the eko which should be ready by 7 or 8 P.M. Many of the Eleko themselves do not hawk about the town in the late afternoon when people buy their evening portions of this food. Instead, they send their children or their wards (girls, and sometimes boys of school age) out to hawk about the town.

These brief descriptions of the work of cooked-food sellers show that their activities, like those of most women, are carried out within the town. Nonetheless, although these women work near their residences, their trading activities occupy much of the day. When they are not actually selling, they spend hours purchasing their raw materials and preparing them for sale.

Some Awe women trade in imported stockfish, dried fish from the

Northern Region or from the Ijebu waterside areas, or in dried meat from the Northern Region. Of the dozen or more women who deal in stockfish, there are only two who buy in sufficient quantities to warrant a trip to Ibadan or Lagos; these women sell to other townswomen who trade in the imported fish. Sometimes women buy stockfish from traders in Akinmorin, a town about three miles south of Awẹ. One of the suppliers at Akinmorin is a woman who twice a month buys about thirty hundred-weight bags of stockfish in Lagos and sells by the bag to traders from Akinmorin, Awẹ, and Ọyọ, or by the dozen in Aiyekale, Imeleke, and Iware markets to women who hawk fish about the villages and hamlets.

Ajagba and Emi-Abata are the markets attended by the three or four Awẹ stockfish traders who frequent the rural markets, however, the majority of stockfish sellers from Awẹ do not attend the rural markets at all except during the main harvest season. Stockfish sellers usually hawk in towns where the consumption of meats and fish is more regular than it is in the farm hamlets. Women from Awẹ often walk to Ọyọ to sell fish, the rationale being that the demand for fish is greater in Ọyọ than in Awẹ. In the early morning, some stockfish traders situate themselves in the market at Bode but by 8:30 or 9 A.M., they leave to go around the town. Those who walk to Ọyọ leave Awẹ about 7:30 A.M. and sell their fish about the daily morning markets and throughout the town. They return to Awẹ around noon.

Sellers of other types of dried fish buy from Ọyọ men or women, some of whom travel to Ẹpẹ or Ejirin in the Ijebu area, and from Hausa traders who bring dried meat and fish from the Northern Region. The Awẹ woman who lives at Igbẹti supplies a type of dried meat (kundi) from the North to one of the women from her natal compound. However, most women who sell dried meat or fish buy it by the denge or by the handful in Awẹ or in Ọyọ and sell in the morning market at Bode or in other places along the main road in Awẹ.

At least three women in the town sell enamelware, bought from Dugbẹ market in Ibadan. These pans of various sizes are purchased by the dozen from Ibadan market women who buy at Lagos. The market for enamelware is very slow, and women do not replenish their stocks for months at a time. One of the enamelware sellers showed me a number of pans which she had had for over a year.

One trader in enamelware regularly attends Emi-Abata and Ajagba and another who lives part of the year in the farmlands sells at Aiyekale. Both women also sell in their compounds; one has a display table in front of the main entrance. The third woman whose residence happens to be in the Bode market area sells in front of the house each morning.

There is in Awẹ one woman who has a patent medicine shop which she stocks by making periodic trips to Ibadan. Several old women in the town sell "native medicines" which they purchase from the local herbalists. Along with these they sell a few kola nuts and other assorted items.

To my knowledge, there are no Awe women who sell any of the types of "traditional" cloth that are woven in various Yoruba towns,[9] nor do any Awe women sell the dyed adire cloth. I know of only one and have heard of two other women in the town who sell the cheaper imported cottons. Probably the major factor accounting for the absence of fabric sellers is the slow rate of turnover for cloth in a town such as Awe. Women who could afford to trade in fabrics would not want to tie up their capital in this item. In any case, there would not be many women in the town who have sufficient capital to trade in the "traditional" Yoruba fabrics. People who buy cloth locally purchase it from Oyo women, but most people buy at Gbagi which is the fabric center of Ibadan.

There are about eight women in town who sell locally made beverages. Two co-wives who are both over 60 years of age have been brewing millet beer (oti oka) for more than 30 years. The two women buy millet from women who trade in the rural markets or directly from farmers. The daughter-in-law of the elder co-wife also assists the old women by securing firewood and millet and by delivering beer to the compounds of those who place orders for it. The palm-wine (emu) sellers are supplied by men whose job it is to tap the trees. Each morning women who work as carriers bring the wine in from the farms. The sellers sit in various shaded areas in the town, and sell throughout the late morning, afternoon, and evening.

There are various women in Awe who sell their services to the townspeople. Of the 12 seamstresses in the town, eight worked in the compounds in which they lived and four had their machines in other compounds. Four women in the town laundered clothes at their residences and at least six women were professional hairdressers, who plaited and tied their customers' hair in the various Yoruba styles.

WOMEN AS PRODUCERS

The manufacture of pottery, soap, and oils is carried on by women in the town. These products are sold to women who resell in the town or in the rural markets. Each type of manufacturing activity has an alloted site (ebu) where it is carried on. All the pottery is made at Ebu Bale, and most women who make pottery are either wives or daughters of Bale's compound. There are five sites where adin (palm kernel oil) is made and women from various compounds work in each ebu.

The work day of the Aladin is long and hard. Women come to the ebu by 5 or 5:30 A.M., start the fires and begin the process of pounding the palm kernels and boiling them to extract the oil. Each batch of kernels is pounded

---

[9] There is one man in Awe who sells a type of cloth (aso oja) which is used by women to tie their babies to their backs. He also sells a type of cloth used by farmers to make the shirts they wear in the fields. This trader buys at the town of Egbe and sells in Awe and in two periodic markets (Ajagba and Olo, near Ogbomosho).

and boiled three or four times until all the oil has been extracted. Forty pans (kongo size, or 1/3 of a denge) of palm kernels (costing 11 d. each) make eight or 10 calabashes of adin, or nearly two garawa (four-gallon tins) of oil. Each calabash sells for 5/6 and each garawa sells for £1.10. It takes three days to extract as much oil as possible from forty kongos of palm kernels. The Aladin buy their palm kernels from women who purchase them in the rural markets, or they buy from women who make red palm oil (epo pupa) from the outer covering of the palm fruit. In the processing of the red palm oil, the kernels are removed and these are sold to the Aladin.

Ose dudu (black soap) is manufactured from a mixture of adin and the ashes of the bark of the cocoa fruit. There are four main ebus for making ose dudu in Awe. Three of these are clustered in one area (at the junction of the Awe-Akinmorin road and the road leading to Sogidi stream); another is located in Basi's Quarter and is referred to as Ebu Afogbonbo after the fact that it is the working place of women from that compound.

Each year during the dry season, the Olose must go to various cocoa farms where they buy the dried cocoa fruit from which the beans have been removed. These hulls are piled and burned in the farms and the ashes put into hundred-weight bags. According to the Olose, they spend from 20 days to one month in the farms. The women often travel in groups of four or five and divide among themselves the ashes they collect. The adin used in mixing the soap is bought by the garawa from the makers and the firewood used in the boiling process is bought daily from women who bring it in from the farms. The women also pay for each pail of water that is brought to them from the streams or water taps.

The Olose's work begins about 5 or 5:30 A.M. By 6 A.M., the old women who carry water arrive with the first supply and the processing begins. Women work at the ebu until dusk.

THE ECONOMICS OF TRADE

Up to this point very little has been said concerning the financial aspects of women's trade activities. This is not only because of the desire to emphasize the physical movements of women and goods, but also because of the difficulties of making precise statements about the size of working capital, commodity turnover, and income. Whereas it was relatively easy to elicit information concerning, and to observe the overall patterns of trade, it was more difficult to get precise information on the financial aspects of women's business enterprises. Most of the provisions sellers, for example, were willing to give prices at which they bought and sold various items and would give the cost of transport to and from the places where they bought their supplies, but declined to give even rough estimates of the rate of turnover on the various items handled. The women who did respond to questions concerning their finances could give only approximate information concerning the frequency of the trips to the source of their supplies and could say only roughly how much they invested in provisions on each trip. Most women who bought and sold farm produce were much more reticent about giving prices at which they *sold* their goods than about stating the cost prices, the transport fees, and other costs involved in their trade. Those who sold produce outside Awe would say precisely how much they had spent for the items which they took to the cities and how much was spent for transport and porterage, but rather than give prices at which they sold the produce, they often would only say that they had "gained" on their transactions.

I should point out, however, that not a single Awe woman whom I interviewed or engaged in conversation refused entirely to discuss the financial aspect of her trade activities. Of course, every piece of information contributed to the total understanding of the economics of trade, and these fragments together with the detailed financial information given by 31 of the Awe women interviewed and 24 of the women from other places provided a picture of the monetary side of trade.[10] Then, too, in 12 months of attending the markets, questioning hundreds of traders, and buying numerous articles, I came to understand many of the processes of exchange that might have remained uncovered or obscure had I worked entirely with informants in the town.

Generally speaking, the working capital of women in the town ranged from less than five shillings to about £40. However, most women traded with capital ranging between £1 and £15. Women who traded in cooked-foods seemed to have the highest rate of capital turnover of any women in town although in general their working capital was very small. Those who traded foodstuffs between the farmlands and the town also had a relatively high rate of capital turnover (many of them, of course, sold to cooked-food sellers) but they often complained that women who bought from them often wanted credit extended them and that instead of paying "in time" these debtors used the money for other purposes.

Because people from the farms did not usually extend credit, the amount of capital a foodstuffs seller had available often depended on her ability to collect from those who were in her debt. The women who traded foodstuffs between the rural areas and city markets seemed to have more liquid capital than any other women in town (including some of the women who had large provisions stores) because they sold their goods quickly and did not usually buy or sell on credit. One of the reasons why on their return trip women who sold produce in the city markets did not bring saleable commodities back to the town was that people in Awe would want to buy on credit and hence would tie up the trader's working capital. The one woman

---

[10] Although only passing references have been made to male traders, I found them extremely willing to discuss all phases of their work.

who did engage in two-way traffic spent much of her "free" time putting pressure on her debtors to pay at least part of the monies owed.

Traders in provisions, especially those who had fairly large stocks, always seemed to be involved in elaborate networks of credit, and while on the face of it they had relatively large amounts of working capital, they reported having small amounts of liquid capital. Stockfish sellers, more than any other group, complained of generally slow rates of turnover, and of having to become involved in debt because buyers could not often pay in cash. Three women reported having gone bankrupt selling stockfish and having turned to collecting and selling firewood to repay their creditors. Afterward they started trading afresh (with credit) in another commodity line.

It should be pointed out that in the circumstances under which Awe women live and work, it is seldom possible for them to separate their trading capital from other monies they possess. They must spend any cash they have as they need it and their capital remains intact or diminishes depending on the financial responsibilities and commitments they have at any given time. Furthermore, because trade is primarily a means by which women can secure the cash to meet financial responsibilities encumbent on them, it is not often that they can substantially increase their trading capital or their net incomes. Even those whose commodities sell at a relatively fast rate and whose capital is mostly in the form of liquid cash are not able to continually reinvest the same proportion or a progressively greater proportion of their incomes. If a woman's average day-to-day living expenses amount to two pounds per month, and she has a net income of four pounds one month, she cannot usually expect to add the extra two pounds to her trading capital. More often than not, children's school fees, obligations to her kinsmen and associates, and other responsibilities require the expenditure of the extra cash and more besides.

With these general remarks as background, some details of the economics of trade as carried on by a few Awe women are presented below. Although information gathered from women from other towns elucidate more clearly some aspects of the financial side of trade, I have chosen not to include any of these cases because it is the data on Awe women that provides the basis for the discussion of the implications of women's economic activities for family organization. The discussion of a few cases should provide the reader with more precise information than would a series of charts in as much as many aspects of the trade situation would be obscured or misrepresented by tabular presentation. In some cases, the women discussed were interviewed many times during my stay in Awe, however, I have mentioned specific dates in order that the reader may know the time of year at which the prices quoted were obtained. It will be noted that where possible I have included information on women whose activities were used earlier in this chapter to illustrate patterns of movement of women and goods.

WOMEN AS TRADERS AND PRODUCERS

1. Gari Seller—Ile Akogun

(January 22, 1962) This trader buys gari from women who live on the farms and who sell at Bode market in Awe, at Ile Gbelekale, and at Akinmorin, a town about three miles south of Awe. Each panful (denge) costs about 2/- and she buys from three to six denges at a time, for which she pays cash. She goes to buy from her suppliers whenever she has sold most of what is on hand. As is the usual practice when buying from the *makers* of gari, she is allowed to put one arm around the rim of the pan when measuring the meal from the seller's pile into the denge. Assuming as one always must in discussing the amount of time women devote to trade, that there are no contingencies or celebrations which necessitate her remaining in her compound or going to another compound for one or more days, this trader takes gari to Oyo five or six days a week. "At times, I don't sell three-pence worth of gari a day; at other times I can carry four pans to Oyo and sell all of them." She walks to Oyo because "there's no regular lorry in the mornings and, too, by trekking, I may meet workers along the road who buy 1d. or 2d. worth of gari." She also sells in her compound. At Awe, each denge sells for 2/-, there being about 1d. to 3d. worth of gari left over from the measure which she bought by putting her arms around the pan. Thus, each denge bought is resold for an amount totaling from 2/1 to 2/3. At Oyo, she sells each denge for 2/3, thus grossing from 2/4 to 2/6 per pan. The trader had only been selling gari for six months, having stopped handling stockfish which she had sold for over 10 years. She said that in the six months, she had sold about two pans of gari every two or three days.

2. Gari Seller—Ile Alagbede-Akinye

(January 23, 1962) This trader also buys with cash from farm women; she goes to one of the roadside buying stations where the makers of gari bring it for sale to townswomen. Each denge costs 2/- and the measuring is done in the manner described above. On the day of this interview, the trader had bought two denges and estimated that it would take at least three days for her to sell them. She sells only in her compound at Awe, and each denge sells for 2/-, her gain consisting of the extra amounts she is allowed when buying from the makers. Usually she sells only two pans in three days during the season when yams and fresh maize are plentiful. When these foods are scarce, she sells about one denge per day but at these times the gari is sold at a cheaper price.

3. Gari Seller—Ile Olode

(May 22, 1962) This trader regularly sells gari at Ayeye in Ibadan. She also deals in lafun, maize, yams, peppers, elubo, and plantain, but except for yams, these are sold in Awẹ. She buys at Ajagba, Emi-Abata, and occasionally at Ajẹgunle and Apara. On non-market days, she buys gari in the hamlets and at various roadside buying stations around Awẹ. All her purchases are made with cash. She gave the following account of a trip to Ibadan on May 17, 1962. She took gari which cost her £4.10 (i.e., 45 denges which equals about one and one-half hundred-weight bags). The fare to Ibadan was 2/6, and the cost of transporting the gari was 3/- (i.e. 2/- per bag). At Ayẹyẹ she paid 1/6 as "owo ile," i.e., as a fee for the use of the market, and 3d. to the man who moved the gari from the lorry to her "stall." As is usual at Ayẹyẹ and in some other markets, the gari was sold by the kongo (a pan about one-third the size of a denge) at a price of 9d. per pan. When I asked the trader how much she gained on her trip to Ibadan, she reported that she made 3/-. My own calculation on the basis of the size of the kongo revealed the following:

Quantity bought	Cost	Fare & Fees to & from Ibadan	Fees at Ayẹyẹ	Quantity Sold	Gross Return	Net
45 denges @ 2/- each	£4.10	8/-	1/9	45 denges =135 kongo @ 9d. each	£5.1.3	1/6

It can be assumed that the trader's report on her returns is correct since the amount of gari measured into the kongo may be less than one-third of that of the denge. In fact, the one and one-half bags of gari may have sold for even more than £5.2.6 (which would yield a 3/- gain) because there was at least one other expense involved which the trader did not mention and which, at the time, I did not remember to ask about, namely the cost of transporting the gari from Emi-Abata and Ajagba where she bought it. In an earlier interview, she had said that from each of these markets it costs 1/- to transport a bag of gari to Awẹ. Presumably it cost her 9d. or 1/- in transport to Emi-Abata (the usual fare) and 1/- on the return. It is standard practice that if traders pay load fees of one shilling or more, they do not pay the passenger fare for the trip when returning from Emi-Abata or Ajagba. The trader walks to Ajagba but it probably costs her 1/- to transport the one-half bag of gari (and herself as well) back to Awẹ. If this trader did not take into account these costs when she calculated that she had gained 3/- on her trip to Ibadan, then it means that she may have gained only 3d. or nothing at all on the trip. Of course, one has to take into account the fact that if she had bought as much gari and tried to sell it in Awẹ, it would have taken a much longer time to dispose of it, she may have lost, in fact, on the transactions, and undoubtedly she would have had to sell some of the gari on credit. As it was, she bought the gari at two markets held within five days of each other and sold all of it at Ayẹyẹ in one day.

The trader reported that she usually takes from £7.10 to £9 worth of gari to Ibadan and that sometimes she takes yams as well. She makes the trip to Ibadan at least once every nine days and gains between three and five shillings on each trip. It should be mentioned that the cost of her fare to Ibadan varies with the amount of produce she takes. If she takes one bag, she pays 2/6 in personal fare; if she takes two bags, the fare is 2/- and if she takes three bags, the fare is 1/6. However, the cost of transporting the loads is constant: she pays 2/- for each bag taken by the lorry.

A final point should be made concerning the "trading capital." While at Ayẹyẹ, the trader uses the money she receives from the sale of gari to pay for her food and to buy anything else she may want. She also buys cloth, trinkets, or anything she may need while she is in Ibadan for the one to three day trip. She reported that she seldom spends less than 6/- (plus one to two shillings a day for food) while she is in the city.

4. Foodstuffs Seller—Ile Balẹ

At the end of November, 1961, I went to see this trader as she was about to make her monthly trip to Lagos. Before her goods were loaded into the lorry, she gave me the cost of the times which totalled £10.9.9. Included were chickens, yams, maize, and a small amount of okra. During the month, she had bought many other foodstuffs but these had all been sold in Awẹ. For this trip, she paid a total of 15/- in transport fees and 5/- for her personal fare. (The usual fare is higher but since she goes to Lagos each month, she is charged only 5/-.) When she returned from Lagos, she reported that some of the chickens had died en route but that the sale of the others and of the yams had allowed her to gain "about £1.10" on the trip. Taken into account in her calculations were all the transport fees paid on the goods (from the periodic markets as well as to Lagos) and her personal transport costs. According to this woman, she has never taken less than £10 worth of foodstuffs and chickens to Lagos and that usually she takes items worth between £20 and £40 each month. She makes at least £1 or £1.10 on each trip and sometimes as much as £3.10 or £4.10 a month, including sales in Awẹ.

5. Ẹkọ Seller—Ile Akogun

(December 13, 1961) This trader pays cash for loose corn which she buys at Bode market by the denge from women who purchase ears of corn. from the farmers. She also buys corn on credit from a woman at Ile Balẹ. Each denge of maize costs 2/6 and she uses two denges of maize each time she makes ẹkọ, which would be two or three times a week, depending on the rate of her sales. Each time she prepares the food, she pays 6d. to the man whose machine is used to grind the maize, and buys 9d. worth of leaves for wrapping the ẹkọ, making her total expenditure 6/3. From the two pans of maize she says she makes ẹkọ worth 7/6. Thus, the yield from the two pans would be 90 portions of ẹkọ which are sold at one-penny each. All of the food is consumed in Awẹ where she hawks about the streets and sells in her compound. Although most of her sales are for cash, she may have extended credit amounting to 5d. or 6d. by the time she has sold each batch of ẹkọ.

6. Ẹkọ Seller—Ile Alagbẹdẹ Akinye

(January 23, 1962) The corn is bought at 2/9 per denge at Bode market or at Ọyọ from women who buy from the farmers. Four or five days a week, she makes ẹkọ in the afternoon and evening and hawks it about Ọyọ each morning. Like the other Elẹkọ mentioned, she cooks two pans of maize each time. At the time of the interview, she said that she had taken ẹkọ made from two pans of maize to Ọyọ earlier in the morning, and that she had sold it for 11/3.

To grind the two pans of maize, she paid the machine owner 6d. The three types of leaves (gẹdu from the "African maple," cocoa, and banana trees) used in wrapping the ẹkọ cost her 1/6. Thus, she spent a total of 7/6 to make ẹkọ which sold for 11/13. Apparently this trader was able to make more ẹkọ from two pans of maize than was the ẹkọ seller mentioned above. Whether she made smaller pieces than the trader referred to above or whether, in Ọyọ, she had sold some of the larger pieces for more than 1d. is not certain. In any case, she reported having sold the ẹkọ for 1d. each. (It could also be that the other woman had understated the returns on her ẹkọ.)

It will be noticed that there is a difference of 3d. in the cost of each denge of maize used by the two Ẹkọ sellers. The price of maize, unlike that of gari, varies very greatly depending on the season of the year. Whereas in this area the price of gari varies between 2/- and 2/6 per denge throughout the year, the price of a denge of maize varies between 1/9 or 2/- and 5/- depending on the season of the year. From June to January, maize costs about £2 per hundred-weight bag and each denge costs from 1/9 to 2/3. Between January and March, each bag of maize costs between £2.15 and £3 and each denge costs 2/6, 2/9, or 3/-1. From March to June, the price of one bag varies between £3.10 and £5, usually costing about £5, and each denge usually costs about 5/-. These prices are those charged by the women who buy maize on the cob, husk it, and sell to "first level" buyers from the towns. If traders in ẹkọ buy directly from the farm women, the price of the denge is always less than if they buy from resellers (alarobo). Since the ẹkọ sellers in Awẹ charge 1d. per portion throughout the year and since they do not substantially increase or decrease the size of the portions regardless of the season, it is

WOMEN AS TRADERS AND PRODUCERS 91

obvious that their returns on the monies invested vary appreciably throughout the year.[11]

7. Ọlọka (Amala Seller)–Ile Asalu

(March 20, 1962) This woman sells amala, ẹba, and three types of stews. For making the amala, she uses yam flour mixed with a bit of cassava flour; ẹba is made from cassava meal. The basic ingredients for one type of stew are beans and condiments; for another, peppers and beef; and the other, peppers and ewedu (a type of greens). The ingredients she uses each day are: elubọ, lafun, gari, peppers, beans, ewedu, pieces of beef, and pọnmọ (beef skin which is boiled and eaten) salt, iru (locust beans), onions, tomatoes, and red palm oil. For making fires, she uses wood, piles of esan (the hard shell which covers the palm kernel) and ogunsọ (another type of fuel made from the fiberous covering which separates the smooth skin of the palm fruit from the shell covering the kernel).

Table 4 gives the Ọlọka's statement of her expenditures for one day and shows the quantities in which she buys various items.

Amala and ẹba are sold in "scoops" (a piece of calabash is used to remove each portion from the pots) which cost 1d. each. Most adults buy 2d. to 3d. portions. The bean stew (gbegiri) is served with each portion and a small amount of pepper stew is added for extra flavor. The pepper stew is served to persons who buy meat which is sold in pieces costing 1d. each. The Ọlọka's returns on her investments vary during the year, depending primarily on the price of foodstuffs. In March, when this interview was given, foodstuffs were scarce, and ingredients that cost £2 at this time of year might cost £1.10 or less during the harvest season, especially during the months from September through December. The Ọlọka could only expect a gain of 2/6 or 3/- on her £2 investment made in March when money is generally in short supply and customers are careful to see that the portions served them are worth the money they spend. During the harvest season, an investment of £2 regularly yields 4 or 5 shillings because (1) foodstuffs (especially elubọ) are cheaper,[12] and (2) customers are served slightly smaller portions than at other times of

---

[11] Of course every discussion of prices should include a reference to seasonality for there is almost no item (cigarettes, matches, and a few other items excepted) whose cost does not vary from one time of year to another.

[12] In discussing the finances of cooked-food sellers some reference should be made to their "overhead" expenses. The akara and amala sellers use enamel pans, the one for frying, the latter for boiling water, which have to be replaced periodically. The Alakara says she uses one pan costing 6/- every two or three months. Most cooked-food sellers buy earthenware pots at the outset of their trade and usually are able to use these for years. Similarly the mortar and pestle used by the Alakara for mixing ingredients last the lifetime of the trade. Stainless steel plated spoons and ladles are used by most women for removing foods (except amala and ẹba) from their cooking vessels.

TABLE 4

AMALA SELLER'S DAILY EXPENSES*

Item	Quantity Usually Purchased			Used Daily (except Firday)			Comments
	£	s	d	£	s	d	
Elubǫ	8	10		1	1		Buys from £6 to £8.10 worth of
Lafun	1	8			2		elubǫ each time, and uses about £1
Gari							(sometimes as much as £1.15) worth
							each day. Included in the estimate
							of £1 to £1.15 is the price of lafun
							which is mixed with the elubo. The cost
							of grinding £1 worth of elubǫ is 1s.
Pepper	2				2		The pepper which costs about £2 from a trader who buys in the rural markets lasts about twenty days. Occasionally the Ǫlǫka buys pepper directly from farmers or farm whoem in which case it is cheaper and she may buy £5 worth. This, she estimates, would last two to two and a half months. The amount of pepper she uses each day varies between 1s. and 3s. worth. During certain Christian and Muslim holidays, when she sells very well, she uses pepper worth 3s.
Palm Oil	1				5		During the rainy season, palm oil
Beans	1	10		2	6		costs 15s for a four-gallon tin.
Onions			3			1	During the dry season the price
Salt		1	3			2	ranges between £1 and £1.10. She
Iru		9	9		9	9	pays 6d. to have each tin of oil
Tomatoes			3			2	transported from the rural markets.
Beef		4			4		
Pǫnǫmo		1			1		
Leaves			1			1	She only uses leaves to wrap some of
Firewood		2			1		the food which is taken out; most people bring pans in which to put their food.
Esan			3			2	*At the time of this interview, she did not have *ewedu* stew and I did not remember to ask about the amount she uses. It would probably be about 1d. or 2d. worth each day.
Ogunso			6			5	In all cases the Ǫlǫka gave the quantity in which she usually buys foodstuffs and the length of time it took to use that which she bought. The figures in both columns, except for those on beans and salt shown in the right hand column, were given by her.

the year. In December, at the time of the major Christian and Muslim holidays when business is brisk, the combination of low food stuffs prices and relatively small servings of the cooked food, might result in a return of 7/6 on an investment of £2.

8. Akara Seller—Ile Elewuetu

(January 24, 1962) This trader uses beans (known in the U.S.A. as black-eyed peas), palm oil, pepper, and onions to make the akara. The beans are purchased in Ibadan by a lorry driver and the palm oil is also supplied from Ibadan by the trader from Ile Sogbo. Peppers and onions are bought in Awẹ from resellers. The Alakara uses the hundred-weight bag of beans as a standard for calculating her expenditures and income. That is, she knows approximately how long it takes to sell akara made from one bag of beans and she knows how much she spends for ingredients used to mix with each bag of beans. Making akara each day except Friday when she goes to mosque, she uses one bag of beans every two weeks and estimates that she gains £1 to £1.10 on each bag. At the time of year when this interview was conducted, her total expenditures for each bag were £7.11 or £8.1, depending on the cost of the beans. The akara sells for ½d. per "cake." The expenditures on each bag of beans are:

Item	Measure	Cost	Transport	Cost of Grinding[13]
Beans	Cwt. bag	£4 or £4.10	2/-	15/- @ 2/6 per day
Palm oil	4-gallon tin	£1.10		
Pepper	denge	14/- @7/- each		
Onions	piles of about 40 each	10/-		

[13] In order to check the information given by the women, one of the men who owns the large grinding machines in Awẹ was interviewed. He supplied the following information:

    cost of grinding 1 denge of maize   3d.
                          1 garawa of elubọ   1s.
                          (i.e., amount contained in calabashes in which it
                          is usually sold)
                          1 denge of beans   9d.

He said that whem "there is not much of a market" for the cooked-food sellers who use these products, he charges 2½d., 9d., and 8d. for the respective items.

    One reason for my having consulted the grinding machine owner was that the Alakara's figure for the cost of grinding beans seemed high. Nonetheless, there can be little doubt that she told the truth when she said that the amount of beans used in the morning usually cost her 1/- and those used in the afternoon cost 1/6 to be ground. She uses a little more than one denge in the morning and about two denges in the afternoon.

9. Stockfish Seller—Ile Bigun

(November 29, 1961) This trader buys stockfish (panla) by the hundredweight bag from an Awẹ woman who makes periodic trips to Lagos to buy the fish. The bag which she was selling at the time of this interview cost her £11.10 which was probably 10/- more than it cost the trader who bought it in Lagos. Stockfish ranges in price from £9 to £13.10 depending on the season of the year and the type of fish. The trader reported that she had bought this bag during the first week of November and had sold only one-third of the fish. She estimated that it might take a total of two months to sell the entire bag. Ordinarily, she said, this was not a bad time for stockfish but the people in the town had little money this year and she had not been able to sell much. (She had an infant of about two months and would not begin to hawk the fish in Ọyọ until the baby, whom she carried on her back, was about five months old and could "stand" the walk.) The trader reported that at times she sells one bag of fish in two weeks and makes about 15/- on the bag. Now she expected to make only one or two shillings or perhaps to lose money on the stockfish since the longer she kept it, the cheaper would be the selling price.

* * *

Because the provisions sellers did not provide detailed information concerning the rate of turnover for their various commodities and often did not specify the quantities in which they bought a various items, I have not included any one of them among the above cases. Eleven of the provisions sellers in the town were interviewed and six of those had stocks with a total value of £20 or more. One woman whose total stock was estimated at between £50 and £60 said that each month she bought about £30 worth of goods, mostly beer and soft drinks, from the United Africa Company store in Ọyọ. She said that she paid the company about £10 to £15 per month and received the other goods on credit since she needed cash to meet her living expenses, to pay the 10/- monthly rent on her store, to pay 5/- per month to her night watchman, and to pay the rent on her Rediffusion box. Occasionally, when she does not sell well during the month, she has to borrow money from her husband (a carpenter) or from other relatives to pay UAC and she repays the loans "little by little" as she collects the money for her next monthly payment to the UAC. She says that when she sells very well, she makes £3.10 or £4 a month but that because she spends the money as she earns it, she cannot give a precise figure for her income.

Very few women in the town were able to put aside any cash in the form of savings. A few of them reported that at various times they had contributed to an *esusu* run by different men in the town. In Awẹ the term *esusu* is used in reference to a form of interest-free savings in which contributors pay a fixed sum of money at stipulated intervals (e.g. weekly or monthly) for a stated length of time after which they receive the amount they contributed minus the sum claimed as fee by the head of the *esusu*.[14]

In one instance, a group of women used their occupational association as an interest-free savings club. The 43 members of the society of women who made and sold adin made voluntary contributions of 6d. per month in 1960 and 1/- per month in 1961; early in 1962, each member received back the sum she had contributed.

Attention in this chapter has centered on the movements of women and goods within and to and from the town of Awẹ. An attempt has been made to cover all the general patterns of trade exhibited by the activities of women of the town, even though not all the commodities handled are mentioned. There are a few occupations engaged in by women of the town which are not directly relevant to this study and which were not mentioned. It should be pointed out that some women teach in the primary and secondary modern schools and one woman is a practical nurse who works in the dispensary.

A NOTE ON MALE OCCUPATIONS

Mention must be made of the occupational activities of men in Awẹ. Most of the men are farmers, some of them deal in services, and others are traders or craftsmen. Seven of the men of the town own shops where bicycles are sold, rented, and repaired. Four men own machines for grinding maize, elubọ, egusi, and pepper; and two others have machines suitable for grinding small amounts of pepper and tomatoes. There are 11 tailors, nine barbers, and six laundry men in the town. Three traditional agbẹdẹ (blacksmiths' work sites) are still in operation in Awẹ but the number of blacksmiths is difficult to specify since nearly all men of the Alagbẹdẹ compounds are blacksmiths. In any case, many of the blacksmiths today earn most of their money by farming. There are about a dozen carpenters in Awẹ, but there is only one who has a large shop in the town. Some young men work under this master carpenter and a few of the adult carpenters work in Ọyọ. A few men of the town work as traders in hardware and men's clothing items, and one trades in a type of Yoruba cloth. Three of the men who live in the town buy and sell fresh beef and two of them have young boys in their employ. The Ajao Bros. provisions store and bakery employs some men as bakers or clerks. There are two professional photographers in the town, and a few men who work as laborers in the Regional Government Departments at Ọyọ or as gardeners for

[14] Another traditional form of interest-free savings is also generally known as esusu in Yorubaland and in the Caribbean (Bascom, 1952) but in Awẹ this is referred to specifically as ajọ, from the verb "to join together." In this form of esusu, a fixed number of contributors pay a stipulated sum at regular intervals; each time the contributions are collected, they are given over to one member of the esusu. The esusu circle cannot be broken until every member has received his "draw."

the churches in Awẹ. Approximately 20 men teach in the six schools in the town. As was mentioned earlier, a number of Awẹ men live and work most of the year in cities throughout the Western Region, in the Northern Region, and in Lagos. In many cases, their wives live and work in Awẹ.

V

RESIDENCE AND KINSHIP IN THE TOWN OF AWE

BEFORE an assessment can be made of the impact of women's economic activities on patterns of behavior within the family and within their wider kin groups, it is imperative that we examine the nature of kin units in Yoruba society. Fundamental to any consideration of kinship is an understanding of the structure of the compound (*agbo ile* or *ile*) which is the basic residential unit in a Yoruba town. Kin groups, defined by descent and by marriage, are based in the compound, and kin ties provide the most important linkage between the various compounds. This chapter sets forth, in broad outline, the physical and social structure of the compound, placing particular emphasis on the position of women within the groups that comprise the residential unit.

THE COMPOUND AS A PHYSICAL ENTITY

The physical structure of the Yoruba compound was described by a number of persons who visited Yoruba towns during the nineteenth century. The compounds of Oshiele (also spelled Oshielle), an Egba community, were described in the following manner by the missionary T. J. Bowen:

> Meroke's house, like others in Oshielle, has a high wall next to the street, on each side. It is built in a square. A gate, carved with the head of an idol, opens into the street. There is a court-yard in the centre, and the rooms are built all around the interior of the square. The sloping roof projecting beyond them forms a verandah. This verandah is the reception place for friends: "The Tortoise," says the Yoruba proverb in alluding to an inhospitable man, "builds his house, and makes the verandah behind it." ... [in hot weather] it is also the bedroom. ... The polished walls and floor shine, as it is said in Yoruba, "like the rain clouds, beautifully black." ... The [floor], however, is not quite even. In one place there is a slight depression of its surface. This marks the spot under which the dead lie (Bowen, 1858:31).

The Reverend R. H. Stone describes the compound in the following manner:

> A "compound" is an enclosed space (generally in the form of a square) bounded by a wall about seven feet high. There is but one entrance to this enclosed space. At night and in times of danger this is closed by strong

double doors well barred. Inside, against this wall, the rooms of the house are built. These rooms are square and are covered by a thatched roof; which rests on the wall on the outside and on posts in the inside so as to give a covering for a piazza extending all around the enclosed space on the inside. In this piazza the inmates mostly live, the rooms being chiefly used for dormitories or for storage... the court of the compound ... is therefore very secure against thieves and beasts of prey prowling about at night....

The compounds of the chiefs are very large sometimes covering several acres of ground. In such cases they are a perfect labyrinth of dwellings.... Away back in these recesses, surrounded by the most trusty of their wives and retainers, the chiefs pass their leisure hours (quoted in Lloyd, 1955:236).

Virtually all compounds in Awe have tell-tale signs which indicate that they once bore close resemblances to the structures described above and represented schematically in Figure 7. Viewed from the outside, the old compounds have the appearance of a fortress. Indeed, the compound, with its wall and gate, open central square, "verandahs" and sleeping rooms, seems a miniature replica of the walled Yoruba town with its customs gates, central market place, and labyrinth of passageways and compounds.

Many of the Awe compounds still form an entire square but some of the dwellings which make up the square are modern houses made of cement or of mud-brick covered with plaster. Such houses may face onto what is now a street but they also have entrances which face onto the central area inside the compound. Thus, many of these new houses give no impression of having a front or a back, rather they have two "faces," one for the outside, one for the inside. In some instances, parts of the old compound, such as one long side or two sides having an "L" shape remain intact. The other two sides of the compound area might be built up with more modern styled houses, but even these retain some of the features of the old compound. Often there is a continuous hallway running the length of the house with rooms on each side of the hall. The first room on the right is the "parlour" belonging to the man who built the house, and there is a door connecting the parlour with the man's bedroom. All other rooms are likely to have only one entrance, namely that from the hallway. Or there may be, within the structure, a number of such "rooms and parlour." Many of the old compounds have cement floors in the main parlour if not in all the rooms. The parlours are outfitted with chairs, tables, and sofas; the more traditional stools being considered inappropriate for such areas. The fronts of compounds which face onto main thoroughfares are often plastered over and painted, and it is only after one has entered that he recognizes the structure to be essentially that of the traditional compound. Figure 8 shows the layout of dwellings that together make up the Bale's compound in Awe.

Each compound bears a name which is derived in one of various ways. Where there is a hereditary chieftaincy title in the compound, the house is

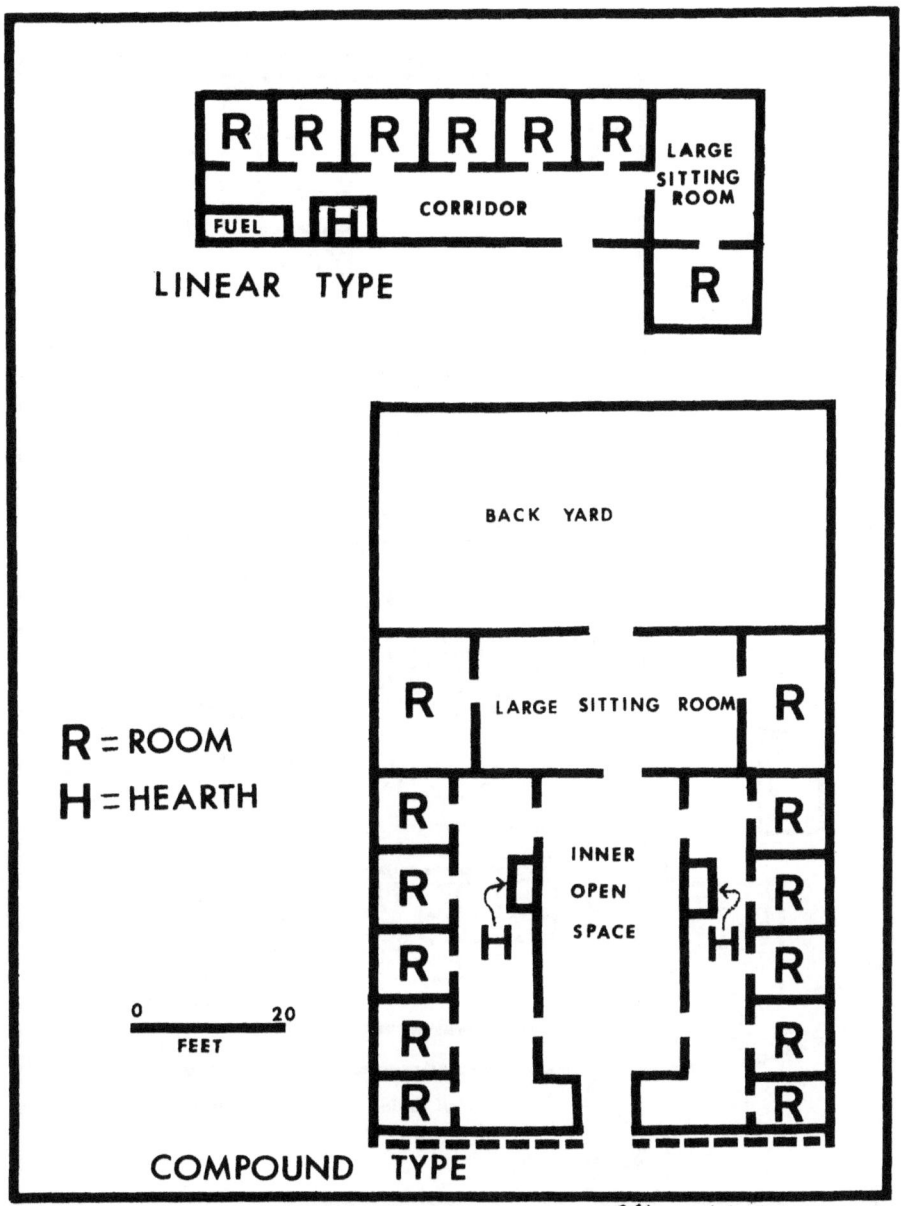

Fig. 7. Yoruba house plans.

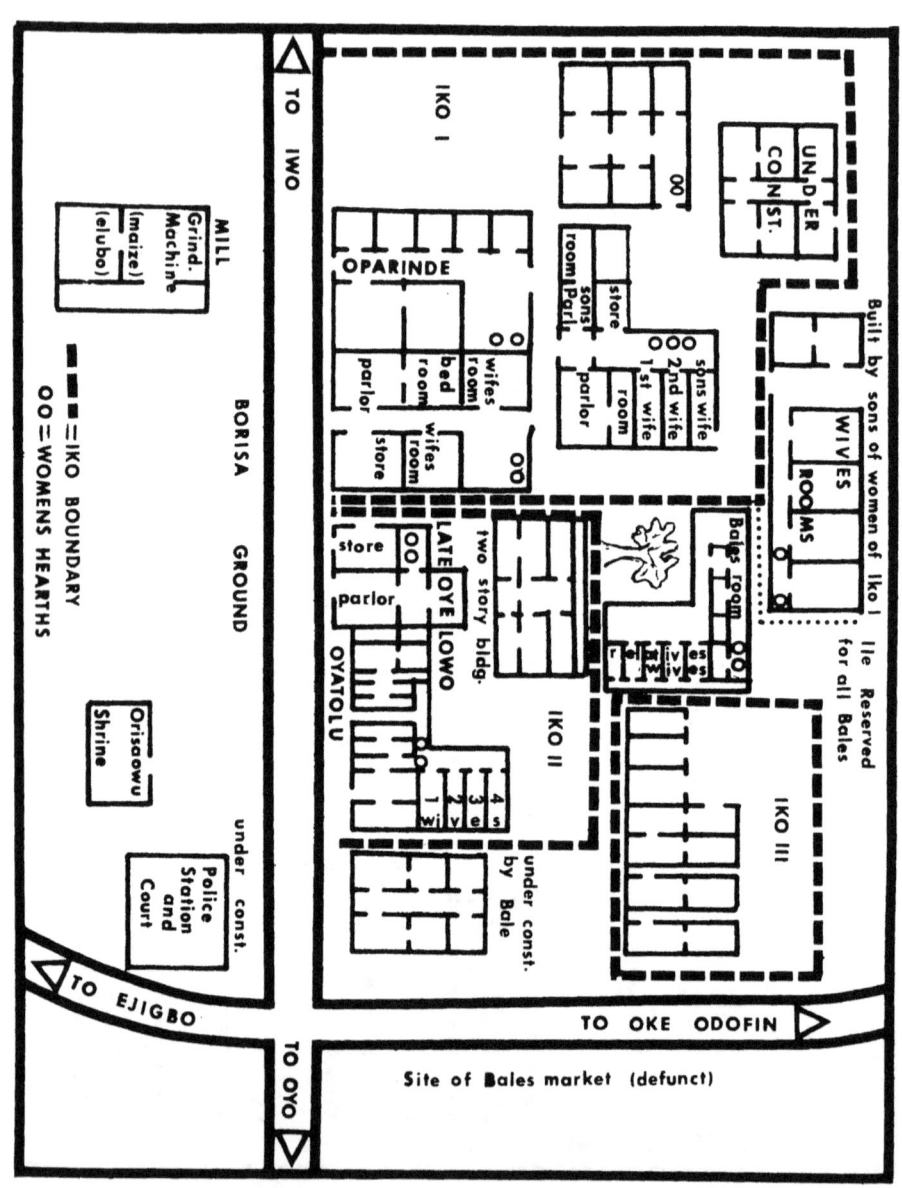

Fig. 8. Sketch of Bale's compound, Awe.

often known by that title. For example, the compounds in which the Quarter chieftaincies rest are: Ile Bale (Bale's house), Ile Onsa, Ile Basi, and Ile Odofin. Even when a man holds a non-hereditary title, his compound may come to be known by that title. The Balogun chieftaincy, for example, is not hereditary (in Awe) yet there is an Ile Balogun in the Basi's quarter and one in the Odofin's quarter. Other houses have held the title, but it is these two houses which came to be known as Ile Balogun during the time they held the chieftaincy and the names became permanently associated with them. The compound of the first woman to be regarded as the Iyaloja (head of the women traders), a non-hereditary title, is still officially known as Ile Iyaloja even though the Agba-Akin title is hereditary in that house. The Agba-Akin title came to rest in the house at a time after the compound became known as Ile Iyaloja and the name was never changed.

A compound may also be named for the craft traditionally associated with the house. There are compounds named for the blacksmiths (Alagbede), hunters (Olode), keepers of birds (Eleiyele), and so on. A number of houses have names that signify something of historical significance about the house. For example, Ile Afogbonebo is so named after the fact that a soldier from the house took 20 men to war and captured 30 enemy soldiers (a fi ogbon dipo ogun).

When the population pressure on the compound's land becomes too great to permit further constructions on the site, "branches" of the compound may be built in other parts of the town. I know of 20 compounds, and there are probably a number of others, that have branches located in various parts of the town. It is not necessary for the offshoots of a compound to be located in the same quarter as the parent compound. At least eight compounds have branches outside the Quarters in which they are located.

THE SOCIAL COMPONENT

The compound is, in many respects, the most basic, though by no means the minimal, unit of social organization in a Yoruba community. It is impossible to understand what kinship entails for a Yoruba man or woman without understanding the compound as a social as well as a physical entity.

Every compound (agbo ile or ile) has associated with it a group of persons who comprise the idi (root) of the house (ile). This idile (rendered as "lineage" in English) is constituted of all persons, male and female, who, by means of a series of accepted genealogical steps, trace their ancestry through a line of males to the founder of the lineage (Lloyd, 1955:240; Schwab, 1955:352-53, 359). Even though every lineage is rooted in and identified with a named compound, lineage and compound are not coterminous (Schwab, 1955:356), for a compound, as will be shown, is made up of persons belonging to different lineages and members of the same lineage often reside in different compounds. Theoretically, each person is a permanent member of the compound and lineage of his father, and can no more change his compound membership than he can his lineage membership. It will be seen that a man may in fact affiliate with his mother's compound and, in some cases, with her lineage.

Each member of the idile of a compound is referred to as an omo ile (see Bascom, 1942:37), i.e., a child of the house, as distinct from an ara ile, a resident in the house. The term omo ile is sometimes applied to persons who are not members of the idile but who have resided in the house for many years. Usually such persons would be descendants of female members of the idile.

The core of the compound is constituted by the adult males of the house. In Awe many of these men are not year round residents of the compound. Those men who are farmers come to the town once a week or once every two weeks. Men working in other towns may come home once a month, once every two months, or even less frequently. In most instances, the male core of a compound is comprised of patrilineal descendants, of the man who founded the "root" (idi) of the house (ile). As was the case in traditional Yoruba society, the seniormost male in the lineage resident in a compound is usually the head of the house and is called the Bale (Baba ile, literally: father of the house). All residents in a compound come under the authority of the Bale.

When a man has been brought up in his mother's compound and resides there with his wives and children, he would usually be regarded as part of the male core of the house even though he belongs to his father's lineage.[1] For example, some men who have lived all their lives in their mother's compound still maintain membership and rights in their father's lineage; they inherit lands by virtue of their lineage membership and could stand for titles which belong to the idile of their father's house. They would, in addition, have certain property rights in their mother's lineage. There is the case of a man in his sixties whose father's compound is Ile Alaran in the Odofin's Quarter but who has lived in his mother's compound (Ile Alagbede at Oke Bata in Onsa's Quarter) since he was a very young boy. This man is a member of his father's lineage, he has property rights which accrue from membership in that idile, and his adult sons may build houses on the land belonging to Ile Alaran. Nevertheless, this man has built a two-story house at Ile Alagbede and is the most influential man in that compound. He is referred to by members of the house as the Bale although he is not the eldest male of the idile of the house. Whenever a member of Ile Alagbede is involved in a dispute with a person of another compound, it is to this man that the Bale of the other compound would look for settlement of the matter.

---

[1] If the man reared in his mother's compound was born out of wedlock and his father did not acknowledge him as his son, he would be regarded as a *de facto* member of his mother's lineage.

When a man resides in his mother's compound, his descendants may come to be regarded as members of that compound and eventually be absorbed into the lineage of the compound. Whether a man living in his mother's compound uses the residence as an entree into her lineage rather than seeks to maintain close ties with his father's compound and lineage seems to depend on the relative gains to be had from affiliation with the lineage of one parent rather than that of the other. In the Bale̩'s compound there is resident a man whose father's mother was an o̩mo̩ Bale̩ (daughter of the Bale̩'s lineage and compound). This man has become a de facto member of the Bale̩'s lineage and compound. He attends the meetings of men of the compound and farms land acquired through that lineage.

Adult females who are daughters of a compound (o̩mo̩ ile) and members of the lineage based in that compound are usually resident in another house, for the post-marital residence rule is one of virilocality, i.e., residence in the husband's home. Since most men reside in their father's compound (i.e., that in which their idile is based), the prevailing post-marital residence pattern is viri-patrilocality. Thus, at marriage a woman moves into the residence of her husband which is usually the compound in which reside the husband's father and other males of the his idile along with their wives and children.

Although viri-patrilocality is the most common form of post-marital residence, some women reside in the compound of their husband's mother's lineage. This viri-matrilocal residence pattern results from the fact that when men reside permanently in their mother's compound, their wives would be brought to live in that compound. The man whose father's compound is Ile Alaran but who resides at Ile Alagbe̩de̩ brought his wives to live at Ile Alagbe̩de̩. The sons of this man (two of whom live with their wives and children in Ibadan, the other with his wife and children in Lagos) regard themselves as members of the lineage based in Ile Alaran even though they will undoubtedly also inherit their father's house and other property rights in Ile Alagbe̩de̩. Interestingly, the wives of these men are regarded as "wives" (awo̩n iyawo) of Ile Alagbe̩de̩ where their father-in-law and his wives reside. When there was a wedding for a daughter of Ile Alagbe̩de̩, the women from Ibadan and Lagos came to Awe̩ to contribute their part, along with the other wives of the house, to the wedding ceremonies.

Implicit in the above paragraph is a most important fact concerning women in the compounds. All women who are married to men of a compound are classed together as wives (awo̩n iyawo) of the entire house. In Awe̩, where many men have at least two wives, the wives always constitute the largest group of adults in the compound. The preponderance of women over men is due also to the fact that many women reside in their husbands' compounds even though their husbands do not live in these compounds most of the year. When, for example, a man spends most of the year in residence at his farm hamlet, one of his wives may live with him while others remain in the compound in the town. In some cases, a man's only wife or all his wives remain in town while he commutes between town and farm. It is also common to find wives resident in the compound while their husbands work in Lagos or other towns. Many compounds are peopled most of the year by women and children, a few old men who do not work, and a few men whose occupations keep them in the town.

I have said that at marriage women move to their husbands' residences. Nonetheless, in almost every compound there are women who are daughters and sisters of the men of the house. Usually these women are widows who chose to return to their fathers' compounds after the death of their husbands. For whatever reasons, they did not re-marry into their deceased husbands' compound and lineage. Divorced women also usually return to live in their fathers' compounds. Women who are not officially divorced but who for one reason or another have left their spouses, can be found in their fathers' houses. This pattern is most common among women whose husbands have a number of wives. If one wife has no children, she might return to live in her father's house.

Besides the adult males, their wives and children, and a few of their adult sisters or daughters, there are other males and females from various lineages to be found living in any given compound. These might be young male or female relatives of one or more of the wives of the house or they might be children of some of the daughters of the house. In addition, there may young women living in the compound by virtue of an economic tie to one or more of the women, either wives or daughters, of the compound.

To summarize: a compound is made up of persons belonging to a number of different lineages. The core of the house consists of males born into the patrilineage associated with the house but it may also include males whose mothers were born into that partrilineage. The men of the lineage, along with their children and their sisters, constitute the idi (root) of the house. Women normally reside in the compounds of their husbands. In any given house one may find people, particularly young people, who are near or distant kinsmen of the wives of the house, or who are there by virtue of economic ties with one of the women living in the compound.

It is only possible to give approximate data on size of compounds in Awe. This is due to the high degree of physical mobility of the men and women who live in the compounds, and, in some instances, to the fact that branches of the same house are scattered throughout the town. The adults actually resident in the compounds throughout the year, including men who commute to the farms, number from 15 to 20 in the smaller compounds to 50 or 60 in the larger ones. The Basi estimated that there are 60 adults living in his compound but hastened to name branches of the house located in other parts of the town and to refer to the hundreds of persons from the house who live in Ibadan, Lagos, Ilorin, Iseyin, Port Harcourt, Kano,

Ogbomosho, and other towns. The Onsa estimated that 40 adults live in his compound but he too mentioned the many members who live most of the time in other towns. One of the young men in Ile Bale counted 50 adults actually resident in the compound and was told by the Elders that this figure represented less than 30 percent of the total number of persons who belong to the house. There are less than 30 adults living in Ile Odofin, making it the smallest of the major chieftaincy compounds. Here again, it was said that most of the members do not live permanently in Awe. In most compounds in Awe, it seems that women comprise two-thirds to three-fourths of the total adult population of the house.

WOMEN IN THE COMPOUND AND LINEAGE

As has been pointed out, the largest group of adults resident in any compound is usually the women who have married into the house. Most often, it is within a woman's *affinal compound* that her day-to-day activities are centered. There she resides with at least some of her children, with her husband's other wives and children, with the wives and children of other men of the compound, perhaps with one or two women born into the idile of the house, and with some of the men of the compound. It is within this unit and from this residential base that women carry on their domestic duties, including their trade activities. Yet, all women have kinship ties with, and assume certain responsibilities in, other compounds. The most important of these is the *natal compound*, i.e., the one in which a woman's idile is based.[2]

A woman's closest relations are affiliated with her affinal and natal compounds. Her husband and children are members of the idile of the house into which she marries; her father, his sisters and brothers, and her own sisters and brothers are members of the idile of the house into which she herself was born. Usually, a woman's natal compound is also the residence of her mother (for whom it is the affinal compound) who, in many respects, is the most important adult in her life.

In order to assess the implications of women's economic roles for Yoruba family relationships, the position of women within their affinal and natal compounds must be understood. I have chosen to begin the discussion with the affinal rather than the natal compound because it is in the former that most adult women reside.

---

[2] Women also have important ties with their mother's natal compound, with their father's mother's natal compound, and, to a lesser degree, with their mother's mother's natal compound but these relationships do not permeate the day to day lives of most women. Nonetheless, the importance of ties with the mother's father's house, the father's mother's house, and the mother's mother's house will become clear in a later discussion of the implications of trade by women for their wider kin groups.

Women's Positions in Their Affinal Compounds

The wives of a compound, irrespective of the men to whom they are married, are considered a single group within the residential unit, and on a number of occasions, they function as a unit. The general Yoruba term for wife is "aya" but the term "iyawo" which, in address and in certain contexts, means "junior wife," is often used in the plural form (*awọn iyawo*) to mean "wives." Each wife of the compound is junior or senior to every other wife depending on the order in which she married into the compound (see Bascom, 1942). On all occasions in which wives participate as a group, their behavior is governed by their relative statuses in the compound. If, as is often the case, wives are given monetary contributions by those observing ceremonies in which they take part, the money is divided according to rank, the senior-most wife receiving the largest share and each junior wife receiving proportionately less than that of the wife immediately senior to herself.

The senior-most wife is the woman who, of the living wives of a house, has been married into the compound for the longest period of time; she may or may not be the eldest of the wives, and her husband may or may not be the oldest man in the compound. In fact, the man to whom she was originally married may not even be alive. The senior-most wife is the "iyale" of the compound. Despite the fact that all wives are ranked according to their seniority in the compound, the wives of each man are also ranked vis-a-vis each other, the senior-most being the iyale to whom all others are iyawo. There can be only one iyale for a compound, and one iyale for a group of wives married to the same man. Distinctions in rank among other wives are made known primarily in forms of address and in non-verbal patterns of behavior.

When wives interact with each other, their behavior depends not only on the relative rank but also on the ages of the women concerned. If there are two women married to the same man, one must be the iyale, other the iyawo. Yet, if there is a difference of only two or three years in their ages, in *most* day-to-day affairs the women behave as if they are peers. They usually address each other by reference to the name of one of their children (i.e., as the mother of so and so), and the iyale would rarely address her co-wife as "iyawo." (In fact, once a woman has borne children, she is almost never *addressed* as "iyawo.") When wives of different men of the compound are of nearly the same age, they also usually interact with each other as if they were peers. Nonetheless, the slight difference in the age and rank of two wives would, as in nearly all other cases in Yoruba society, be reflected in the pronoun used in direct address if not always in pronoun used in reference. Where the senior of the two is also the older, she would be addressed in the second person plural. She may, however, be referred to in the third person singular rather than in the third person plural.[3] If perchance the senior wife is slightly *younger* than the iyawo, both women are likely to use reciprocal forms of address, either the singular or plural depending on the degree of the fondness for each other. In almost no cases would an iyale be *considerably* younger than her iyawo for man does not take a woman older than his first wife to be a junior wife. Where he inherits the widow of a brother, the widow would not be an iyawo but would occupy the same position she has always occupied in the compound (see Bascom, 1942:39). If the newly acquired widow is senior in rank to the man's iyale, she would not after the marriage refer to herself as the man's senior wife, nor would she be considered as such even though the man's iyale would show her the respect appropriate to her higher status among the wives of the compound.

When a generation separates any two wives of a single man or of different men of the compound, the younger is likely to behave toward the older much as she would toward a woman whom she calls "mother." In fact, the term *iya* (mother) or, in cases where the woman is very old, the term *iya agba* (literally, elder mother) which is used for grandmother, would be used in address. In greeting the elder co-wife and when making requests of her, the younger woman would kneel and, as Yoruba speakers always do, she would use the second person plural in addressing the older woman (see Mabogunje, 1958).

The status of "wife" with respect to a given compound, does not necessarily terminate when the woman no longer lives in the compound. If the wife is not officially divorced from her husband, she remains a wife of the house even though she may reside in her father's house or even if she has gone to another town in pursuit of her trade activities. Several Awẹ women living and working in other towns are officially married into compounds in

---

[3] Whether the third person plural would be used in reference to such an iyale would depend on the age of the person to whom the iyawo is speaking, for the relative age of the person spoken to vis-a-vis the iyale would be crucial. When speaking of the iyale to a person senior to her in age, the third person *singular* would be used because the senior person would refer to the iyale in the third person singular and because the iyawo would show respect for the senior person by placing *herself and her iyale* in a lower position than the person being spoken to.

For example, if the iyawo is speaking to a person of a generation above herself and the iyale, she says: *o ni ki n' sọ fun nyin.* . . . "She (third person singular) says that I should tell you (second person plural) . . ." In such cases, the person spoken to would be addressed in the second person plural.

On the other hand, if the iyawo is speaking of the iyale to a person junior to her in age, the third person *plural* would be used. The person spoken to would also use the plural form in reference to the iyale, and might, depending on their relative ages, use the plural form in addressing the iyawo. In any case, the iyawo would say: *"nwọn ni ki n'sọ fun ọ.* . . "she (literally, "they," third person plural) says that I should tell you (second person singular). . ."

When the iyale referred to, the person spoken to, and the iyawo are all of nearly the same age, the singular forms would be used. Iyawo: *o ni ki n' sọ fun ọ* . . .

Awẹ. Whenever they return to the town, they are accepted as wives of the house, but the extent of their participation in affairs of the house depends on the reasons for their having left and the type of relationship that has been maintained between them and their husbands. Even though a widow may be officially inherited by one of her deceased husband's brothers, if she is a middle-aged woman who has borne children for her deceased husband, the husband's brother may not consider her an appropriate sexual mate and she may return to live in her father's house. Nonetheless, she is, until she remarries, a wife of her deceased husband's compound.

Wives who reside outside their husbands' compounds have various responsibilities to the other wives of the house and, in fact, one of the means by which a non-resident wife maintains her connection with the compound is through participation in those activities in which all wives are expected to take part.

There are various settings in which interaction among wives takes place. Co-wives of the same man share domestic duties, including the upkeep of their section of the compound, and the preparation of meals for their husband. The senior wife is responsible for allocating household tasks among the wives. She would, for example, make arrangements for the preparation of the husband's meals. In Awẹ, when a man has more than two wives, most often each wife takes turns in preparing the husband's meals when he is at home. Where there are only two wives, the junior wife may shop for the provisions, undertake the task of grinding pepper or attending to other preliminary processing while the cooking itself is done by the senior wife. The senior wife is also responsible for making the arrangements by which each wife would take her turn in sleeping with the husband. As Mabogunje (1958) has pointed out, when there is a misunderstanding between the husband and one of the junior wives, it is often to the senior wife that her junior would turn with the request that the older wife intercede to settle the matter.

All the wives of a compound have certain responsibilities on such occasions as weddings, funerals, and naming ceremonies for newborn babies. Since these activities all involve the wives as independent wage earners, they will be discussed at a later point, along with the various forms of economic cooperation and competition that take place among wives.

Whereas there are many situations in which wives constitute a cohesive group within the compound setting, it is important to note as Lloyd (1955) and Schwab (1955) have done, that wives form the basis for "segmentation" within the polygynous family. Each "domestic family" (Schwab, 1955) within the compound consists of a man, his wife, and children or a man, his wives, and children. The minimal unit within the polygynous family is constituted by a woman and her children; there are as many sub-groups within the polygynous family as there are wives with children.

Even though each of a man's wives and her children constitute a sub-unit of the polygynous family, and although each woman's major responsibilities are toward her own children, as a wife of the compound a woman has a responsibility to all the children in it. The children of one man, and indeed all the children of one compound, in their daily lives, relate to each other in terms of the order of their birth, *not* in terms of their separate mothers. Irrespective of the woman who gave birth to a child, insofar as his father's other children are concerned, he is either an *aburo* (junior sibling) or an *egbọn* (senior sibling). In fact, *all* children of the compound are ranked according to their relative age and each is the aburo or the egbọn of every other child of the house. Because all the children of the compound are of slightly different status, each wife must see to it that her children's behavior toward the others is appropriate to their relative statuses.

All children in a compound relate to each of their father's wives—and to each of the other wives of the compound—in a fashion befitting the status of the wife. Indeed, a child may take liberties with his own mother that he would not take with the other wives of the house. Women who are senior to his mother must be accorded the utmost respect, and even though any wife who married into the compound after a child was born may not address that child by his given names but must coin pet names for him (see Bascom, 1942), this child would not, unless he were senior in age to or of the same age as the wife, treat her as an equal or as a junior.

Women who are married into a house are the "out-group" with respect to the adult men and women born into or "adopted"[4] into the lineage of the house. Wives cannot participate in lineage affairs but they often know as much or more about these affairs than do the daughters of the house, for the wives get news from their husbands and they are in a position to see much of what goes on.

The nature of the relationship between wives and adult daughters of the house depends largely on the relative ages of the women concerned. When a wife is of the generation above the daughter of the house, she treats the younger woman as a daughter; the younger woman in turn would behave toward the older in a manner appropriate to the latter's status among the wives of the former's mother's generation. If, however, a wife is junior to or of nearly the same age as a daughter of the house, the latter woman is, in some ways, treated as if she were a man; i.e., she is given the respect that a wife would accord a male member of the lineage who is of an age comparable to that of the woman concerned. A daughter of a compound is addressed by her given names by wives of the house who belong to her own mother's

---

[4] I placed the word *adopted* in quotation marks because, as has been said earlier, most of the ọmọ ile who were not actually born into the lineage are descendants of founders of the lineage. They are not adopted as such but over a number of generations come to be accepted as members of the house.

generation, however, the younger wives would address her as "the mother of so and so" or as a "mother of [or a child of] such and such a house." A daughter of Ile Alagbede Akinye, a woman in her late thirties or early forties, returned to live in her father's house after the death of her husband who was a Bale of Awe. She is referred to and addressed by name by all the wives of her mother's generation; those older women who came into the house after she was born address her by various pet names; all the wives younger than herself refer to her and address her as "Iya Ile Bale" (literally, mother from Bale's compound).

There are times when adult daughters of the house take precedence over all the wives of the house. When, for example, there is a celebration which concerns the lineage, the daughters, whether resident in their father's house or in their husband's house, are the women responsible for preparation of food, and they may have special roles to play in the observances. During the Ogun festival of 1961, I attended the ceremonies at one of the Alagbede (blacksmith) compounds in Awe. The woman who was reponsible for securing provisions for the feast was a daughter of the house who was also a resident in the house. She reported that the wives of the house had made contributions of food and money and had rendered assistance in the preparations but they had done so *on behalf of* their children who were, of course, members of the lineage of the compound.

Details of the relationship between wives and their husbands will be discussed in the following chapter. At this point, I only want to draw attention to some aspects of this relationship. Each "domestic family" occupies a specified area within the compound. Ideally, a man and his wife or wives have adjacent rooms; the husband has a room and each wife has her own room which she shares with all or some of her children. In practice, men have their own rooms, wives who have been in the compound for a number of years have their own rooms, but a wife of one or two years residence in the house ofter shares her husband's mother's room.

Within each family, it is the duty of the wives to respect and defer to their husband. Husband and wives do not usually take their meals together. The husband's food is set before him by the wife whose turn it is to cook for him and after he has eaten, the wives eat with their children. Women kneel as a sign of respect when greeting their husbands in the morning. They also see to it that each of their children kneels or prostrates when greeting his or her father.

The husband's privacy within the compound is respected and no wife would enter her husband's room without his permission nor would she take any of his possessions without being told to do so. The husband usually has a parlour in which he entertains his friends and receives his guests, and as a rule wives do not use this parlour.

In Awe, husbands do not usually address their wives by name. A young wife without children may be called "Iyawo" but most wives with children would be called "mother of so and so." For example, a woman might be called "Mama Funṣo" or "iya Funṣo" rather than be addressed by name. Women never refer to or address their husbands by name; a man would be referred to as "my husband," and would usually be addressed as the "father of so and so."

Women do not have much occasion to deal with men of the compound other than their husband. The other men of the husband's lineage, i.e., his actual or classificatory brothers, are given the utmost respect; one of them could, on the death of his brother, become the husband of the widow. Wives must show great deference toward males senior to their husbands; they regard men of their husband's generation as they would their own husbands. However, elderly wives often adopt a playful attitude toward young adult males of their husband's lineage, teasing them by referring to them as "husband" (ọkọ mi or bale mi).

Wives of a compound, like all other persons resident in that compound, are officially subject to the authority of the man who is head of that compound. Most wives of a compound do not usually have extensive day-to-day dealings with the Bale, but inasmuch as this man is responsible for settling minor disputes which break out among the residents of the house, the wives may be brought before him in times of conflict. If a wife quarrels with another wife and neither the Iyale of the compound nor the husband of the women concerned is able to effect a settlement, the women may be brought before the Bale who, in conjunction with the Iyale and some other elders of the house, settles the matter.

If a wife has a dispute with her husband such that she leaves for her father's house, the father and some men of his lineage bring the bride back to her husband's house where they and the Bale, attempt to effect a reconciliation between the husband and wife.

Women's Positions in Their Natal Compounds

Women, it has been noted, are life-long participants in the affairs relating to their natal compounds even though after marriage their day-to-day activities usually center in their affinal compounds. The foregoing section discussed some aspects of the position of women within the affinal unit, thereby setting the stage for a later consideration of the effects of women's economic roles on their behavior within, and on the structure of, the affinal compound which, as has been shown, includes the "domestic family." The lasting ties that a woman has with her natal compound are those accruing from her membership in the lineage (idile) of that compound. For a female youth who grows up in her natal compound, the entire social unit, including affinally as well as consanguineally affiliated members, constitutes the most important group of kinsmen in her life. The social life centers in the compound. As an adult woman, the links to her natal compound are primarily with persons who constitute the idile of the compound and most females of the idile, of whom she is one, do not reside in the natal compound. It is mainly through her mother that a woman maintains ties with the females resident in her natal compound. Thus, as a background to the effect of women's economic roles on behavioral patterns within that segment of their kinsmen constituted by persons belonging to their natal compounds, it is important to consider the position of women within the lineages to which they belong.

Strictly speaking, rank within the lineage is determined by order of birth without regard to sex. Thus, an elder sister is a senior sibling (egbon) deserving of as much respect as an elder brother. Before boys and girls of a lineage reach adulthood, their relative order of birth is *in fact* the chief determinant of their statuses. Nonetheless, as adults, *in general* men of the lineage exercise more influence over lineage affairs and *in general* men rank higher than women. This does not mean that certain indicators of respect (use of plural pronouns in address and reference, prostrating when greeting) are no longer shown an elder female sibling by a junior male sibling. Quite the contrary: throughout their lives the patterns of deference dictated by relative order of birth would be observed by lineage mates, but in many affairs, women, regardless of age, defer to men.

A woman's active participation in some types of lineage affairs begins during her early youth. As a child, she is taught the history of her lineage, ofttimes by her mother, who is a wife of the compound, as well as by the men of the lineage. A girl child, like her brothers, is exposed to the lineage praise names (*oriki*) and to the ritual chants (*rara*) associated with that lineage. A mother often addresses her young children by the praise name of the children's lineage, implanting in their minds this important part of lineage history and at the same time conveying to them her highest endearment by associating them with the heroic past of their ancestors. As children of a lineage, the girls as well as the boys are observers at some of the important ceremonies which go on in the compound. For example, as soon as they are able to walk, children follow at the side of a wedding procession, often making their appearance in places where they are not supposed to be. From their mothers and from the adult members of their lineage, they learn of the family *orisa* (gods) and are permitted to observe some of the propitiation rites. By watching their elders, they learn the dances and songs associated with various ceremonies and from the drummers who beat out the tones of their oriki, the children learn to recognize and respond to these praise names.

As a young woman of marriageable age, the extent of a female's exposure to and participation in lineage affairs is less than that of her brothers. If a young woman lives in the compound, she would be aware of the issues relating to inheritance of properties but she would not be directly involved in any of the deliberations that might take place. She might be well-informed concerning on-going intra-lineage disputes but would not necessarily be informed as to the background of the controversies. If she is not attending school, she would have begun some type of money-making enterprise, hoping to save enough so that she might be somewhat financially secure at the time of her marriage. Her orientation is toward the marriage that she will enter and hence toward a move out of her natal compound into that of her prospective husband. Young men, on the other hand, would be preparing to take their places among the men of the lineage and compound.

For young women who grow up in compounds other than those of their fathers, active participation in and knowledge of lineage affairs might be minimal. If, as often happens, a young woman lives and works with a female relative who lives in a house other than the girl's own father's house, she would grow up more or less like an omo ile (daughter of the house) of the compound in which she resides rather than of the house into which she was born. This does not mean, however, that she is no longer regarded as an omo ile of her father's house.

As has been said, when a woman gets married, her day-to-day concern is with the affairs of her husband's lineage and compound rather than with those of her own lineage and compound. If, as is the case with most Awe women, she lives in the same town in which her natal compound is located, she would pay regular visits to her mother who lives in that compound but on such occasions she is likely to learn more about matters relating to the wives and children of her natal compound than of affairs relating to men of the compound. She and the other adult daughters of the house would, however, remain in close touch with one another and exchange news of their lineage and natal compound. When there is a meeting of all members of her lineage, a woman would attend and thus remain abreast of matters pertaining specifically to her lineage as well as of those relating generally to her natal compound.

The older a woman gets, the more important is her position within the lineage, for as a senior member of the lineage she would be consulted by men and women of the lineage about many kinds of affairs. In cases of property disputes, she might be called upon to remember important events that took place during her early life or to recount important facts of lineage history; she may have pivotal roles in the rites of passage through which her lineage members must go. If a woman is the oldest child of her father, she would be consulted by her brothers before any decisions regarding the father's properties would be made.

When a woman's father dies, she is entitled to a share in any properties, including land, that are left to be divided among his children. If there is any movable property, a woman would take that share to which she is entitled.[5]

---

[5] This general picture of women's property rights was obtained from informants in Awe; however, many of the points raised have been discussed by Lloyd (1962).

The most valuable properties, however, are usually unmovable ones: the father's house in the compound or the section of the compound that was occupied by him and his wives, his land, and his rights to titles being the most important.

The father's house would be left to his male children and depending on the size and type, one or more of the sons would usually reside in the house with their wives and children. The daughters would have a place of residence in their husbands' compounds but if any one of them left her husband's house, her brothers would provide living quarters for her in her father's house.

Traditionally, the rights to land which are inherited by children of a deceased man are usufructuary rights. The land would be divided into a number of parts equal to the number of wives with children or, in rarer cases, into as many parts as there are children. In the former case, the children of each wife would divide the land allotted to their *origun*.[6] If the land in

---

[6] The term "origun" (literally corner) has been variously defined by Schwab (1955) and Lloyd (1955; 1962). Schwab speaks of it as a "major matri-segment" of the idile. In those parts of Yorubaland where the lineage is a patrilineally defined group (such as in the area where Schwab conducted his field work and where my own work was carried out), *there are no major matri-segments of the lineage*; there are only major patri-segments. Lloyd understood this when he noted that in reciting genealogies people always *presume* different maternity for the founders of lineage segments because it is *assumed* that "children born of the same mother would not have acted in opposition to one another" (Lloyd, 1955:243). It is *only* on any single generational level that there are, within each polygynous family, matri-sections, each comprising those children which one wife bore for the husband. The transgenerational segments of the lineage are always defined by reference to a *male* ancestor. Any person, male or female, will claim the right of membership in the segment, *not* on the basis of descent from the *woman* who mothered the founder of the segment but on the basis of descent (usually through males, occasionally through females) from the *male* founder of the segment. Segments of the lineage are termed iko (perhaps an elided form of Schwab's isoko), idi, and ojumu in various parts fo Yorubaland.

The concept of origun comes to the fore when there is something—usually land or titles—that must be shared among a group of people who are acknowledged as having a right to a share in the particular item. Just as there are "corners" of the earth, or "corners" of a compound, so there are, for purposes of equitable distribution of inherited commodities, "corners" or divisions of various kinship units.

In Yorubaland, there are two kinship units in which the concept of origun comes to the fore. These are: (1) the polygynous family and (2) the corporate descent group constituted by living members of the lineage. (This may not apply exactly to those parts of Yorubaland where, according to Lloyd, there are cognatic descent groups.)

The polygynous family is divided according to "maternal affiliations"; there are as many divisions as there are wives with children (Lloyd, 1955; Schwab, 1955). A group of children of identical parenthood (one father, one mother) are referred to in Yoruba as omo iya (literally, children of one mother). Thus, within the polygynous family the children which each wife bears for the husband would be referred to as "omo iya." (The term omo iya is often extended to cover other groups but these extensions do not concern us here.) *For the purpose of equitable division of any property possessed by their father, each set of children (omo iya) constitute an origun*. Where the origun principle is invoked, properties are divided equally among the omo iya, not among the individual children.

The living members of the lineage constitute a corporate descent group which is divided into segments (iko) founded by deceased male members of the lineage.

question is farmland, those males of the family who are farmers would each use a portion of the land, sometimes including portions belonging to their other brothers and their sisters. The rights of the women may be waived in favor of their brothers so long as the women have no adult male sons who require the use of the land. However, if a woman's son were in need of land, she could activate her claims to the land inherited from her father, and her brothers would be obliged to grant usufructuary rights to the son.

When a woman dies, however, she cannot bequeath any *dormant* usufructuary rights to land on to her son. That is, if the son had not been using the land during his mother's lifetime, and if his mother had not invested any money in the development of the land, the son could not legally lay claim to that land. If he were in need of land, however, he might appeal to his mother's brothers or to their sons to be permitted to use a portion of that land.

On the other hand, if a man activates his mother's rights to land during her lifetime, he may pass this land on to his sons. In principle, the land should not pass out of the lineage but in fact it does so in this very manner. If, for example, a man and his unmarried son are farming land the use of which was acquired through the man's mother, upon the death of the older man, the son would continue to farm this land. When the son then passes the use of the land on to his son, the land *in effect* belongs to the lineage of the men using it. When, however, any portion of the land is allowed to lie fallow so as to re-vitalize the soil through natural growth, the men of the lineage to which it originally belonged might challenge the right of men of the other lineage to start again to use the land. If the man who permitted the land to revert to natural growth is still alive, he might maintain that the land is rightfully his to use whenever it is fit to be put into use. If this man dies while the land is in disuse, there could ensue a suit between the two lineages as to who should have a right to the land. Depending on the detailed evidence presented, the judges could be justified in supporting the claims of either party.

Generally speaking, if there is no pressure brought to bear by young men of the original lineage that owned the land, a man could go on using the land acquired through one of his female ancestors and eventually the original ownership of the land might be forgotten.

Serious disputes concerning land ownership do arise when there is an attempt to alienate the land. If a man wanted to sell land belonging originally

---

Members of each iko̜ trace their descent from a *male* ancestor. For *purposes of equality of access to indivisible properties (such as titles) or for equity in distribution of divisible properties (such as compound land), each lineage segment (iko̜) constitutes an origun.*

The Yoruba way of insuring equity in division is to separate persons into groups (o̜mo̜ iya in one instance, iko̜ in another) and each group constitutes an origun, the members of which have, vis-a-vis other origun, equal access to the properties concerned.

to his mother's lineage, the members of her lineage would maintain that this could not be done because the man in question only had usufructuary rights to the land. The same thing might happen, of course, in attempts to sell land belonging to the would-be seller's own lineage.

With respect to rights to titles, the position of a woman is analogous to her position with regard to land. Of considerable note is the fact that where inheritance of titles is concerned, it is the iko (lineage segment) and not the idile that is the crucial kinship unit. For inasmuch as the idile embraces *all* patrilineally related descendants from the original founder of the compound and lineage, and since titles which rest in a compound should circulate among the partrilineal segments of the lineage that forms the core of the compound, persons who want to claim the right to a title are concerned about asserting their rights to affiliation with given iko. If they can justify claims to *rights* in the iko, they are not too concerned that people will know that they do not belong to the idile.

This fact makes easier to understand how men who are not members of a lineage sometimes come to hold titles reserved for the house in which that lineage is based. Since women as well as men are part of the iko, their sons can claim right to properties of their mother. When there is a meeting of her lineage or of her segment of the lineage, a woman might send her oldest son to represent her interests. In time, the son could come to be a *de facto* member of the group; this is especially true if he contributes substantially to the upkeep of the group by virtue of being well-educated or successful in business. In other words, a man may affiliate with his mother's iko even though he is a member of his father's idile (lineage) and of his father's ile (compound). Thus, when it falls the turn of the iko to select a person to fill a vacant chieftaincy, the persons contending that title may be male offspring of *women* of the lineage as well as male offspring of males of the lineage. If the son of a female member of the iko is able to win the support of the majority of men within the iko, then it is he who would assume the vacant title.

The Bale (senior-most chief) of Awe, for example, is not a patrilineal descendant of the idile that provides the Bale for the town and technically he can not be referred to as an omo ile of Ile Bale. His father's compound is Ile Eleiyele. But when it came the turn of his mother's iko to provide the Bale, it *is said* that none of the males of the iko were "capable" of holding the title and that the present Bale contested it on the basis of his mother's membership in the iko. Most of the members of his mother's iko gave him their support even though some are said to have done so grudgingly. To this day, some members of the house—including some of those from his own iko— contend that the Bale should have been chosen from among the patrilineal kinsmen of Ile Bale. Yet, no one contests the *principle* involved, namely that a man may come into property through his mother's membership in a lineage.

From the above discussion it should be clear that even though the rights of women of a lineage may be given over to their brothers or sons, women do constitute a group to be reckoned with in matters relating to inheritance. One of the real sources of conflict in the system of inheritance is the fact that it is through women that important shifts in lines of ownership can take place. In a patrilineal system that is as flexible as that of the Yoruba in the area where I worked, women can, in effect, cause properties to pass from their patrilineages to other patrilineages.

In many cases, the rights of women born into a lineage may be temporarily waived without their necessarily being permanently relinquished. Where a political office is at stake, the sons of a woman may press claims to their mother's rights long after the mother is deceased for no one could deny that the woman was a member of a particular iko nor could anyone, on principle, bar the sons from claiming the right of association with that iko. On the other hand, if there is land at stake, the sons of a deceased woman seem to have less chance of securing rights that could have been claimed by their mother. (This is true, of course, only if the woman had not, during her lifetime, activated her rights in the land.) Those male members of the lineage that owns the land in question could rightfully insist that the land should pass through the fatherline only and as a further measure they could maintain that the woman's rights were extinguished at the time of her death.

This raises an important point concerning the rights of women within the lineage. In principle, the rights of men of a lineage cannot be extinguished. However, when the rights of a woman remain dormant during her lifetime, they are likely to be extinguished forever. This is not surprising in as much as patrilineality is the dominant principle governing inheritance and since, for the most part, a woman's children inherit from their father.

The extent to which a woman's rights can be usurped or extinguished depends in large measure on the woman's position outside the lineage and, with respect to her own father's properties, on the extent of his regard for her. If a woman is a chief—such as an Iyalode (head of women in the town) or one of her lieutenants—if she is an Iyaloja (head of the women traders), or even if she is a highly prosperous trader, she would usually have great influence within the lineage and could in fact function more or less like a man of the lineage with many of the prerogatives this entails. I know of two cases where women exercise great influence over their fathers' properties as a result of the man's wishes. One woman manages the cocoa farm left by her deceased father because he designated that she should have the farm. However, this woman does not regard the farm as her exclusive property and she uses the returns from it to help her brothers' children. In this case, the woman has no male issues so that, upon her death, the farm will probably go to a brother or a brother's son. In the other case, the old man is still alive but most of his affairs are managed by his eldest daughter and her eldest son. It appears that this daughter will have the most influential voice in any of his affairs after his death.

It should be noted that in no case would *all* the sons of a woman lay claims to rights within their mother's lineage. If there is land at stake, any son who needs the land could seek the right of usufruct, but a junior son is not likely to do so without consulting his oldest brother as well as his mother. Where there is a title to be contested, it is almost invariably the oldest son who would lay claim to the title. Hardly ever would a junior brother be so presumptuous as to contest the title. The senior son might, however, waive his claim of rights to the title in favor of a junior brother who is felt to be more capable of bearing the responsibilities, financial and otherwise, that fall to chiefs.

The above discussion of the position of women with respect to their natal and affinal compounds should make it apparent that in any given compound there are two sets of women (wives and daughters) who exercise influence over its affairs. The wives of a compound are principally concerned with safeguarding the rights of their children within the lineage of that compound. The principle of seniority is such that after a man's death certain of his properties and prerogatives pass to his junior brothers rather than to his sons, but nevertheless a wife would seek to insure that her sons were ranked fairly vis-a-vis other men of the lineage and would stand with them against any attempt to undermine their positions. At certain times it might be necessary for her to render monetary assistance to her sons; at other times she would provide counsel. As outsiders, the wives cannot directly intervene in their husband's lineage affairs but they can prompt their sons to action. If a woman remains in her affinal compound after her husband dies, and if, as is so often the case in small towns today, her sons are living and working in another town, the sons may depend on her to keep them abreast of affairs of the lineage. If the mother learns of some development that could possibly affect her son, she would notify him that he should come home to look after his interests.

In both their positions as wives of one kin group and daughters of another, Yoruba women have as their first concern the welfare of their children. Where inheritable properties are at stake, it is most often the sons whose interests must be guarded. In addition to providing their sons with access to properties other than those of the sons' own lineages, women seek to insure that their sons will not be discriminated against within the lineages to which these men belong. Thus, even though women may not exercise their claims to properties in their own lineages and even though they have no claims to properties in their husbands' lineages, they can be instrumental in securing the property rights of men.

VI
FEMALE EMPLOYMENT AND FAMILY ORGANIZATION IN YORUBA SOCIETY

ADULT females in Yoruba society regard employment in trade or other money-making occupations as a necessary component of their role as women. To be a "complete" woman in Yoruba society is, first of all, to be married and to have children. Most women work *because* by so doing they fulfill their roles within the family. The aim of this chapter is to explore some dimensions of the interplay between women's economic roles and their roles within the family. It will examine some ways in which the structure of the family and patterns of behavior exhibited by persons within it are related to the involvement of women in trade.

In discussing the implications of Yoruba women's economic activities for family life, an attempt shall be made to consider their roles within the various kinship groupings to which they belong: (1) the immediate family constituted by a man, his wife or wives, and children; (2) the group of persons with whom a woman has affinal ties—namely, with the persons of her husband's lineage and compound; and (3) the group of persons to whom a woman is related by birth—namely, those persons who constitute the idile of her father's compound, her father's mother's compound, her mother's father's compound, and her mother's mother's compound.

Within the immediate family, a woman is a wife and a mother; the dyadic relationships that may be isolated are: (1) the husband-wife relationship, (2) the mother-child relationship, and (3) the co-wife relationship. The discussion that follows will deal first with these three sets of relationships and then with the relationship of women traders to the wider kin groups to which they belong.

WOMEN IN THE ROLE OF WIFE

When a woman gets married, she usually begins to trade on her own, even though before her marriage she may have been working for or with another woman. A husband is expected to give each bride a sum of money to help her begin her trade but only a few of the Awe women interviewed had received part of their initial trading capital from their husbands. When asked to specify the amounts received, the women said they could not remember. One woman said that her husband gave her "a large amount" and when questioned as to the amount, she said "about £5." In only two cases did a woman say that her husband had entirely financed the beginning of her trade activities, and the amounts mentioned were £2 and "about £3," respectively. Most of the women had begun their trading with money which they had saved while working with their mothers or with another woman trader. In other instances, the women had begun trading by purchasing their initial stock on credit.

Even though they started out with their own funds, women often received assistance from their husbands in the building of the stalls or shops in which they displayed their goods. In one case, the husband was a carpenter and had built the shop with materials he himself supplied. Another woman's husband had made available for her trade a room in the compound in which they lived. Some men had made the arrangements whereby their wives could rent shops in compounds that faced onto the main street or that were situated in other favorable locations in the town. In every instance, the upkeep of the shop, including the rent if there was any, was the wife's responsibility.

Whether men contribute to their wives' trading capital or not, the business is not regarded as a joint enterprise. Each wife is responsible for investing her capital as she sees fit and the returns on it are her own. In rare cases, a woman enters into partnership with her co-wife but, here too, the two women concerned control the trade, and the proceeds are shared between them.

From the time a woman begins to trade, her husband has little to do with her operations. He does not, unless consulted, offer any advice concerning the trade. In emergencies, he may help by extending to her a gift or a loan to help replenish her trading capital. Whether he does so would depend, in part, on whether he judges her to be a good businesswoman. In any case, whatever a husband gives his wife is her own; a woman trades on her own account, not on behalf of herself and her husband.

It might be argued that because trade activities often demand on-the-spot decisions as to allocation of capital, the system fosters independent rather than joint operations. It would be impossible for a trader to consult her husband each time she wanted to make an investment. Theoretically, a husband *could* invest in his wife's trade and allow her to make the decisions concerning the allocation of their resources. To my knowledge, such does not happen among the Yoruba. In a sense, by undertaking separate investments, the husband and wife minimize the risks involved for if one of them loses money in his economic endeavors, the loss does not entail the money belonging to both, and the successful partner may help sustain the other's loss.

Of the Awẹ women traders and producer-traders (makers of palm oil, palm kernel oil, soap, and pottery) interviewed, 70 provided information concerning their husbands.[1] Actually, reference was made to 65 men since of the women formally interviewed, five pairs were each co-wives of one man. Fifteen of the husbands were deceased, 33 were living in the town or on the farms (23 farmers, four traders, one teacher, one baker, one gardener, one clerk), and 17 were living and working in other towns. In all cases, the money-making enterprises of the husband and wife were entirely independent undertakings. In one instance the husband had a shop in which he sold hardware and a few provisions and in which his wife also sold provisions. The woman reported that she sometimes gave her husband money to purchase various commodities for her in Ibadan but that their businesses were carried on separately.

Even though many women who trade in foodstuffs are married to farmers, those women who live in the town do not usually buy directly from their husbands. The men sell to women who go about the farms buying foodstuffs and their wives buy from various of these women. Of course, in some instances, the women deal in items that are processed before they reach the town and much of the first-level processing of foodstuffs is done by women in the hamlets who buy the raw materials from the farmers. A gari seller in the town said that her husband grew cassava but that because she herself did not make gari, she had no occasion to buy from him. Like other gari sellers, she buys from women who make the cassava meal. This trader reported that she had seen her husband's farm only about a half-dozen times in 10 years, and on those occasions she had gone there because her husband needed her help in bringing foodstuffs to the town.

When a woman lives in the farmland with her husband and buys foodstuffs for resale to women from various towns, she buys from her husband as she would from any other farmer. When gari makers were questioned as to the source of their supply of cassava, they reported that they bought from various farmers, sometimes including their husbands, sometimes not. When farmers were asked if they would sell to their wives on the same basis as to other traders, they replied in the affirmative. One man explained that a farmer expects his wife to make a fair offer for any foodstuffs he had to sell; however, if she offered a price which unacceptable, he would sell to

---

[1] Eighty-five women traders and 38 producer-traders were interviewed. The conditions under which I talked to these women were such that not all of them had time to answer all the questions I wanted to ask. Whereas they all answered questions concerning patterns of trade, and most of them discussed the uses to which their earnings were put, some of them made only passing references to their husbands. Of course, much of the data used in this chapter was obtained not only from formal interviews with the women, but from interviews with male traders and farmers, through daily conversations with people about the town, and from visits to compounds and to farm hamlets.

another woman who came around the farm. "There is no question here of responsibilities toward a wife; that is a different matter. Here it is a matter of trading."

Farmers sometimes ask their wives to take crops to the market for them since it is generally felt that men are more easily cheated in the bargaining process than are women. Similarly, when a man brings foodstuffs to the town for sale, he might ask his wife to call a trader who deals in foodstuffs and he would bargain with this woman in the presence of his wife. By so doing, he feels that he will get a fair price for his crops. When farmers sell directly to women in the markets or in the fields, they set their prices according to information on the state of the market supplied by other farmers or by their wives who live in the hamlets.

Because their wives' money-making activities are independent of their own, men do not expect to be given free of charge items in which their wives trade. Of course both husbands and wives make gifts to each other but trading is one thing; gift-giving is another. A man who smokes *buys* cigarettes from his wife who sells them; one who drinks palm wine buys the quantity he wants. Of course, husbands often purchase items on credit but no man is expected to put his wife in an embarrassing position by asking for more credit than she can afford to extend.

A woman's income is kept separate from that of her husband. There is no common budget for a man and his wife. Husbands and wives subscribe separately to the upkeep of the family unit but there is no clear-cut division of responsibility. The husband, according to the men and women interviewed, is expected to "do whatever is within his power" for his wives and children, and the wives must strive to do the rest. In actuality, with respect to the financial upkeep of themselves and the monetary contributions to their children, the women do whatever they can, and, when necessary, they call upon their husbands' assistance.

All the same, *ideally* there are certain responsibilities that rest upon one or the other of the spouses. Men are said to be responsible for the upkeep of the dwelling in which their families reside, for the major expenses associated with educating the children (payment of school fees and purchase of text books), and for supplying the children with clothes. They are also supposed to buy the major staples for meals or to supply them from their farms. Wives are expected to buy most of their own clothing, some of the clothing for their children, and to supply the foods that supplement the main staples.

In fact, the major expenses associated with the upkeep of the family dwelling are always met by the husband. This is true whether the family resides in a section of a compound or in a separate house in the compound area. Men see to it that the roofing is kept in good repair; they pay the carpenters who build furniture for the parlors and, where furniture other than mats are used, for the bedrooms; they undertake to have the walls plastered or to put in a floor of cement. If they can afford it, they build a new house during their lifetime. The prestige attached to owning a large and attractive house is very great, and a man saves as much money as he can in an effort to build an impressive house for his family.

The extent of a man's contribution to the education of his children seems to depend as much on the income of his wives as on his own income. If a woman can afford to send her children to school, her husband might make only a token contribution to the children's education; in such a case only when the wife is in financial difficulties, would her husband pay the school fees. Usually it takes both the husband and wife to keep the children in school; the earnings of most men are not sufficient to enable them to send all their children to school therefore each wife usually has to bear part or all of the expenses for educating one or more of her children.

In every conversation with women whose children were of school age, the subject arose of school fees and the hardships which women endure in order to give their children the best education they could afford. Thirty of the women formally interviewed had children in primary or secondary modern school and all of them reported that they and their husbands were jointly paying for the children's education. A dozen of these women gave details concerning their children's education. Where the children were attending secondary modern school, it was the husband who paid the school fees and bought books for one or two terms of the year while the wife bought school supplies, paid at least one term's fees, and assumed responsibility for day-to-day expenses. In each case, the fees per term were approximately £6.10, making a total of £19.10 per year, and books cost about £4 per year. Only two women who each had two children in senior primary school reported that their husbands paid all the fees which amounted to £4 per year for each child. The other four women who each had two children in primary school and the woman with one child in primary school paid the fees themselves. For the children in classes between Infant I and Standard II (junior primary) they paid £1.10 per year and for those in senior primary, the mothers paid £4 per year. Whenever women mentioned sons who were in secondary grammar school, they said that their husbands paid most of the expenses.

Women whose children had reached adulthood often mentioned that they had spent most of their younger years trying to give their children at least a few years of formal education. Eight women reported having sent their children through primary school, modern school, or, in a few cases, to higher institutions. With the earnings from traffic in foodstuffs between Awe and Lagos, and without financial assistance from her husband, one woman had sent her four sons through primary school. One son had subsequently gone through trade school, another completed secondary grammar school, and the other two were in the process of completing their secondary school education. Another woman reported having sent her two daughters through Primary VI.

Her first husband had died in 1921, two years after their marriage and four months after the birth of her first daughter. After her husband died, she went to join her mother, a trader in cloth, who had moved from Awe to Lagos to Aba in the Eastern Region. The woman herself began to trade in cloth and beads in Aba and in Port Harcourt.[2] In 1923 she married her second husband for whom she bore her second daughter. This man died in 1926 when the child was one year old. In 1927, her mother returned to Awe with the two girls, and enrolled them in school. The woman herself remained in Port Harcourt where she sold cloth, beads, and ready-to-wear dresses which she sewed herself. Most of her earnings were sent to her mother in Awe for the support of her daughters and for their education. Due to a series of misfortunes that befell her in the mid 1930's, her trade declined and she was unable to give her daughters more than a primary school education. A third woman reported that her three daughters were in primary school when her husband, a Baptist minister, died in 1944. She paid her daughters' school fees by sewing and, after the machine which she had had for over 20 years broke down, by making and selling egusi oil (from melon seeds) and robo, a type of food made from the melon seeds after the oil is extracted. She sold in the rural markets, hawked about the farm hamlets, and in the town.

Whereas husbands did contribute to their children's education whenever they could afford to do so, whether they did so or not, women were always entirely responsible or almost entirely responsible for feeding themselves and their children; all of them supplied some of their husbands' meals as well.

Men who worked on the farms came home once a week, once every two weeks or, in a few cases, every evening. When their husbands were on the farms, women bought food for themselves and their children out of the money they earned in trade. They also bought the ingredients for most of the meals that they prepared for their husbands when the men were at home. Occasionally the husbands brought home yams, greens, or other foodstuffs which they had grown, but most of the foodstuffs are grown *for sale* on the market not for home consumption. All the members of a farmer's family who live in town buy most of the food they consume. The women and children in the farms hamlets get more of their food from the fields but even they buy much of what they consume.

---

[2] The life history of this trader is a fascinating one. Before her marriage in 1919, she had served as a housegirl and apprentice trader to a Lagos woman whose trade operations extended to Togo and Ghana. As a housegirl, this woman had sold mats and cloth in Cotonou, Lome, and "Eweland" in the Gold Coast. On return trips, she brought dried fish from Cotonou for sale in Lagos.

She was in Aba during the market women's riots of 1923 and 1928. She had been a participant in the 1923 uprising although she reports that the Aba women instructed all "foreign women" (mostly Yoruba) that they should not participate in the actual fighting but should carry sticks during the demonstration. This trader had vivid memories of the events leading up to the riots and of the destruction of properties which took place.

Women living in the town bought breakfast for themselves and their children from cooked-food sellers. School children and those left in the compound while their mothers went to their places of work, were given money ranging from 1d. to 6d. to purchase their noontime meals. When a woman took her children to her shop or to the market, she bought whatever food they ate during the day. Women bought (or used from the foodstuffs they sell) the ingredients for the main meals they and their children ate during the afternoon. They also bought the ẹkọ which is usually eaten as the evening meal.

Women who lived in the farm hamlets, bought ẹkọ for breakfast as the morning meal or prepared a mixture of pounded maize and water (ogi) for themselves and their children. Women who prepared gari for sale to the townswomen, might take some of this food as the afternoon meal for themselves and their children. Women in the hamlets who made palm oil, soap, palm kernel oil, or who engaged in any type of work other than the preparation of gari had to buy the gari consumed by themselves and their families. During the times when yams were plentiful, farmers often gave their wives a yam or two from which would be prepared the main meal for one or two days.

When men are working in the fields surrounding the hamlets, for breakfast they eat ẹkọ or akara which they buy for cash or on credit from the women who hawk about the farmlands. For their midday meals, some farmers boil and eat one or two slices of yam in the fields. Occasionally women cook for their husbands during the day, however, since they are often working in different places, the husbands do not usually expect their wives to prepare any meal except that which they eat in the late afternoon after returning from the fields.

Even when men and their wives live together in the town all the year, the women assume responsibility for most of the meals (see Table 5 for sample food budgets). Since the men and women very seldom work in the same places during the day, the men often buy their foods from women who sell near their place of work: they buy hot foods from the cooked-food sellers, or bread, or gari which they mix with water and drink in liquid form. Their wives purchase or prepare foods for themselves and the children. The main meal of the day is usually prepared by the wife from money which she earns.

Women not only assume almost complete responsibility for feeding themselves and their children, they also buy their own clothes and most of their children's clothes. This is particularly true in the case of girl children. Some women reported that their husbands bought cloth for the shirts and trousers worn by their school-age sons but nearly all the women bought the cloth for their daughters' dresses. Women do not ask for, nor are they given, a "clothing allowance" for their children. Whenever they have the means, they

TABLE 5

EXPENDITURES FOR FOOD: FOUR EXAMPLES
(All data collected in March, 1962)

I[1]	S	M	T	W	Th	F	S
Morning	Amala (FS) 1½d. (made from yam flour)	Beans (FS) 1½d. Bread 1d.	Beans (FS) 3d.	Amala (FS) 1½d.	Beans (FS) 1d. Bread 1d.	Amala (FS) 1½d.	Beans 1½d.
Afternoon	Bread 6d. Meat 1s. Chicken 1s Tomatoes & pepper 1d	Iyan (FS) 3d (pounded yam)	Bread 2d. Iyan (FS) 6d Meat 6d Tomatoes & pepper 1½d.	Iyan (FS) 4d	Iyan (FS) 3d Palm oil 3d. Onions ½d. Tomatoes 1d.	Iyan (FS) 6d. Pepper Tomatoes ½d. Palm oil 2d Meat 1s. 6d	Bread 3d. Iyan (FS) 3d.
Evening	Ekọ (FS) 3d	Ekọ (FS) 3d	Ekọ (S) 2d Akara (FS) 1d	Ekọ (FS) 3d	Ekọ (FS) 4d	Ekọ (FS) 3d	Ekọ (FS) 3d
	2s. 11½d.	8½d.	1s. 9½d.	8½d.	1s. 1½d.	2s. 10d.	10½d.

[1] FS=Bought from Cooked-Food Seller. The woman who supplied the information in example I buys breakfast for herself and for a six year old niece who lives with her. In the afternoon she cooks for herself, the girl, and her aged husband. In this example, as in those that follow, the meat, chicken, oil, tomatoes, condiments, etc., listed for the afternoon meals are used in cooking various types of stews.

Table 5 cont'd

II[2]	S	M	T	W	Th	F	S
Morning	Amala (FS) 3d Ogi (FS)2d (from maize) Alapa (FS) 3d (made from ground melon seeds and beans)	Beans (FS) 5d Bread 6d	Bread 6d Beans (FS) 6d	Amala (FS) 8d	Beans (FS) 4d Ekọ (FS)2d	Ekọ (FS)3d Beans (FS) 4d	Ọle (FS)2d (from beans) Ekọ (FS) 4d
Afternoon	Iyan (FS)9d Bread 3d Pepper 4d Palm oil 6d Tomatoes & onions 2d Ewedu 1d (type of greens) Iru (locust beans) 1d	Iyan (FS)9d	Iyan (FS)1s Meat 3s2d Palm oil 6d Onions, tomatoes & pepper 5d Igbalo (FS) 1 d (similar to alapa)	Boiled Yams (FS) 3d Iyan (FS)6d	Iyan (FS) 9d Alapa (FS) 3d	Iyan (FS) 11d Bread 2d Pepper 2d Onions 1d Palm oil 3d Roasted maize 1d	Amala 6d Eba 3d (from gari) Meat 4s Pepper 6d Palm oil 6d Egusi 6d (melon seeds) Bread 2d Groundnuts (FS) (roasted) 2d Igbalo (FS) 2d
Evening	Ekọ (FS)4d	Ekọ (FS)4d	Ekọ(FS)4d	Ekọ (FS)4d	Ogi(FS)3d	Ekọ(FS)4d	Ekọ(FS)4d
	3s 1d	2s	6s 6d	1s 9d	1s 9d	2s 7d	7s 7d

[2] The trader in example II buys breakfast for herself, her two year old daughter, her five and one-half year old son, and her eight year old housegirl. Her husband who works in Ọyọ also eats part of the afternoon meal of stew and a staple. In the evening, she buys ekọ for herself and the children. Like many women, she does not prepare stews each day because she sometimes has some left over from the previous day. This trader is one of the most prosperous of the women who deal in foodstuffs. It is she who buys maize (by the hundred-weight bag) and other foodstuffs at Igbeti and Ajawa for resale in the town. Even so, it appears that she spends most of her earnings on food. Her income is probably between £6 and £7 per month.

Table 5 Cont'd

III[3]	S	M	T	W	Th	F	S
Morning	Ekọ (FS)3d	Ekọ(FS)1d Food for niece(FS)2d	Ewa (FS) 1½d Food for niece(FS)2d	Ekọ (FS) (from that bought previous eve) Food for niece 2d	Ekọ 1d Food for niece(FS) 2d	Ọsan ½d (a fruit) food for niece(FS) 2d	Ekọ 3d
Afternoon	Eba meat for stew 1s	Iyan Meat for stew 1s	Iyan 1s (for herself & two other women)	Gari (mixed a portion of gari bought in market with water consumed in market)	Iyan (FS)3d Meat for stew 1d	Iyan (FS) 9d Meat for stew 1s. 6d	Amala Stew
Evening	Ekọ(FS)2d	Ekọ(FS)2d	Ekọ(FS)6d	Ekọ(FS)2d	Ekọ(FS)2d	Ekọ(FS)3d	Ekọ(FS)3d
	cash:1s5d	cash:1s5d	cash:1s9½d	cash:4d	cash:8d	cash:2s 8½d	cash:6d

[3] Whenever the trader in example III cooks the staples which she and her thirteen year old niece consume, she uses part of those foodstuffs which she buys for resale. Se does not keep records of the amount of food they consume but simply cooks as much as they eat. All the ingredients for the stews, except meat and salt, are taken from the commodities in which she trades. She cannot stipulate what foods her niece buys: she simply gives her 2d to purchase whatever she wants.

FEMALE EMPLOYMENT AND FAMILY ORGANIZATION   127

Table 5 cont'd

IV[a]	S	M	T	W	TH	F	S
Morning	Amala (FS)2d	Agbalumo 1½d (Osan-type of fruit)	Ogi (FS)1½d	Eko(FS)1d	Eko(FS)2d	Ogi(FS)1½d	Ogi(FS)1½d
			Igbalo (FS) 1d	Igbalo(FS) 1d		Ole(FS)1d	Akara 1½d
Afternoon	Amala Meat 2s Ewedu 2d Iru 2d Egusi(gift) Palm oil Pepper Salt	Eba	Amala Meat for stew 2s	Eba	Amala Stockfish for stew 1s	Eko(FS)2d	Iyan (FS)4d
Evening	Eko(FS)2d	(Eko(FS)2d	Eko(FS)2d	Eko(FS)2d	Eko(FS)2d	Eko(FS)2d	Eko(FS)2d
	cash:2s 8d	cash:3½d	cash:2s 4½d	cash:4d	cash 1s. 4d	6½d	9d

[a] The trader in example IV feeds only herself; her husband is dead and her only son lives in Lagos. The ingredients for Amala and Eba are taken from the foodstuffs which she sells.

purchase whatever wearing apparel their children need and it is only when they cannot afford a necessary item that they approach their husbands.

With respect to the budget, one general remark msut be made. From the conversations with women and men in the town, it appears that neither sex expects the major financial responsibility for the day-to-day upkeep of a woman and her children to devolve upon the husband. In fact, it is expected that since women earn money and in many cases during much of the year have more cash than their husbands, they should use their money to support themselves and their children. When there are major periodic expenses to be met, it is expected that the husbands will help to defray these expenses. It is the mothers who is constantly in touch with her children's needs and who informs her husband of the children's requirements.

It should be stressed that, from the evidence given by Awe informants, men do not have substantially higher cash incomes than women. In fact, the farmers reported that they often have smaller year-round incomes, although during the main harvest seasons they might earn more than any of their wives. Fifty pounds per year was reported as a high *total* cash income for a farmer, and £20 to £30 was given as a common cash income. On the average, the farms are no more than two or three acres in size. Although Awe is outside the main cocoa farming belt, many men devote some of their land to this crop; however, even those who plant as much as an acre of cocoa harvested only about four hundred-weight bags of the beans. During the 1961 season, the Awe Cooperative Produce Marketing Society paid £4.10 per hundred-weight bag of cocoa. A man with one acre of cocoa would receive only about £18 for the season. Most Awe farmers depend on cassava, yams, maize, and other food crops for the bulk of their income and over the year, the sales of which might yield £30. Men who worked as traders, repairmen, bakers, etc. in the town also had small monthly incomes. Generally, their estimated earnings ranged between £1.10 and £4 per month. Those men working outside the town probably did not earn much more than £3 to £6 per month. Thus, it can be seen that this is not a situation where men put upon their wives expenses that they themselves could undertake. Women have to virtually support themselves if they are to be supported at all.

From their meager earnings, men have a number of expenses in addition to their daily expenditures on food and on the occasional outlays for clothing. In February, 1962, I met with a group of 40 farmers to discuss their work and on a number of occasions I had interviews with various farmers and male traders. In every instance, the major expenses encumbent upon men were listed as follows: (1) taking a wife, (2) building and repairing houses, (3) sending children to school, (4) contributing to ceremonies: naming ceremonies for newborn babies, weddings, funerals, etc. Also included in the list were expenses associated with their work: whenever farmers cleared plots of land, they hired laborers (identified as Hausa men) to help with the work; when they called together a group of men to roof a farm house or to help in some other way on the farms, i.e., when they called for an ọwẹ (cooperative work group), they had to supply food for the helpers; male traders often employed young boys who helped with porterage and performed other tasks. Most men also had to buy some equipment for their work (farmers bought hoes, cutlasses, and a heavy type of cloth known as "kijipa" to wear in the fields); keep their bicycles in good repair, and buy yearly licenses for them; and pay taxes.

What is of special importance is the fact that men list as their major expense the procurement of wives. The nature of the division of labor is such that men and their wives often reside in different places for most of the year. This residential pattern, the high value placed on having children, the fact that men more than women are expected to have frequent sexual gratification, and the fact that women do not cohabit with their husbands for at least seven months of their pregnancy nor during the period of lactation (which extends from one and one-half to two and one-half years), serves to foster polygyny and involves men, at different points in their lives, in the expenses entailed in taking a bride. Most men have at least two wives during their lifetime although they *may* have only one of their wives living with them at any particular time.

A woman who is the only wife of her husband may herself suggest to him that he take another wife to help with the household duties so that she can devote more time to her trade activities (see Mabogunje, 1961b). This is particularly likely if a woman has borne a number of children who have passed infancy, for she would want to be able to earn as much as possible in order to provide for her children's material needs. This is a different situation from the one in which a wife, because she had had no children or no children who survived infancy, suggests to her husband that he take a second wife. However, in both instances the more senior wife might subsequently devote more of her energies to trade. When it is necessary for a woman's husband to reside in the farmlands much of the year or in a town other than the one in which she carries on her trade activities, she might also suggest that her husband take another wife who could look after him so that she herself would not have to move to the farm or to another town.

Even in cases where a wife does not suggest that her husband take another bride, her trade activities might be one of the factors that account for his doing so. When a woman is established in her trade, she might choose not to "follow her husband" to the place where he lives and works. In such cases a husband would not try to force his wife to join him. Rather, if he were away for long periods of time, he would take a second wife or establish a temporary liaison with another woman.

While it is here suggested that a wife's engagement in trade activities may be a factor in her husband's decision to take another wife, it is not suggested that this is the only factor in such a decision or that in every case it is a consideration at all. Furthermore, it is not always that a man who lives and works in the farmlands or in another town takes a second wife when his wife is not with him. There are cases where a husband has only the wife who lives in Awe while he himself lives and works in another town. Of course, it cannot be said with certainty that these men do not have alliances with other women in the towns in which they live.

Whereas many women trade in the town while their husbands work in other places, it is also true that Awe women, like women in other parts of Yoruba areas, may move to the town in which their husbands work. Whether they do so seems to depend on the conditions under which they would have to live and on whether the new place of residence promises better trade opportunities for the wives. Some Awe women are living in Kano, Ogbomosho, Lagos, Ibadan, and other places throughout West Africa where their husbands have found employment.

It should be pointed out, however, that even if a woman changes her residence in order to be with her husband, she may not follow him on a subsequent move. Some women who had gone to Kano remained there as traders even after their husbands had returned to work in the South. These women had established trade niches as "suppliers" of Northern Region produce to traders in the South. Some of them remained in Kano for years after their husbands had left; others stayed behind until such time as they could make the necessary adjustments in their trade relations.

The fact that husbands and wives often have separate residences for much of the year means that many husbands cannot oversee their wives' day-to-day behavior. Yet, in Awe both men and women assume that so long as a woman is living in her husband's house, she will not carry on a love affair with another man and it is definitely expected that all her children will be borne for her husband. In fact there seem to be very few cases in which adultery occurs. One of the women who was most often pointed out as being an immoral person was a woman who, while her husband worked in Lagos, had conceived a child by one of the men who worked as a cocoa buyer in the Awe area.

When questioned concerning their sexual lives during the absence of their husbands, young women maintain that they engage in sexual activities primarily because they want to have children and point out that so long as they are pregnant or nursing they do not engage in sexual intercourse. One woman put it this way: "as soon as I have stopped giving this baby the breast, and I have rested for a little while, my husband will come to me as often as possible because both of us want to have children. That's how it is. What more is there to be done?"

In the few cases where I questioned women in their mid-thirties concerning their sexual activities and Yoruba sexual norms, they all maintained that women were far less interested in sex *per se* than were the men and that once a woman had her children, she "would not worry" about sex. However, one of these women pointed out that she would definitely have to sleep with her husband when he paid his monthly visits to Awẹ because as theirs was a monogamous union, she alone would have to satisfy her husband.

These statements are not meant to imply that women have no regard for sex other than as a means to an end. It does seem, however, that women who must be separated from their husbands for fairly long periods of time appear far less anxious about their lack of sexual activities than are the Westerners who usually inquire about them. However, any woman who was not pregnant or nursing would want sexual access to her husband. She would have legitimate grounds for leaving a husband who would not cohabit with her. In such a case, the woman would return to her father's house, marry into another compound, or move to another town.

It seems that one of the restraints on women who might be tempted to enter into illicit affairs is the fact that most married women live in their husbands' compounds. Their movements are observable by men and women who live in the house. Often young wives actually sleep in the same room with their mothers-in-law and they always live in the same area of the compound. Under these circumstances, it is much more difficult to carry on an illicit love affair than it would be in places like Lagos where couples often rent rooms in compounds where there are no kinsmen to supervise a wife's behavior.

It should be made clear, however, that neither men nor women assume that the independence women enjoy as a result of their involvement in trade makes them loose or immoral. In fact, this could hardly be the case in a society where virtually all women are engaged in trade, and apparently have been for hundreds of years. Even when women are engaged in long distance traffic, it is not assumed that this automatically makes them "loose" although it *is* recognized that women who leave their husbands entirely to pursue their trade activities are likely to enter into alliances with men in the places in which they live and work.

Generally speaking, men appreciate the fact that from their earnings, they cannot entirely support their wives and children, and they justify their wives' relative independence by reference to this fact. When asked about his views on the subject, one man replied: "What can be said when a wife has her work to do just as her husband has his? If the women stop trading, the men won't be able to meet all the responsibilities. To give an example: one of my children was entering school this year and I had no money. My wife in Lagos paid the £18. If she hadn't been working, nkọ?"

So long as the wife contributes her share to the household expenses and so long as she does not flagrantly overstep the bounds placed on a married woman (i.e., as long as she does not openly commit adultery or behave in an unseemly manner), the husband is not expected to object to her trading activities. Since men recognize the need for women to work and to take care of their children, they do not place undue demands on the wives' time or attention. They accept as part of their lives the fact that they, like women, must buy on the market many of the services which their wives could perform, provided they were not engaged in trade.

Once a woman has embarked on a particular line of trade, she is virtually free to go wherever her work leads her. If the husband raises objections and cannot himself supply the wherewithal for his wife to remain at home, a woman may in fact leave him entirely so that she will be free to support her children. An example is supplied by the trader who, having had disagreements with her husband over her prolonged absences from the compound, left Awẹ entirely to spend most her time living and working in Igbẹti. Awẹ women say: "the man who does not ask what food I will eat cannot shower me with abuse."

WOMEN IN THE ROLE OF MOTHER

The relationship between women and their children is adjusted to the realities imposed by women's economic roles. The involvement of women in trade has meant that responsibility for the care of children cannot devolve entirely onto the mothers. They must rely on other women and on housegirls to assist them in various ways.

However, the fact that others share in the upbringing of the children does not mean that the mothers are neglectful of their offspring. Women value their children more than anything else and they place importance on securing for their sons and daughters the best opportunities they can provide. The children are a woman's "main gains from the marriage she [has entered] into and their achievements are her only happiness" (Mabogunje, *Odu* 5:29).

Mothers are warm and affectionate toward their children; they are expected to be understanding and somewhat indulgent toward them. It is the mothers who are expected to be the first persons to teach their children to be obedient and respectful to their elders, to be generous and unselfish with their peers, and to be shrewd but fair in their assessment of the motives and behavior of those with whom they come in contact. Yet, to be a good mother involves more than the display of affection or the supervision of behavior. It also entails the provision of the material means by which children can have food and clothing, get an education, and learn a profession in order to be able to support themselves when they become adults. In fact, whereas Yoruba mothers do not consider themselves to be the only persons capable of bringing up their children in such a way that they will acquire those personal qualities most valued by the society, they do feel that no one would work as hard as themselves or sacrifice as much to provide for their children's material well-being.

In their lifetime, women must assume some responsibility for the upbringing of their own children; they must be prepared to assist other women with *their* children; and they must carry on some type of activity by which they earn money. Thus, it is necessary that there be a regularized pattern of accommodation between women's occupational life cycles and their domestic life cycles. In fact, such a pattern can be distinguished.

During the early years of her marriage, a woman's main aim is to have children, and her energies are largely devoted to caring for her babies. Trade activities are definitely subordinated to child care and other domestic duties that fall to young brides. When a woman gets married, she tries to conceive her first child as soon as possible. She usually lives with her husband and cohabits with him as often as possible in the hope that she will conceive during the early months of her marriage. If a man has other wives, their sexual access to him is limited during the first few months after he takes a new bride. When the husband is a farmer, the Iyawo (most recently acquired wife) may go to live with him in the farms while the other wives live and work in the town. If the bride remains in the town compound with her husband's mother, she sleeps in her husband's room when he makes weekly or fortnightly visits to the compound.

Some brides have less frequent access to their husbands but whenever they see them, they try to become pregnant. A young woman of 20 years of age was married during the Christmas holidays of 1961. Prior to the wedding, the groom returned to Awe from Lagos where he worked as a carpenter. About three or four weeks after the marriage he had returned to his job in Lagos and the bride subsequently saw him only at the time of his monthly visits to Awe. When she was interviewed in August, 1962, she reported that she had conceived and that her pregnancy was in the fifth month.[3] Another expectant mother of about 18 years of age, who became a bride in December, 1961, reported that her husband, a lorry driver, had lived in Ibadan since 1959 and had continued to live there after their marriage. He came to Awe shortly before the wedding and remained in town for a few weeks. Between January and August, he had paid her two visits and he sometimes called at the compound en route from Ibadan to Ilorin.

Before a woman's first child is born, she engages in some type of money-making activity, but young brides usually trade on a relatively small scale. Many women reported that they made and sold cooked foods (especially ękǫ), gari, or a few provisions in the early period of their marriages. Women try not to engage in any strenuous work during the first five months of a

---

[3] Yòruba women are reticent about giving the approximate length of their pregnancy, and since this young woman was interviewed at the maternity clinic held at the Awe Dispensary, where it was not possible to conduct an entirely private interview, it may be that she was in fact less than five months pregnant.

pregnancy (especially of the first pregnancy) for fear that they might have a miscarriage. Those who must use the mortar and pestle in making soap, palm oil, or palm kernel oil curtail their activities until after the fifth month when the pregnancy has become "strong" in the womb. In the last four months of her pregnancy, a woman can carry on virtually any type of work or trade activity as it is felt that hard work makes for easy delivery.

Ideally, for 40 days after delivery, a woman remains within the compound and does not engage in any type of trade. Some women said they had waited one month before resuming any type of trade activity. However, the length of time a woman takes off from her work seemed to depend on her financial situation. On a visit to some of the aba (farm residences) around Awẹ, a group of women and myself called at a house to see a woman and her two-day old baby. When I expressed surprise at the fact that the mother was walking around and attending to a few light tasks, another woman from the aba exclaimed that the mother was now strong enough to pound yams for iyan or to pound eyin (the palm fruit) for making red palm oil. All the women present, including these from the town, agreed that the mother was strong enough to work and the mother herself said she would resume normal work after the naming ceremony for the baby.[4] A woman who lived in Oshogbo with her hsuband returned to Awẹ three months before her baby was born. She did not engage in any trade while in Awẹ but she did help her sisters with their trade. For 40 days after the child was born, she remained in her natal compound with her mother and did not cook or engage in other housework. At the end of the 40-day period, she dressed in expensive clothes and jewelry and called at various compounds to greet her relatives. She and her mother had prepared akara which was distributed to those on whom she called. When the baby was three months old, she returned to Oshogbo to resume her trade in provisions.

Women do not often leave in the care of others babies whom they are nursing, although their older children, their mothers, mothers-in-law, sisters, or housegirls may hold the babies while the mothers themselves are around. Wherever the mothers go, they carry their babies tied to their backs. Women who sell in shops, stalls, or markets in the town carry their babies with them and keep them on their backs while they are trading. Women who must work in the sunlight drape cloths from their heads onto their backs to avoid exposing the babies to the sun. Those who make soap, oil, or pottery take their babies to the worksites and keep them on their backs throughout almost all their manufacturing operations. If the children are old enough to walk, they may be placed on the ground at the mother's side while she carries on her work.

---

[4] Naming ceremonies are held on the eighth day after delivery for boys and girls, or they are held on the seventh day for girls and the ninth for boys.

When a woman usually engages in a type of activity that can not be carried on with an infant on her back, she curtails her activities until the baby is old enough to be taken to her place of work, or to be left in the care of someone else. One of the stockfish sellers who usually hawked about Ọyọ did not resume trading for about a month after her baby was born. From September, 1961 to January, 1962, she sold fish in front of her compound in the Bode market area. In February and succeeding months, she walked to Ọyọ each morning and returned to Awẹ around noon.

In the sections that follow are detailed daily routines for three women each of whom has an infant or small baby.

---

1. Routine of Mother of 2½-month baby

6 A.M.	Arises at 6 or earlier if baby wakes up. As soon as she awakes, arouses baby who sleeps on mat with her and her five year-old daughter. Bathes baby with warm water. Rubs his body with coconut oil. Gives him *agbo* [a broth made by boiling in water certain leaves, a dash of palm oil, and eru ("Ethiopian pepper"). Different women report using different types of leaves and some did not mention palm oil.] Puts baby on her back.
7 A.M.	Buys breakfast for herself and five year-old daughter. Usually they eat ẹko. Sweeps the part of the compound in which she and her mother-in-law live.
8 A.M.	Eats breakfast with her daughter. The girl eats about a half leafful of ẹko (c. ½d.) while the mother eats the other half and one whole portion.
9 A.M.	Washes baby's clothes.
Rest of Morning	Sits in stall where her mother-in-law sells provisions. She herself made and sold ẹko until about three days before her delivery but she has not resumed her trade since she had the baby. She said that she will begin to make ẹko when the child is about five or six months old and would not be bothered too much by the heat. Now she sells pepper in small piles on a tray in her mother-in-law's stall. Her daughter plays near the stall; all this time the baby is strapped to the mother's back. He sleeps whenever he likes, and when he wakes up, she gives him the breast. If he cries, she also gives him the breast.
c. 12 Noon	Returns to compound. Gives baby agbo. Puts him on her lap for a while but does not lay him on mat. Daughter might put baby on her back for awhile "for fun"; she wants "to practice" holding baby.
1 P.M.	Puts baby on her back. Grinds pepper, prepares stew which she, her daughter, and her mother-in-law will eat in the afternoon. Her husband lives and works in Lagos; he comes home "from time to time."
2 P.M.	Eats ẹko and stew for lunch. Daughter eats from separate leaf, takes stew from same pan. Mother-in-law would eat with them if she is at home. Washes pans and pots.

3 P.M.	Rests. Puts baby beside her as she lies on mat. Daughter goes about compound playing. Bathes baby and rubs him with coconut oil.
c. 4 P.M.	Might return to mother-in-law's stall, or she simply plays with baby in the house. Sometimes visits a sister in nearby compound.
5:30 P.M.	Supervises her daughter's bath. She helps her by scrubbing her back but girl can bathe herself.
7:00 P.M.	Buys eko for daughter's supper and sends her to bed.
8:00 P.M.	Gives baby agbo. Eats eko. Goes to bed by 9.
c. 1 A.M.	Gives baby agbo when he wakes up at night.

About once every five days, the woman washes for herself and her daughter. The daughter helps her by bringing water in a small bucket.

2. Routine of Mother with Nine-Month-Old Baby

c. 5–5:30 A.M.	Arises from mat on which she sleeps with nine-month-old son and four-year-old son. Wakes baby if he has not awakened by himself. If husband has not left for farm, goes to husband's room to greet him. If he leaves before she gets up, he will first come to say good morning to her. Feeds baby agbo. Bathes him in water which she has warmed on the fire. Uses soap (ose dudu) and sponge. Bath given in large enamel basin placed in sleeping room. Rubs body with coconut oil and osun (red dye made from bark of "African rosewood" tree). Dresses him. Ties him on her back.
c. 6:30 A.M.	Sweeps area in front of the sleeping rooms and parlor in their part of compound.
c. 6:45 A.M.	Goes to food sellers to buy eko (1d. but child doesn't eat all of it) and beans (1d.) for her four-year-old son, and amala (2d.) or beans (2d.) for herself. (Women who hawk eko may bring it to the compound.)
7 A.M.	Starts to pound millet used to make a type of beer (oti oka). If there is no millet to be pounded, goes to farm area to collect firewood for cooking. (The wood used to make beer is bought in large bundles from women who bring it to town.) When she goes to the farm, leaves food for four-year-old with her mother-in-law who looks after him whenever she is out.
8 A.M.	(when at home) Gives four-year-old his breakfast. He eats by himself from leaves in which foods are wrapped. (He awakes about 7 or 7:30 A.M., comes to greet her, his father—when he's at home—and any other people whom he sees in the compound. Before breakfast, she washes his mouth with a hydrogen peroxide solution; he puts on the slipover shirt that he wears during the day.)

Rest of Morning	(when at home) Pounds millet. Delivers beer to compounds of men who send someone to order it. When she goes to farms, usually takes until about 11:30 A.M. to collect wood and transport it to town. [All during morning, keeps child on her back—whether collecting firewood or pounding or delivering beer. Child sleeps on her back. She gives him the breast whenever he wakes up or cries.]
c. 12 Noon	Takes bath. Suns sleeping mats. Starts to prepare lunch. Grinds pepper, tomatoes, and onions on stone. Usually cooks stew every other day. Cooks. Feeds four-year-old and herself. (Also husband when he is at home. She is the only wife of husband so there is no one else to cook for him.) Washes pots and pans used for cooking and eating.
c. 2 P.M.	Rests. Lies on mat; puts baby on mat for a while.
c. 3 P.M.	Washes clothes for baby. When there is only a little to do in mornings, she might wash clothes at that time. (Does general laundry once a week: usually in late morning.)
c. 4 P.M.	Lights fire, puts on water to boil for beer. (Her mother-in-law and mother-in-law's co-wife attend to the beer.)
c. 5 P.M.	Bathes four-year-old son.
7 P.M.	**Bathes baby.**
7:30 P.M.	Feeds herself and four-year-old (She buys ekọ for both of them.)
8:30- 9 P.M.	Sleep.
c. 12 Midnight	Baby wakes up. She gives him agbo.

The mother said that no one besides herself carries the baby, feeds him, or bathes him. If he is on the mat for a while, his older brother or a cousin (c. three and one-half years old) might play with him. However, the baby does not like to be put onto the mat and seldom is. When she goes visiting she takes the baby with her.

The woman happens to live in a compound (Alagbẹdẹ Akinye) which I visited on the average of three times a week, and I knew this woman very well. From the time the baby was born I never saw anyone other than the mother carry him. When her mother died, the woman carried the baby all during the funeral ceremonies. On each occasion that I met her at her home or in the streets, she had her child on her back.

---

3. Routine of Mother of Child Aged 1 Year, 3 Months

6 A.M.	("at the latest") Arises. Takes maize to mill to be ground. Leaves child asleep on mat with his sister (c. seven years old). Returns home with ground maize.

7 A.M.	Bathes son [in warm water with agbo added. Uses soap (ọṣẹ dudu) and sponge.] Rubs his body with coconut oil. Washes his mouth with a mixture of alum and iyere (a spice). These are ground together and the powder is put on cotton to wipe mouth. Puts son on her back. Gives daughter money 1 d. or 1½d.) to buy food. (Girl leaves for school at about 7:30 A.M.)
8 A.M.	Gives son breakfast—beans bought from cooked food seller. (He feeds himself.)
Rest of Morning	Sifts maize, drinks ground maize stirred in boiling water for her breakfast. Washes large pot used for making ẹkọ. Draws water and starts to boil water for cooking ẹkọ.
c. 1 P.M.	Finishes preparing ẹkọ which she sells in afternoon and in evening market. Bathes.

While mother is preparing ẹkọ, son plays in the area near the place where she cooks. She can usually see him at all times. If he moves out of sight and is not with an older child, she calls to him or goes to look for him. If son gets hungry between meals, she gives him the breast or agbo.

Starts stew for afternoon meal.

2 P.M.	Feeds son and daughter. Usually they eat ẹkọ (cold) or amala (buys from food seller or prepares it herself). Prepares eba for her own meal. She often cooks for her iyawo (junior wife) and always for her husband when he comes home from the farm. Iyawo washes pots. Daughter washes pans.
3 P.M.	Rests. Daughter plays with the little boy.
4 P.M.	Puts son on her back and goes around town to sell ẹkọ.
6 P.M.	Returns to compound. Gives daughter ẹkọ or money for food.
7 P.M.	Takes son on her back as she goes to sell in the evening market.
9 P.M.	Returns home. Eats ẹkọ or amala. Goes to bed.

She says that whenever she has a chance during the day, she washes clothes for the baby. On Saturday she washes for herself and her daughter. Her iyawo does most of the sweeping and washes for the husband.

The mother is the only adult who takes care of the child. Her daughter helps a bit but most of the time the woman takes care of him herself. She is the only one who bathes or feeds the child.

A woman who is fortunate enough to conceive during the first year of her marriage usually tries to have a second child as soon as possible. During at least seven months of the pregnancy and throughout the one to two and one-half year period when she is nursing her child, she does not cohabit with her husband.[5] However, as soon as possible after the first child is weaned, she would want to become pregnant again. Usually the same thing holds after the weaning of the second child.

During these early years of her marriage, when a woman has only pre-school age children, there is not much pressure on her to expand the scale of ther trade activities. Her expenses are small in comparison with those of later years: most of her babies' food comes from her breast; the food for herself and her older child or children would be relatively cheap; the cloths needed for diapers and the clothes worn by young children are not expensive. Generally speaking, a woman can afford to subordinate her trade to the upbringing of her young children.

It is after a woman has a child in school and younger ones approaching school age that she starts to devote much of her attention to trade and this is precisely because, in order to support her children, she must earn more money than in previous years. It is at this point and in later years that she enters into the intricate Yoruba system of child-rearing whereby children are dispersed and responsibilities for their upkeep diffused among kin and non-kin in various parts of the compound, the town, and the country. In order that mothers can trade, and the children can become educated, acquire a profession, or learn the skills associated with some occupation by which they can earn a living as adults, women (and men) help each other in the upbringing of the children. Elder sisters take children from younger ones and by so doing are supplied with children who can help them with their domestic chores and trade activities; grandmothers look after their grandchildren while they themselves receive some assistance from their own children; prosperous women take in the children of less fortunate relatives while some of their own children may be with kinsmen who are more educated than themselves; childless women take in the children of their more fortunate female kinsmen, thereby helping themselves as well as the mothers concerned; elder women who are not caring for grandchildren take in housegirls who help them with their trade and whom they help to acquire some formal education and whom they instruct in the art of trade; young women who must trade and look after their own children take in an additional child who assists with the children while the women attend to their money-making pursuits. Some concrete manifestations of the system in operation are supplied by women who live in Awẹ.

The woman who buys foodstuffs in Ajawa and Igbẹti has three children: her eight-year-old son lives in Ibadan with his father's mother (i.e., with the woman's mother-in-law); her five-year-old son and her two-and one-half year-old

---

[5]Nowadays, most women nurse their children for a period of one and one-half to two years. They report that "in the olden days," babies were nursed for two and one-half or three years.

daughter live with her in Awẹ. Also living with her is a girl of about eight who is the daughter of one of her classificatory brothers. Her older son had gone to live with his grandmother when he was about five years old. This woman, who engages in trade in Ibadan, feeds the boy, buys his school supplies, and most of his clothes. The boy's father sends his mother money to help support herself and the child whenever she requests it. Both he and his wife buy some of the boy's clothes. The two younger children are at present supported largely by their mother (she buys their food and most of their clothes) but the woman expects that when the five-year-old boy begins school, his father will pay part of the school fees, buy some of the books, and buy his clothes. At present, the woman is also supporting her niece who recently came to live with her, and she expects to enroll the niece in primary school. On the days when this trader goes to Ajawa and Igbẹti, she takes her daughter, on her back, to the markets. The little boy is left in the compound; there is no adult who looks after him. His mother tells him where she leaves his lunch money (c. 2d.) and she gives him instructions to play in the compound area until she returns home. Of course, the girl who lives with his mother and helps her with household chores would be around to keep an eye on him.

It is not only after a woman has begun to have children that she has with her a girl who helps her around the house. At the time of her marriage, a bride may be given a child (usually a girl, sometimes a boy) who would be brought up more or less as her own and who would assist her by carrying water from the taps located in various places about the town, running errands, sweeping, etc. In most cases, the child is the son or daughter of a sibling or a near relative.[6] Thus, there is added to the immediate family of husband and wife a child who is attached to, and the responsibility of, the wife, rather than of both husband and wife. This does not mean that the husband does not contribute in any way to the girl's upkeep. When a farmer gives his wife foodstuffs he has grown or when a man provides any money for food, he is contributing to the girl's living expenses for she would eat of the foods prepared. In a monogamous household, or in cases where there is only one wife living with the husband, and there is usually only one girl, or perhaps two such girls, living with the family and the husband as well as the wife would treat them as daughters. Sometimes minors who are added to the family are relatives of the husband, often a brother's daughter, brought in to render assistance to the wife. In such cases, the wife would still undertake to provide food and some clothing items for the girl but the husband's responsibilities toward her would be greater than if she were not one of his own relatives.

[6] I was told that in former times it was customary for a young bride to be given such a child but that nowadays when the rearing of children entails more cash outlay, the practice is not so prevalent as before.

The young Awẹ woman who returned home from Oshogbo for the delivery of her baby reported that ever since her marriage she has had her husband's 10-year-old sister living with her. The girl attends primary school and is supported entirely by this woman and her husband. On her return to Oshogbo, this woman would have the assistance of the young girl in caring for the baby.

Women who themselves have school age children might also assist with the upbringing of their siblings' children. One of the provisions sellers had three teenage children and a pre-school age child whom she kept with her in the shop throughout the day. Her two teenage sons were attending secondary school at Lagos, their major support coming from her husband who traded between Kano and Lagos. This woman supported her teenage daughter who attended secondary modern school in Awẹ. In addition to her young son and teenage daughter, she had living with her a boy and girl who were the children of her younger sister who lived in Lagos. Both these children attended primary school and their fees were paid by their mother in Lagos. The woman in Awẹ fed the children and provided them with school supplies from her shop. She reported that her sons in Lagos received some of their spending money from her sister and that they sometimes lived with her sister during the school holidays.

In addition to their children or the children of relatives, a few Awẹ women employ housegirls who help them with their trade. The Ọlọka (seller of amala), to whom reference has been made earlier, has four children, one of whom is married and lives in Lagos with his wife and baby. In Awẹ, she has a son attending secondary modern school, and a son and daughter in primary school. Also living with her is the five-year-old daughter of an elder sister and a girl of about 12 who is employed to help her with her trade. All these children are supported by the Ọlọka. She said that her husband "does not have the power (resources)" to send the children to school so she must do everything herself. The housegirl who comes from Iware is paid 15s. a month for her work and is fed by her employer.

The woman who is the only patent medicine shop owner in Awẹ supports two of her children: a daughter in secondary modern school at Iseyin and a son at the Baptist Boys High School in Ọyọ. Her oldest son graduated from Awẹ High School and had a teaching job in a government school in Igbeti. Living with this woman is a younger brother borne by one of the women married to her father, a girl of four or five who is the daughter of one of her brothers, a year-old baby whom her daughter had borne before she entered modern school, and a housegirl of about 14 or 15 years of age. This woman paid the school fees for her daughter at Iseyin and her younger brother who attended secondary modern school in Awẹ. She explained that the boy's mother was a trader who had not been very successful and who could not afford to send him to school. The woman's own son who had just entered the high school in Ọyọ would have his fees paid by her for the first year, after which time her husband would pay them. Her brother's little girl had been sent from Ogbomoshọ to live with her because the child had a congenital limb disorder. For two years this woman had taken the girl to a health center in Ilora, a town near Awẹ. This little girl and the woman's grandchild were fed and clothed by her. The girl who lived with her as a house servant had been sent from Igbẹti by the woman's son. This girl helped to care for the children and hawked medicines around the town. For her services, she received food and about 3s. per week.

When their own children have reached adulthood, women often take care of their grandchildren or the children of junior relatives, thereby sharing with these mothers some of their responsibilities and/or allowing them to devote more time to their trade pursuits. Grandmothers expect to assist their daughters or daughters-in-law with the children. It is often the grandmothers who volunteer their services, and once they begin to take care of their grandchildren, they make the necessary adjustments in their own trade activities.

The woman from Ile Alagbẹde Akinye who made and sold millet beer with her co-wife, had living with her the three and one-half year-old son of her daughter who lived in Awẹ. The daughter's older son of primary school age lived with his parents. Caring for him was not a problem because by the time he came from school, his mother was home from the periodic markets or roadside stations where she bought foodstuffs. However, had she not had her mother's help with the three and one-half year-old, this young woman probably would have had to curtail her trade activities. The senior co-wife from Ile Alagbẹde Akinye took care of the four-year-old son of her daughter-in-law, referred to earlier in this chapter as the "mother of a nine month old child," whenever the younger woman was away from the compound. Because the daughter-in-law had a baby who demanded much of her time and attention and because she delivered beer and engaged in other work that took her outside the compound, most of the time it was the mother-in-law who looked after the four-year-old.

Two of the old women interviewed reported that they had given up most of their trade in order to look after their grandchildren. One of these women sold a few provisions in front of her compound. This trade was not so much to make money as to have something to do while the children were in school.

The trader from Ile Balẹ who sold foodstuffs in Lagos had living with her the 13-year-old daughter of her younger sister who lived in Kano. This trader's own daughter was married and living in Lagos; two of her sons had jobs and were self-supporting; one son was in his last year of high school and the other lived in Lagos with his brother who worked there. The niece had come from Kano to attend school in Awẹ and to help her aunt with household duties. While the mother in Kano paid the girl's school fees and bought her books, the aunt in Awe took care of her day-to-day expenses and bought most of her clothes.

The childless women known to me and interviewed by me each had at least one child living with her. In most cases, these were children of female relatives who were being helped by the women concerned. One provisions seller was supporting two youngsters, one of whom was enrolled in primary school. The children were treated as if they were her own and in ordinary conversation, she referred to them as her "children."

The examples cited above give some indication of the degree of mobility of children in this society, and of the extent to which women, in order to carry out their roles as mothers and traders, must rely on the assistance of one another. The examples also indicate something of the way in which domestic cycles and trade cycles are accommodated to one another. Generally speaking, if a woman has children during the first six years of her marriage, her trade activities are subordinated to her domestic duties. From the time her children reach school age until they reach the various points at which they become independent adults,[7] a woman must maximize her efforts to earn money to support her children. In effect, trade becomes the most important domestic duty. If the woman herself continues to bear children during this period, and even in some cases where she does not, she must depend on her older children, on house girls, or on her female relatives (usually older women) to help with the day-to-day task of earning for those children who live with her. During this period in her domestic cycle, she often must enter into arrangements of mutual assistance, financial or otherwise, with women who have no children. For example, a woman living and trading in Lagos might send her own children to live with a female relative in Awe and to attend primary or secondary modern school there, while she helps to support her female relative's children who are attending school in Lagos or elsewhere. Not all the arrangements are symmetrical at any one time nor are they always mutual exchanges between two parties. However, over the years, most of those women who receive assistance will be called upon to render assistance. While their children are growing up, most women do not realize *personal* benefit from their increased trade activities; the financial support which they provide for their children and the other children dependent on them constitutes their major investment. In fact, most of the returns on their labor are spent on their children.

When a woman's children reach young adulthood, if she has been fortunate over the years and has acquired a firm footing in a line of trade, she

---

[7] The point at which a child becomes self-supporting is often in part a function of his parents' financial position and of the amount of assistance his parents receive from other kinsmen.

may devote her energies to the "expansion" of her business. Of course, the extent to which she can expand the business is limited by the fact that basically she is poor; her operations still remain those of a "petty trader." In any case, her financial obligations are sure to persist even though they may not be as urgent as those of past years. She may have to assist with the education of her siblings' children; she may have to support an adolescent relative who comes to live with her so as to make lighter her day-to-day household duties. She might be called upon to support her aging mother; the death of a parent, particularly of her mother, would necessitate the outlay of large sums of money as would the marriage of a son or daughter.

By the time a woman becomes the grandmother of children who have passed infancy, she must expect to be called upon, if necessary, to help care for her grandchildren. Women who throughout the years of hard work have "just managed" to support themselves and their children must now take care of their grandchildren while depending on the parents of the children for their own support. These old women do not give up trade altogether. They buy and sell on a small scale, often using as capital monies given them by their children (they would not use monies earmarked for the grandchildren's upkeep). Grandmothers who have been relatively successful traders might themselves continue in their work even though they have grandchildren living with them. They could afford to hire a housegirl or take in a young relative to help them with the children. A woman who is engaged in a line of work which would not enable her to take care of the children, might adopt a new pattern of trade while continuing in the same commodity line. For example a trader in farm produce might sell in the town rather than travel to other cities.

Children in this society learn early the "blueprints for behavior" that are aimed at facilitating their adjustment to the world of the market which permeates their lives. Although there is a fairly long perod (from birth to about the age of two) when children are physically and emotionally close to, and almost entirely dependent upon, their mothers, from the time they are weaned and taken from their mother's back,[8] they are taught to be relatively independent.

From the time children are old enough to walk, they are allowed and encouraged to play around the compound with other children without constant adult supervision. Children of about three years of age can play in any area of the compound without reporting to their mothers or guardians each time they move about. Often times there are no adults supervising these play groups. Children of three years of age are sent on "small errands" within

---

[8] After a young child is weaned, a mother does not regularly put him on her back. However, if he is sick, in discomfort, or uneasy in any situation, she would put him on her back.

the compound. Those of five or six run errands in many parts of the town. They know many of the compounds in their Quarter and they know the compounds of their mother's relatives and friends in other parts of town. They know the main market, Orita Merin, and other important areas of the town. The mother can send them to buy items that are already measured into quantities with stipulated prices (e.g., tomatoes and peppers). Young children go to the store to buy packaged or canned foods which have more or less uniform prices throughout the town. They learn by the age of five and sometimes earlier to buy eko, akara, and other cooked foods from the women who sell them. When sent on errands, children are told to make up songs about their mission so that they will not forget. Those who do not do as they are told are sent out again to rectify their mistakes. For an errand well done, a boy child is rewarded with sweet-sounding phrases in which the mother refers to him as "my husband"; other terms of endearment are used with girls. Sometimes children are rewarded with a small amount of cash to buy goodies.

A child of five or six years can sweep the floor, go to the tap for water, and wash the pans in which he or she eats. He or she can get dressed in every-day clothes without help. In general, children are taught at an early age to look after most of their needs in case there is no adult to whom they can turn for assistance.

From the time they are able to speak, children learn that obedience is the most important virtue in a child. When the mother or father gives instructions as to what should be done in any situation, the child is expected to obey. A disobedient child is often spanked and reprimanded for his misbehavior. Children repeat instructions given them to make sure they understand, and for the most part they obey their elders. Because they are taught obedience and respect for their elders, they can be left in the care of others or left to play without any special supervision. For, if a child is told by an adult that he must refrain from some particular activity, he usually responds accordingly. The children would be reported to their mothers or guardians if they have been disobedient or have misbehaved. The mothers would apply whatever punishment is commensurate with the offense.

When children are of school age, it is not necessary to have an adult in the compound to look after them. If the mothers have shops or stalls in the town or if they work at any one of the ebu in the town, the children would stop at their mother's place of work after school. The mothers give them instructions as to what should be done when they return to the compound. Most children have regular chores (such as replenishing the family's water supply) which they attend to after school is out. They complete any school work assigned them and may return to their mothers to play or help around the shop.

Children who are eight or nine years old often help their mothers with their trade activities. After school, young boys and girls can be seen hawking about the town. Usually they are children of women who sell eko, groundnuts, or some other food that has been measured into quantities with given values. Others help with household chores while their mothers attend to the trade.

Some teenage girls carry on their mothers' or guardians' trade while the women are trading in another place or attending to other affairs. These girls know the prices and measures for all the items sold. Women who sell gari, for example, can leave these girls to measure the denges, kongos, and other smaller measures in which gari is sold.

Boys of 10 or 12 do not usually help their mothers with trade activities. Some of them go to the farms to help their fathers. The younger ones harvest pepper while the older ones help with the weeding. Some of them collect green vegetables (efo) which are sold to the women traders. The farmers complain that nowadays many boys, especially teenagers, do not want to help in the farms but those who will become farmers do work with their fathers, learning the occupation.

Throughout this disucssion, emphasis has been given to the material support given children by their female parent or guardian and to the assistance rendered to these females by the children concerned. Nonetheless, it must be stressed that men contribute to the material support of children, and even in cases where they cannot give financial support, they directly or indirectly provide much of the guidance and care given children. It must also be pointed out that although the patterns of child-rearing can be analyzed in terms of their accommodation to economic patterns, the relationship between children and their parents or guardians cannot be fully understood in terms of economics. Children are highly valued for the pleasure and emotional satisfaction they give and no man or woman wants to be without this satisfaction.

WOMEN IN THE ROLE OF CO-WIFE

Turning to an examination of the woman in the role of trader and of co-wife, it must be recalled that the co-wife category contains not only women who are married to the same man but includes all women who are married into the same compound. Therefore, the discussion of women as co-wives of the same man is a logical link between the discussion of women in the immediate family and that of women as wives within the larger kin group constituted by members of their affinal compound.

It will be recalled that the wives of any man, like all the wives in a compound, are ranked according to the order of their marriage. It was pointed out that the older wives are usually freer to trade than is the junior-most wife who has more responsibilities toward the husband and more domestic duties within the compound. This latter point must not be over-stressed, however, because even the junior-most wife engages in some type of money-making activity. The major difference between herself and her older co-wives is that her range of movements is more restricted and hence the type of trade in which she might engage is somewhat circumscribed by her position. A young woman in the status of iyawo would not normally be found trafficking foodstuffs between Awe and Ibadan or Awe and Lagos. Her trade orbit would extend from the town to the surrounding farmlands or would be entirely within the town.

In the types of households found in Awe, the major tasks which might fall to the iyawo are cooking, washing, sweeping, and mopping. Usually children of the house draw water from the taps and streams in the town. Since each wife cleans her own room, at most the iyawo would only have to sweep and mop that part of the verandah in front of the rooms occupied by herself, her husband's mother, her husband, and her co-wives. Usually each wife prepares meals for herself and her children, but in those cases in Awe where there were only two co-wives, they often cooked and ate their meals together with their children while the husband ate separately. In any case, as I have pointed out, much of the "preparing of meals" is done for the wives by those women who specialize in the sale of cooked foods.

Undoubtedly, the main reason why a recently married woman remains close to her husband and restricts her trading activities is not so much that she has a great deal of *housework* to do but because she wants to have children.

Women married to the same man may or may not carry on cooperative economic activities. As a rule, the women's trades are carried out on an independent basis. However, wives who engage in the *production* and trading of certain commodities sometimes join together in their work and share the proceeds. Again, I must stress that this type of cooperation between co-wives of one man seemed the exception rather than the rule. In one case referred to earlier, two women who had been co-wives for over 30 years, along with the daughter-in-law of the senior wife, brewed oti oka (millet beer) for sale and shared the proceeds. In another case, the women made and sold red palm oil on a partnership basis.

Sometimes wives of the same man carry on independent trade but render assistance to each other when necessary. Two wives of Ile Elewuetu said that, prior to my arrival in Awe, both had sold enamelware in front of their compound. By the time I had made their acquaintance, the senior wife had given up her trade in enamelware and only sold akara which she cooked under a stall adjacent to that of her iyawo. Both women worked independently but each would look after the other's trade if for some reason her co-wife had to leave the compound.

As a rule, wives of the same man do not handle the same commodity line. Except for the cases referred to above and two cases where co-wives sold eko, the women dealt in different items. When the women attend the same markets, they travel together but since their commodities are different, they sit in different parts of the market. The co-wives who sold ekọ reported to me that they sometimes walked together to Ọyọ and hawked about the streets there.

The extent to which wives of the same man assist each other in trade activities depends on their general disposition toward each other. Wives are said to become jealous if one among them becomes unusually prosperous. This is especially true if it is felt that her success was due to preferential treatment by the husband or if in pursuance of her trade, she had shirked some of her responsibilities in the compound. Several women related stories about particular wives who in their jealousy over the prosperity of another had left the compound and had gone to trade in Lagos. The jealousy reported to exist, and which was sometimes obvious, between various co-wives living in the town was usually traced to differential treatment of the wives by the husband, rather than to economic factors. Actually in the few cases known to me where co-wives were definitely hostile toward each other even though they often appeared together in public, neither woman was appreciably better off economically than the other. In one case, one had more children than the other and this was considered one proof and cause of the husband's preferences for the more prolific wife. There was only one case known to me in which the co-wives displayed an unusual degree of competitiveness in their trade. One of the co-wives was a successful foodstuffs seller and her iyawo, it is said, "did not rest" until she had secured a provisions shop. Although both women were polite to each other, they never patronized each other's business.

Generally speaking, when wives are married to the same man, if the women concerned respect each other's position within the household and if the man of the house shows no obvious preference for one over the other, there is a minimum of friction between them in most situations, including trade. The wives, although they are mindful of their interests and especially of their children's interests, display a cordiality toward one another. In the five cases where I knew personally two women who were wives of the same man, they appeared to be friends. These might have been exceptional cases but that cannot be stated with certainty.

As could be predicted from all that has been said concerning women's economic activities, the money earned by each co-wife is her own. When co-wives eat from the same pot, either they each contribute part of the ingredients used, or they contribute equal amounts of money for the purchase of the ingredients. Each co-wife is responsible for the financial support of her own children. Only in cases where the wives regularly cook together would a co-wife have her children fed by her mate. Even in cases where this happens, the mother of the children is usually present. However, in one compound which I frequently visited, one set of co-wives often served food to their respective *grandchildren* regardless of whether both women were present. Yet, most of the time the food had been purchased by each woman for her own grandchildren. Nonetheless, there were occasions when either one of the women bought or prepared food for the children.

No woman ever reported having borrowed money from her co-wife to either replenish her trading capital or to make necessary purchases. Some did, however, mention instances in which they had borrowed from women who were wives of the same compound but who were married to husbands other than their own. For example, a woman who was a wife in Ile Bale but who had not lived in that compound since her husband died, reported that on different occasions she had borrowed money from another wife of Ile Bale who still lived in their affinal compound.

On occasions when her co-wife is celebrating a funeral, holding a naming ceremony for a new born baby, or preparing for the wedding of a son or daughter, a woman contributes money to her mate (or co-wife) and/or spends money on various items of food or clothing for the ceremony. In explaining why she bought salt by the denge rather than by the 40 pound bag and why she bought many other items in small quantities when larger ones were cheaper, a cooked-food seller pointed out that, within the two months prior to our discussion, she had had to spend a considerable sum of money. Among other things, her co-wife's daughter had gotten married in Lagos and this required the expenditure of about £5 for aso ebi ("family dress") and in contribution to the bride and her mother.

WOMEN AS WIVES WITHIN THEIR AFFINAL COMPOUNDS

In some compounds within the town, a number of wives engage in the same productive activity. These wives would not necessarily be married to the same men. At various compounds, the women make adin (palm kernel oil), epo pupa (red palm oil), pottery, or ose dudu (black soap). The sites at which these are made (ebu) are located on the land belonging to the compound in which most of the women working at the ebu live. The women who make oil or soap at a site belonging to a particular compound are usually wives or daughters of the compound. In some instances the sites are situated independently of any compound and women from various houses work there. Most phases of the manufacturing processes require the cooperation of at least two women. Although each woman has her own raw materials and does not share the proceeds from the finished product, there is a great deal of cooperation among women who work at the same site, regardless of whether they are wives of the same house. In fact, on my first visit to an ebu at which ose dudu was being made, I was under the impression that the enterprise was a cooperative one, for the women assisted each other with all phases of the work and no one seemed to feel that she should carry on with her own task at the expense of her neighbor.

On several occasions when I visited the ẹbu at Ile Afogbonbo, there were at least three or four women (who identified themselves as wives of the house) making soap. Each woman usually pounds her own mixture of ashes and oil but they assist each other in stirring the soap, removing it from the fire, transporting raw materials, etc. All the women who make adin at the ebu at Ile Arinago and most of those working in the ẹbu at Ile Asalu and Ile Onṣalapeleke are wives of these compounds. Again, the women were observed helping each other whenever necessary. Sometimes two women would pound together the kernels used by one of them. Any woman could be asked to keep an eye on a boiling pot when the owner had to leave the site for a short time.

In Awẹ, I did not encounter any instance in which wives of a particular house necessarily traded in the same goods, but in two instances, in Ọyọ, I was told that women of a particular house traded in certain items. On a survey of Akesan market, it surprised me to see three women selling hardware made by local blacksmiths. When I remarked that I had never seen women handling this line of wares before, I was told that they were wives of "awọn Ologun" (blacksmiths who worship Ogun, the god of iron) who live at the *Afin* (the compound of the king) and that in this house the wives sell these items. During an interview with a woman who sold cloth (the type known as ọja) at Emi-Abata and at Akesan, she reported that she had sold "ankara" (imported printed cotton) when she lived in her home town of Ejigbo but when she married into a compound at Isale Bashorun in Ọyọ, she was told by her husband that the wives of this house sold ọja and she had since been selling this type of cloth. It might be that this represents an old Yoruba pattern in which at least some women sold the craft goods produced by the men (or women) of the house.

The financial responsibilities of women as wives within a compound are quite distinct from the responsibilities of their husbands who are members of the idile of the compound. When there are ceremonies of any type within the compound, the wives make their own contributions out of the money which they earn as traders. Whether the fact that women have independent earning power can be said to account for this pattern is not certain. But, in the compound as in the immediate family, husbands and wives make independent contributions in those situations that require the outlay of money or goods.

When there are naming ceremonies, weddings, or funerals within the compound, each wife contributes money to the person who is in charge of the ceremony. A wife is particularly careful to give generously of her time and money to activities in her affinal compound for she is subject to criticisms from two sources: her husband might point out that she expects him to help her with her "family activities" but will not give equally to his "family's activities," and the other wives of the house will criticize her as being miserly. They might hint that she is hoarding money in order to increase her trade.

One of the major parts of any ceremony is the preparation of food for the feasting which takes place. Wives of a house are usually responsible for the cooking and they usually purchase, on behalf of themselves as wives or of their children as members of the compound, at least part of the raw materials which they prepare. When a woman trades in foodstuffs, she would prepare some of these as part of the repast or she would give foodstuffs to the women in charge of the preparations.

Women do not attend market, go to their shops, or work in their ẹbu when there is a celebration in their affinal compound. Nor would they all do so when one of their co-wives has an important occasion to be celebrated in her natal compound. Throughout the period of the celebration in the wife's natal compound, she would be helped by the women married to the same husband as herself and by her special friends among the other wives of her affinal compound. Each of the wives of her affinal compound would assist her on at least one day of the celebration.

By contributing money to a woman or women who are holding a ceremony, wives, like other participants and observers, help to defray the expenses which would otherwise make serious inroads into trading capital. At the time when any of the three important Yoruba *rites de passage* (naming ceremonies, weddings, funerals) are being held, and especially in the case of the long celebrations associated with death, a number of women and men are involved in considerable expense. The major outlays are for clothes worn on the occasion and for food given those who come to participate in the celebrations. Since nearly everyone who partakes of the food gives the celebrant a small amount of cash and since some of the women of the same affinal or natal compound give substantial sums, the celebrant is relieved of some of the financial burden of the occasion.

One notable feature in the relationship between wives and other members of the compound and among wives themselves is the extent to which the market economy permeates these relationships. There are occasions for gift-giving on the part of those who live in the compound, but in everyday affairs, most items which exchange hands are bought and sold. Because it is recognized that traders must earn a fair return on their investments, members of the household do not expect to be treated substantially differently from any other customers. Men and women of a compound buy from each other, and they give their children money to purchase items from the other women of the house. Of course, occasionally members of a compound may be given a bit more for the same price paid by outsiders, or they might be given the same quantity for a lower price than that paid by others but this is not an everyday occurrence. Since traders are related to a great number of people, in order to protect themselves against losses on their investments, they must, in a real sense, keep business relationships apart from kin and convivial relationships.

The economic activities of wives of a compound may serve as bonds that foster friendship rather than animosity among them. In Awẹ where there is not as much diversity in the goods handled by women as there is in some larger towns, many wives of the compound (though not of the same husband) deal in the same items. They are thus linked together by trade associational ties as well as by affinal kin ties; for all women who deal in the same line "know themselves" regardless of whether they belong to a formal trade association. When one of their number dies or has a death in the family, they contribute to help defray the funeral expenses. When they meet, they discuss matters relating to their children and their work, and generally maintain cordial relationships. The same obtains whether they are wives of different houses or wives of the same house. In the latter case, the trade link adds an economic dimension to the social ties involved in the wife-to-wife relationship.

WOMEN AS DAUGHTERS WITHIN THEIR LINEAGES AND NATAL COMPOUNDS

From birth, women are members of a patrilineal descent group. They also have relatives in the lineages of their mother's father, their father's mother, and their mother's mother. Both the responsibilities which women have toward their descent group and their position within this group depends in part on their success as traders. Generally speaking, the more successful a woman becomes, the more demands are placed on her by her kinsmen and the greater is the contribution she will be expected to make to her less fortunate kinsmen and to ceremonials.

A close relationship usually exists among sisters and between sisters and brothers regardless of whether they share one or both parents in common. Women exhibit a concern for the welfare of their sisters' children which is sometimes indistinguishable from that which they have for their own children. Because women control the allocation of their resources, they can and do contribute materially to sisters who are less fortunate than themselves. As has been pointed out, many of the Awẹ women had their sisters' children living with them or were contributing whatever they could to help with the cost of educating one or two of these children. When their own children had not yet begun school, the women would take whatever they could from their earnings to help support a nephew or niece who was in school. After a woman's own children had completed their education or had gone as far as they could, she would help her sister's children to get at least a primary and secondary or secondary modern education. When women had junior brothers and sisters, whether by the same parents or by the same father, they would often help to secure an education for these younger ones. These junior siblings lived with the sister in her husband's house and were supported entirely or almost entirely by her.

Women, just as much as men, must contribute to the ceremonies undertaken by members of their descent group. When a woman's niece or nephew gets married, she aids the mother in making preparations for the ceremony. The woman contributes part of the money which her sister uses to entertain her friends. She must buy the aso ebi (family dress) chosen for the occasion and give money to the bride herself.

On the night when the bride goes from her father's house to that of her husband, the bridal party—consisting of the bride, her "best friend" (maid of honor), her egbe (those young unmarried and married girls who constitute her "association" or informal age set), most of the wives of her natal compound, some of her brothers, drummers, and spectators—calls at each compound in which her close relatives live. They invariably call at the compounds in which her mother's sisters live and the sisters, like others on whom they call, give money to the bride, to the wives of her natal compound, and, usually to the drummers who accompany the procession. If the mother of the bride has died before the girl gets married, usually one of the mother's sisters (sometimes her mother's "best friend") would "do the mother's share" of the wedding celebrations.

Where there is a death in the family, usually the deceased's surviving children, and adult grandchildren, are responsible for planning the final rites. His or her sisters and brothers also have a share in the obsequies but it is the children who are in the forefront. Each man or woman who is financially able to do so would plan a separate celebration, involving the purchase and preparation of food and drink for those who come to greet the mourners, and the engagement of drummers for the occasion. As a member of the lineage, a woman must share in the responsibilities for a funeral, and her obligations do not descend onto her husband, although he would always render some financial assistance to his wife.

As would be expected, the closer the relationship of a woman to the deceased, the greater the financial outlay which must be made. On the death of a parent, particularly of her mother, a woman must be prepared to spend as much as she could possibly afford (many older women would have made an effort to put aside some money towards this event) to give the deceased a proper funeral. An Awe woman in her late forties, whose earnings as a trader average about £4 per month, spent over £100 during the 40 days of feasting and ritual which followed the death of her mother. Her elder sister, a woman about 60 years old, spend roughly the same amount. The adult grandchildren of the deceased each spent from £15 to £20 entertaining their friends.

Depending on the age and financial position of her parents when any one of her grandparents dies, an adult woman may have to take major responsibility for the funeral or she may only entertain her friends (her egbe) while the parent concerned would bear most of the expense. A woman must give money for the funeral of any member of her own lineage and of her mother's lineage. Upon the death of a person of her father's mother or her mother's mother's lineage, a woman may contribute only a small amount of money but she would usually help with the preparation of the food to be served.

In all these matters, the financial standing of the woman is expected to determine the size of her contribution. If a trader is considered to be prosperous, she would expected to contribute more than a less successful person who stands in the same relationship to the deceased. Furthermore, since all of the funeral celebrations are not completed at the time a person dies, years after the death of her parents or grandparents, a woman may decide to celebrate part of the final obsequies. She would consult her brothers and sisters and together they would undertake the ceremonies.

In the family grouping into which they are born as well as in that into which they marry, Yoruba women—as daughters, sisters, wives, and mothers—have placed upon them responsibilities that are independent of those placed on the men in these groups. It is through their trade activities that women are able to meet these obligations. This chapter has shown that, in turn, women are supported in their economic endeavors by a system of reciprocity and mutual assistance that exists among kinsmen.

VII

CONCLUDING SUMMARY

IN Yoruba society, the world of the market is primarily a woman's world. Apparently this has been the case for as long as the Yoruba have lived in towns and the available evidence indicates that they have been town dwellers for at least six centuries. Traditional Yoruba towns were based on internal economic specialization, there being farmers, craftsmen, producer-traders, and non-producing middlemen among the inhabitants of each town. Most of the men cultivated the fields that stretched for miles outside the town. The processing of foodstuffs was entirely in the hands of women; both men and women engaged in craft productions. The degree of specialization necessitated the exchange of goods[1] among the various producers and each town had at least one market place in which this exchange was carried on.

Nearly all the trade within a town market was in the hands of local women, most of whom were producer-traders, i.e., they were women who manufactured soap, pottery, oils, and cloth, who prepared beverages, cooked foods, etc., and who marketed the goods they produced. In addition to selling the items which they themselves produced, some women had the responsibility of marketing those of their husbands' crops that were not consumed by members of the household. At least as early as the nineteenth century, some women were non-producing middlemen who purchased commodities from farmers and craftsmen and re-sold these goods in the markets.

Even though most women traded in markets located within the towns where they lived, women as well as men were engaged in trade between towns. When the first Europeans visited Yorubaland in the nineteenth century, they found women trading in places located hundreds of miles from their home towns. The only writer to remark on the age of women engaged in long-distance trade (Lander, 1833; Vol. 1:122) reported that the more than

---

[1] When used with reference to the traditional economy, "exchange" refers to the fact that goods "changed hands." During the nineteenth century, the *exchange principle* appears to have been the mechanism by which the economy was integrated; however, it cannot be said with certainty that the pre-nineteenth century economy was an exchange economy.

100 women whom he encountered in one group had all "passed the bloom of life." This suggests that in traditional Yorubaland (as in the present day society) it was *mainly* women past the age of child-bearing who engaged in long-distance traffic which necessitated their being away from their homes for weeks or even months at a time. Those women who had responsibility for their children traded in the local markets; some of them may have undertaken journeys to markets in neighboring towns.

During the period of the Yoruba civil wars, most of which post-dated the Landers' visit to the country, women still engaged in both local and long-distance trade. Bowen (1857:307) could write of this period:

> A good many men, and still more women, are engaged in traffic. Some are engaged in exchanging commodities of the interior, chiefly ivory and carbonate of soda from the desert, for the imports of the low country, as salt, tobacco, cotton cloth, beads, guns, etc., and others in trading from town to town, in the various productions of their own country. All these commodities being carried on peoples' heads, in loads of sixty or seventy pounds weight, give employment to a great number of carriers.

It has been suggested in this study that contrary to what some writers have proposed, it was not because they enjoyed immunity from kidnappers or marauders that women engaged in long-distance trade. No trader, male or female, dared venture too far from his home town without the relative protection offered by travel in caravans. Women endured the risks of long-distance trade because most men were either employed in farming (which, owing to the location of the fields, exposed them to even greater risks) or they were engaged in actual warfare.

It has been proposed that two main factors served to perpetuate the traditional division of labor in twentieth century Yorubaland. On the one hand, the introduction, during the early colonial era, of export crop farming, the expansion of the internal market for farm produce, and the dearth of employment opportunities in non-agricultural pursuits, served to keep men engaged in agriculture. On the other hand, the expansion of the distributive sector of the economy meant that women, experienced as they were in the art of trade, could take advantage of the new avenues opened in this sphere. The tasks of collecting, bulking, and transporting goods from the farmlands to the towns fell to women as did the job of distributing the non-agricultural goods produced in the country and those imported into the country by the expatriate firms.

Yoruba women operate mainly within the internal marketing system of Nigeria. Their trade activities are mostly carried out through the system of daily and periodic markets located throughout Western Nigeria. Today, as in the past, both daily and periodic markets are found in the towns. However, the twentieth century trend has been toward urban daily markets and rural periodic markets. Even though periodic markets, like daily markets, are *indigenous* Yoruba institutions, their existence in *rural* areas is a recent phenomenon, reflecting the demands of the modern economy. Their proliferation has been a concommitant of the growth of villages in a society where the permanent traditional settlements were towns.

The involvement of women in the world of trade and markets entails varying degrees of mobility. Some women are engaged in trade that requires movement within a radius of 10 miles of their home town; some work almost entirely within the town; and others move between nearby markets and those in towns and cities 100 or more miles away. Some of the patterns of trade, including the complex of movements, transactions, and associations entered into in the procurement and disposal of goods, were illustrated by reference to the activities of women in the small Yoruba town of Awe.

Statements have been made to the effect that in rural markets "older women [aged fifty-five and over] deal with most of the imported goods [including cloth and provisions], or with goods of high value in relation to bulk" while younger women (under 25) deal in local food items, calabashes, mats, etc. (Hodder, 1962:113-114). After 12 months of regular attendance at six rural markets, of visits on more than three occasions to two others, of attendance at over a dozen others on at least one market day, and of frequent visits to markets in Ibadan, Oyo, and Awe, it seems to me that any statement linking *age* of women to *commodity line* is bound to be subject to so many qualifications as to be vacuous. Women of all ages deal in farm produce and all types of imported goods. Even trade in local medicines, herbs, and religious or magical objects is carried on by women whose ages span a very wide range. The amount of capital at a woman's disposal will determine the scale on which she can trade in any commodity but it appears that the only commodity lines that exclude women with less than £10 to £15 working capital are cloth and gold jewelry. Both these lines are handled by women in their early twenties as well as by women in their late sixties or perhaps older. Women of all ages deal in imported provisions, dried meats, and fish, cooked foods, etc.

What is apparent from the study of women traders is that the physical range of a woman's trade activities depends to a great extent on her domestic status. That is, it depends on her age, her marital status, and on the ages of the children for whose care she is responsible. The trading orbit of women who have to care for young children is of necessity more restricted than that of women whose children are old enough to be left in the care of others or who can take care of themselves when their mothers are away. If a woman's child is too young to be left with another woman or an older child, she must engage in trade which can be carried on while the child is with her during the day. Such a woman has a variety of possible commodity lines, but there is restriction on her mobility. She can sell in her compound, in a shop, or depending on the age of the child, can hawk her wares over a total of as much as about six miles a day, carrying the young one on her back. However, she can not engage in traffic that requires frequent trips to distant towns.[2]

Thus, it can be said that there are certain *types* of trade activities that are not carried on by a woman taking care of her young children. Since such a woman does most of her trading in the community where she resides, it also means that the choice of commodity line will be dependent to a great extent on the nature of the consumer demand in the place in which she *lives*. If a woman with young children is trading in a small town like Awe, and has the capital to deal in cloth, she is more likely to invest it in provisions for which the demand is greater and more constant throughout the year. However, if such a woman lives in Ibadan, she could just as well trade in cloth as in provisions because in either case, hers *could* be a relatively sedentary line of work.

Because women cannot spend much of their time performing a number of household tasks for themselves and their familes, some women (and men) have specialized in these occupations such as sewing, ironing, washing, cooking, hairdressing, etc., thereby carving out a means of earning a living and at the same time freeing other women to devote their energies to their particular specialties which are also sold on the market.

Women (and men) regard the employment of women in trade or productive activities as an integral part of their roles as wives and mothers, and such employment accounts for some features of Yoruba family organization. Husbands have virtually nothing to do with the management of their wives' trade activities. Although men sometimes assist their wives by making contributions to their trading capital, married women trade on their own account and the incomes they receive are theirs to dispose of as they see fit. Each spouse makes a separate contribution to the maintenance of the family unit and in many instances the responsibility for the wife and her children falls almost entirely on the woman herself. The pattern of separate employment by each spouse might result in their physical separation for weeks, months, and sometimes years at a time.

---

[2] Even here one cannot make facile statements. A woman who buys produce in Igbeti, about eighty miles from Awe, takes her two year old daughter when she goes to the market every five days. She keeps the girl tied to her back throughout the night, stopping occasionally to allow the child to rest and to eat. However, her round-trips to Igbeti are made within a twenty-four hour period; she leaves for the market in the afternoon and returns to Awe early the following morning. Her five year old son is looked after by her husband who returns from work shortly after the trader has left for the market. On days when she goes to Ajawa in the mornings, the boy is left to play in the compound until his mother returns in the afternoon. Still this trader has to adjust her movements to the demands placed on her by her two young children. She does not attend market on days when either of them is not feeling well; but then no woman leaves a sick child in the house while she goes off to trade.

CONCLUDING SUMMARY

Despite the relatively high degree of independence of movement and the nearly complete economic independence of women in the Yoruba town studied, the women do not regard themselves as having equal authority with their husbands in respect to certain family matters. Women are free to work as hard as they may for their children; many of the decisions concerning the children's welfare are made by the mothers alone when the children are young and by the mothers in consultation with the children themselves when they reach young adulthood. However, husbands are always kept abreast of their wives' plans for the children and in cases where they disagree with a course of action decided upon by the wife, it is the woman who must defer to her husband's wishes. A man is still the official head of his household and ultimately if a woman defies her husband's authority, she must leave his house, thereby involving herself and her kinsmen in expense and, if she has children, laying herself open to criticism for being irresponsible.

The socialization process reflects the fact that women cannot assume full responsibility for the upbringing of their children. Through an intricate system of "child-exchange" and sharing of responsibility for the financial upkeep of their offspring, women are able to attend to their trade activities and fulfill their responsibilities as mothers. At an early age, children are taught to be relatively self-reliant. They also learn to obey and respect persons senior to themselves. Being relatively independent youths who are obedient to their elders, children can be left on their own or in the care of adults other than their parents.

In discussing the co-wife relationship, most writers tend to stress the frictions that are reported to exist in polygynous households. It might be expected that where women compete for a share of the market as well as for the attention of their husbands, there would be much hostility among co-wives. The point was made that wives of the same husband do not usually trade in the same items unless they do so on a partnership basis. In effect, the economic competition among the wives is minimized, for although they compete for a share of the same general market, the women do not regard themselves as competing for the same customers. The fact that each wife of one man is ranked according to the relative length of time she has been his spouse helps to minimize the possible areas of friction among the women. Senior wives by virtue of their position are expected to have more freedom to engage in trade than has a junior wife who has more responsibilities, sexual and domestic, within the family unit.

Observation of the dynamics of family life reveals that a man, his wife or wives, and children often do not share a common residence throughout the year. Nor does the "immediate family" assume sole responsibility for socializing the children born into it. Yet it cannot be said that the relatively small "immediate family" it is an artificial construct of the anthropologist or one that has no reality for the Yoruba themselves. To appreciate the continuity that this unit has for the Yoruba, one must refer to the social entity of which it is a part, namely the compound. Every man, no matter where he resides, is an official member of a compound. Usually it is the compound of his father but it may be that of his mother's father. The compound is the residential base of every man, his wife or wives, and children, regardless of the places in which they reside. The "immediate family," though often not a co-residential unit at any particular time, is regarded by the Yoruba as a co-residential unit *over time* and this is considered more important than the fact that the members are temporarily dispersed.

Within their affinal and natal kin groups, Yoruba women have financial responsibilities that are independent of those of their husbands or brothers. From their earnings as traders, women as wives of one group and daughters of another are expected to contribute to ceremonials and to render assistance to their kin groups. Members of these groups provide women with help in rearing their children and they can be a resource to whom women turn for help in emergencies. Thus, those wider kin groups, like the smaller "immediate family," must be listed among the important structural supports that facilitate trade by women.

APPENDIX

A COMMENT ON THE QUESTION OF FEMALE TRADE AND SEXUAL LICENSE

The relationship between women's roles as traders and their roles within the family and community have been discussed by a number of students of African societies (Nadel, 1942; McCall, 1956, 1961; Ottenberg, 1959; Southall, 1961; Izzett, 1961). The point is always made that the employment of women in trade involves a degree of independence of movement not accorded women whose societies relegate to them the task of cultivating the soil. Most writers go on to state that employment in trade affords women a relatively high degree of economic independence from their husbands. It was Nadel (1942) who first explicitly linked this economic independence and physical mobility to sexual independence and immorality on the part of women. He pointed out that professional (long-distance) Nupe traders were usually women past the age of child-bearing or barren women, many of whom no longer lived with their husbands. According to Nadel's informants, virtually all women engaged in trade in the Bida market were also engaged in prostitution. Nadel reports having known Bida women in Lokoja and Ibadan, who were well-known traders and equally well-known prostitutes.

Ever since Nadel's provocative formulations concerning the implications of trade by women for their overall position within the family and within the society, there has been a tendency for anthropologists to assume sexual independence and immorality wherever there is female trade and economic independence. At least it seems to be expected that the incidence of adultery is in some way attributable to the women's economic activities. It should be noted that Nadel's hypotheses referred to a certain type of trader, namely those he designated as "professionals," and that most of these women were found in large towns, not in the outlying areas. In Yoruba society, Lagos included, trade by women is not automatically linked to sexual immorality. In fact, since virtually all women are traders, one cannot explain the deviant sexual behavior of a relatively small proportion of women in the society by reference to their trade activities. If one undertook to account for the incidence of *prostitution* in contemporary Yoruba society, he or she would have to begin by examining those features which distinguish the more Westernized urban centers from the more traditional towns; for it is in the more Westernized towns that one would encounter features which contribute to the fact that some women, a number of whom may be traders, turn to prostitution as a source of income. By and large, it appears that even though women in small towns like Awẹ enjoy a high degree of physical and economic independence, their behavior usually conforms to that expected of respectable married and unmarried women. In Awẹ adultery seems to be rare and prostitution is virtually non-existent.

BIBLIOGRAPHY
(Updated as of 1972)

Adediran, J. A.
    1960   The Urban Geography of Ibadan.
              Unpublished paper submitted for B. A. Honors Geography. University College. Ibadan

Ajayi, Jacob
    n.d.   The Ijaye War, 1860-1865: A Study in Yoruba War and Politics in the mid-19th Century. Unpublished manuscript

Ajayi, J. F. Ade and Robert S. Smith
    1964   Yoruba Warfare in the 19th Century. Cambridge University Press and the Institute of African Studies, University of African Studies, University of Ibadan

Ajisafe, A. K.
    1924   The Laws and Customs of the Yoruba People. G. Routledge. London

Akinyele, I. B.
    1959   Iwe Itan Ibadan. James Townsend & Sons. Exeter, England

Baker, T. and H. Bird
    1959   Urbanisation and the Position of Women. *In* Urbanism in West Africa (Special Number of Sociological Review: July) University College of North Staffordshire

Bascom, William R.
    1942   The Principle of Seniority in the Social Structure of the Yoruba. American Anthropologist 44: 1:37-46
    1951   Social Status, Wealth and Individual Differences Among the Yoruba. American Anthropologist 53: 4:490-506
    1952   The Esusu: A Credit Institution of the Yoruba. Journal of the Royal Anthropological Institute 82:63-69
    1955   Urbanization Among the Yoruba. American Journal of Sociology 60: 5:446-454
    1962   Some Aspects of Yoruba Urbanism. American Anthropologist 64: 4:669-709

Bauer, P. T.
    1954   West African Trade. Cambridge University Press

Beier, N. U.
    1955   The Position of Yoruba Women. Presence Africaine 1/2 39-46

Biobaku, S. O.
    1955   The Origin of the Yoruba. Federal Ministry of Information. Lagos
    1957   The Egba and Their Neighbors. Clarendon Press. Oxford

Bohannon, Laura and Paul
    1957   Tiv Markets. The New York Academy of Science. Series II 19: 7:613-621

Bohannon, Paul and George Dalton
    1962   Markets in Africa. Northwestern University Press. Evanston, Ill.

Bowen, T. J.
    1857   Central Africa. Southern Baptist Publication Society. Charleston, S. C.
    1858   Meroke: or Missionary Life in Africa. American Sunday School Union. Philadelphia

Burns, Sir Alan
    1955   History of Nigeria. George Allen and Unwin Ltd. London

Campbell, Richard
    1861   A Pilgrimage to My Motherland. London

Červenka, Zdenek
    1971   The Nigeria War 1967-1970, Bernard and Graefe, Frankfurt

Cohen, Abner
    1965   The Social Organization of Credit in a West African Cattle Market. Africa 35: 1:8-19
    1966   Politics of the Kola Trade. Africa 36: 1:18-36

Coleman, James S.
    1958   Nigeria: Background to Nationalism. University of California Press. Los Angeles

Comhaire-Sylvain, S.
    1950   Associations on the Basis of Origin in Lagos. American Catholic Sociological Review 11: 4:234-236

Crowder, Michael
    1962   The Story of Nigeria. Faber and Faber. London

Dewey, Alice G.
    1962   Peasant Marketing in Java. The Free Press. Glencoe, Ill.

Dike, K. O., ed.
    1960   Eminent Nigerians of the Nineteenth Century. Cambridge University Press
    1959   Economic Survey of Nigeria. Federal Government Printer. Lagos

Ellis, A. B.
    1894   The Yoruba-Speaking Peoples of the Slave Coast. Chapman and Hall. London

Fadipe, N. A.
    1970   The Sociology of the Yoruba. F. O. Okediji and O. O. Okediji, eds. Ibadan University Press

Forde, Daryll
    1951   The Yoruba-speaking Peoples of Southwestern Nigeria. Ethnographic Survey Part IV. International African Institute. London

Federal Government of Nigeria
    1959   Economic Survey of Nigeria. Federal Government Printer. Lagos
    1962   Handbook of Commerce and Industry. Lagos

Galletti, R., Baldwin, K. D. S., and Dina, I.O.
    1956   Nigerian Cocoa Farmers. The Nigerian Cocoa Marketing Board. *By* Oxford University Press

Goddard, S.
    1965   Town-Farm Relationships in Yorubaland: A Case Study from Oyo. Africa 35:1:21-29

Harris, Jack
    1940   The Position of Women in a Nigerian Society. Transactions of the New York Academy of Sciences. Series II 2: 5:141-148

Herskovits, Melville J. and Mitchell Harwitz
    1964   Economic Transition in Africa. Northwestern University Press. Evanston, Ill.

Hill, Polly.
    1970   Studies in Rural Capitalism in West Africa. Cambridge University Press.

Hodder, B. W.
    1961   Rural Periodic Markets in Part of Yorubaland, Western Nigeria. Transactions and Papers of the Institute of British Geographers. Publication No. 29:149-159
    1962   The Yoruba Rural Market, *in* Markets in Africa. Bohannon, P. and G. Dalton, eds. Northwestern University Press. Evanston, Ill.

Hodder, B. W. and U. I. Ukwu
    1969   Markets in West Africa. Ibadan University Press

International Bank for Reconstruction and Development
    1954   The Economic Development of Nigeria. Federal Government Printer. Lagos

International Institute of Differing Civilizations
    1959   Women's Role in the Development of Tropical and Sub-Tropical Countires. Brussels

Ita, Ndunteui O.
    1971   Bibliography of Nigeria. Frank Cass. London

Izzett, A.
    1961   Family Life Among the Yoruba in Lagos, Nigeria. *In* Social Change in Modern Africa. A. Southall, ed. International African Institute. Oxford University Press

Johnson, Samuel
    1921   The History of the Yorubas. O. Johnson, ed. CMS (Nigeria) Bookshops. Lagos

Jones, William O.
    1969   Marketing of Staple Food Crops in Tropical Africa: Overall Analysis and Report. Prepared for U.S. Agency for International Development by The Food Research Institute, Stanford University

Katzin, Margaret
    1959   The Jamaican Country Higgler. Social and Economic Studies (Jamaica) 8: 4:421-40

1964 The Role of the Small Entrepreneur. *In* Economic Transition in Africa. M. J. Herskovits and M. Harwitz, eds. Northwestern University Press

Lander, Richard and John
    1833 Journal of an Expedition to Explore the Course and Termination of the Niger. J. and J. Harper. New York. 2 vols.

Leith-Ross, S.
    1956 The Rise of a New Elite Amongst the Women of Nigeria. International Social Science Bulletin (UNESCO) 8: 3:481-488

LeVine, Robert A.
    1963a Child Rearing in Sub-Saharan Africa: An Interim Report. Bulletin of the Menninger Clinic 27: 5:245-256
    1963b Sex Roles and Economic Change in Africa. Paper read at meeting of American Anthropological Association. San Francisco

Lloyd, P. C.
    1953*a* Some Modern Changes in the Government of Yoruba Towns. Proceedings of the Second Annual Conference (Sociology Section) of the West African Institute of Social and Economic Research. University College, Ibadan
    1953*b* Craft Organizations in Yoruba Towns. Africa 23: 1:30-44
    1954 The Traditional Political System of the Yoruba. Southwestern Journal of Anthropology 10: 4:366-384
    1955 The Yoruba Lineage. Africa 25: 3:235-251
    1959 The Yoruba Town Today. *In* Urbanism in West Africa (special number of Sociological Review: July) University College of North Staffordshire
    1960 Sacred Kingship and Government Among the Yoruba. Africa 30: 3:221-237
    1962 Yoruba Land Law. Nigerian Institute of Social and Economic Research. Oxford University Press

Lloyd, P. C., A. L. Mabogunje, and B. Awe, eds.
    1967 The City of Ibadan. Cambridge University Press and the Institute of African Studies, University of Ibadan

Lockwood, William G.
    1972 Periodic Markets: Source Materials on Markets and Fairs in Peasant Society (A Bibliography). Council of Planning Librarians Exchange Bibliography No. 341. Monticello, Illinois

Mabogunje, Akin
    1958 The Yoruba Home. Odu: Journal of Yoruba and Related Studies. Number 5. General Publications Section. Ministry of Education. Ibadan
    1959 The Evolution of Rural Settlement in Egba Division, Nigeria. Journal of Tropical Geography. (University of Malaya) 13:65-77
    1961*a* Some Comments on Land Tenure in Egba Division, Western Nigeria. Africa 31: 3:258-269
    1961*b* The Market-Woman. Ibadan (University College Ibadan) 11:14-16
    1962*a* Yoruba Towns. Ibadan University Press. Ibadan
    1962*b* The Growth of Residential Districts in Ibadan. The Geographical Review (American Geographical Society) 52: 1:56-77
    1963 Urbanization in Nigeria: A constraint on Economic Development. Paper read at Conference of African Studies Association. San Francisco.
    1968 Urbanization in Nigeria. University of London Press

Mabogunje, Akin and M. O. Oyawoye
    1961   The Problems of Northern Yoruba Towns: The Example of Shaki. Nigerian Geographical Journal 4: 1:3-10

Marris, Peter
    1961   Family and Social Change in an African City. Routledge and Kegan Paul. London

Marshall, G. A.
    1962   The Marketing of Farm Produce: Some Patterns of Trade Among Women in Western Nigeria. Proceedings of 1961 Conference of Nigerian Institute of Social and Economic Research, Ibadan.
    1963   Yoruba Periodic Markets. Paper read at Conference of African Studies Association. San Francisco.
    1970   In a World of Women: Field Work in a Yoruba Community. *In* Women in the Field, Peggy Golde. ed. Aldine Publishing Co. Chicago

McCall, Daniel F.
    1956   The Effect on Family Structure of Changing Economic Activities of Women in a Gold Coast Town. Unpublished Ph.D. dissertation. Columbia University
    1961   Trade and the Role of Wife in a Modern West African Town. *In* Social Change in Modern Africa. Aidan Southall, ed. International African Institute. Oxford University Press.

Mintz, Sidney W.
    1955   The Jamaican Internal Marketing Pattern. Social and Economic Studies (Jamaica) 4: 1:95-103
              The Role of the Middleman in the Internal Distribution System of a Caribbean Peasant Economy. Human Organization 15: 2:18-23
    1971   Men, Women, and Trade. Comparative Studies in Society and History 13: 3:247-269

Miracle, Marvin P., ed.
    1970   Markets and Market Relationships, Part I and Part II. African Urban Notes. Summer 1970 and Fall 1970. Center for African Studies. Michigan State University. East Lansing

Mitchell, J. Clyde
    1961   Social Change and the Stability of Marriage in Northern Rhodesia. *In* Social Change in Modern Africa. International African Institute. Oxford University Press

Morton-Williams, Peter
    1960   The Yoruba Ogboni Cult in Oyo. Africa 30:4:362-75

Murdock, George P.
    1949   Social Structure. The Macmillan Company. New York.

Nadel, S. F.
    1942   A Black Byzantium. International African Institute. Oxford University Press.
    1952   Witchcraft in Four African Societies: An Essay in Comparison. American Anthropologist 54: 1:18-29
    1957   The Theory of Social Structure. The Free Press. Glenco, Ill.

Nypan, Astrid
    1960   Market Trade: A Sample Survey of Market Traders in Accra. African Business Series no. 2. Economic Research Division. University College of Ghana.

Ojo, G. J. A.
    1966   Yoruba Palaces: A Study of the Afins of Yorubaland. University of London Press
    1967   Yoruba Culture: A Geographical Analysis. University of London Press

Ojo, S. O.
    n.d.   Iwe Itan Oyo, Ikoyi ati Afijio. Published for the author *by* Atoro Printing Works, Oyo.

Okigbo, P. N. C.
    1962   Nigerian National Accounts, 1950-1957. Federal Ministry of Economic Development. Lagos.

Oyenuga, V. A.
    1959   Our Needs and Resources in Food and Agriculture. Federal Ministry of Information. Lagos.

Ottenberg, P. V.
    1959   The Changing Position of Women Among the Afikpo Ibo. *In* Continuity and Change in African Cultures. University of Chicago (cited Phoenix Edition 1962).

Pedler, F. J.
    1955   Economic Geography of West Africa. Longmans, Green. London.

Pitts, Forrest R., ed.
    1962   Urban Systems and Economic Development. School of Business Administration, University of Oregon. Eugene, Oregon.

Polanyi, Karl, C. M. Arensberg, and H. W. Pearson
    1957   Trade and Market in the Early Empires. Free Press. Glencoe, Ill.

Price, H. L. Ward
    1939   Land Tenure in the Yoruba Provinces. Government Printer. Lagos.

Rosman, Abraham
    1959   An Analysis of a Kanuri Market in Northern Nigeria. Presented at the Annual Meeting of the American Anthropological Association. Mexico City

Schwab, William B.
    1955   Kinship and Lineage Among the Yoruba. Africa. 25: 4:352-374

Service, Elman R.
    1962   Primitive Social Organization. Random House. New York.

Smith, Robert H. T.
    1972   Periodic Markets in Africa, Asia, and Latin America (A Bibliography). Council of Planning Librarians Exchange Bibliography No. 318. Monticello, Illinois

Smith, Robert S.
    1969   Kingdoms of the Yoruba. Methuen. London

Smith, Mary
    1954   Baba of Karo. Faber. London.

Southall, Aidan
    1961   The Position of Women and the Stability of Marriage. *In* Social Change in Modern Africa. A. Southall, ed. International African Institute. Oxford University Press.

Talbot, P. Amaury
    1926   The Peoples of Southern Nigeria. Crown Agents for the Colonies. Oxford University Press. 4 vols.

Thodey, Alan R.
    1968   Marketing of Staple Foods in Western Nigeria. Draft Report (3 Volumes). Prepared for the U.S. Agency for International Development.
    1969   Analysis of Staple Food Price Behavior in Western Nigeria. Ph.D. Dissertation. University of Illinois, Urbana

Ward, Edward
    1937   Marriage Among the Yoruba. Catholic University of America Anthropological Series No. 4. Catholic University of America. Washington, D.C.
    1938   The Yoruba Husband-Wife Code. Catholic University of America Anthropological Series No. 6. Washington, D. C.

Wescott, Joan
    1962   The Sculpture and Myths of Eshu-Elegba, the Yoruba Trickster: Definition and Interpretation in Yoruba Iconography. Africa 32: 4:336-354.

Willett, Frank
    1960   Investigations at Old Oyo, 1956-57: An Interim Report. Journal of the Historical Society of Nigeria (Ibadan) 2: 1:59-77

Plate 1. A lorry, of the type used throughout West Africa, Loading passengers in front of Ile Akajewale in Awe.

Plate 2. An Olǫka (amala seller) from Awę moves her business to Apara market on market day.

172 PLATES 3 AND 4

Plate 3. Awẹ panla (stockfish) sellers at Apara market.

Plate 4. Gari (cassava meal) buyer at Apara puts her arm around the rim of the denge (enamel pan) as she measures gari into calabash on her right.

Plate 5. Elubo (dried yam slices) and yams displayed at Apara. Farmers and market elder (with umbrella) in foreground.

Plate 6. Traders exchanging greeting at Apara. Basket of chickens (left foreground), local pottery, elubo, and yams on display.

Plate 7. Ife Odan market: research assistant (back to camera) chats with young orogbo ("bitter kola") and kola nut seller as her stall-mate looks on.

Plate 8. Male "produce buyers" (with female visitor) in Ife Odan at scale used to weigh cocoa and palm kernels that are bagged and sold to the Western Region's Marketing Board.

Plate 9. Young Eastern Nigerian male at Ife Odan sells second-hand clothes (termed "Bosikona," signifying that customers might prefer to "sneak into a corner" to buy such items). A denge is held by trader in foreground.

Plate 10. Calabash sellers under shade tree at Ife Odan.

Plate 11. Young girl watches photographing of cloth (type known as oja) sellers walking through Ife Odan market.

Plate 12. Gari, lafun (dried cassava), elubo, peppers, etc. are bagged, basketed, and ready for transport from Ife Odan market.

www.ingramcontent.com/pod-product-compliance
Lightning Source LLC
Jackson TN
JSHW070313120426
100741JS00007B/44